# A TEXTBO(
## Fundamentals, D
## and Problem Solving

**E. KARTHIKEYAN**

Assistant Professor (Computer Science)
Karpagam Arts and Science College
Coimbatore

**PHI Learning Private Limited**

Delhi-110092

2016

$ 4.87

**A TEXTBOOK ON C: Fundamentals, Data Structures and Problem Solving**
E. Karthikeyan

ISBN-978-81-203-3424-3

The export rights of this book are vested solely with the publisher.

**Second Printing**  ...  ...  **February, 2016**

Published by Asoke K. Ghosh, PHI Learning Private Limited, Rimjhim House, 111, Patparganj Industrial Estate, Delhi-110092 and Printed by Raj Press, New Delhi-110012.

# Contents

# *Preface*

C is one of the most widely used high level programming languages since its birth in the early 1970s. Even today, C's power and flexibility, make it a powerful language suitable for developing several operating systems, graphical applications, hardware interfacing, device drivers, and embedded and mobile applications.

This book has been prepared after carefully evaluating the merits and demerits of many standard books available in the market on C programming, in an attempt to provide the best content to the student. Since, the numerous applications of C programming make it essential for all the students of computer science to learn this language in detail, in this book, fundamental concepts such as data types, input and output statements, looping statements, etc. are clearly explained in a simplified manner that could be understood by all.

I have written this book with focus on MCA/B.E./B.Tech./B.Sc. (Computer Science) and Diploma courses. Since most of the MNC recruitments are based on proficiency in C/C++, this book has been organized with special focus to aid the students in interviews and tests, and the key points are highlighted as *Notes*.

This book covers not only the mechanics of the language but also the style. The topics covered in this book are taken from a broad spectrum of discrete algorithms, their design and analyses.

In the first part, basic concepts are explained with necessary examples and sufficient number of programs. One of the key topics, *Data structures* associated with C language, is covered in the second part of this book. The concepts are presented with examples, diagrammatic representations, and programs are written following the step-by-step procedures. The linked lists, the heart of the data structure part, are very well illustrated. The third and final part of this book consists of a collection of solved programs to support more understanding.

The text provides more than 200 programs and examples, and covers the syllabi of almost all the universities. All the essential concepts of C language are presented in the compact form of one single textbook.

E. Karthikeyan

# Chapter 1

# *Introduction*

## 1.1  NEED OF LANGUAGES

Every living object in the world needs a language which may include signs, gesture, sounds, symbols, signals, verbs, etc., to communicate with each other. People speak many *Natural Languages* all over the world. These languages are called Natural Languages because they evolved naturally with the time since the creation of the world; nobody created them. In order to convey our ideas and feelings to another person or group of people, the medium used is the language.

Similarly, if we want to communicate with the computer, we need a language. There are different languages to communicate with the computer, which are known as *Computer Languages.*

## 1.2  CATEGORIES OF THE LANGUAGES

In the same way as there are different categories and kinds of languages there are many computer languages. The following figure shows a broad division of such languages.

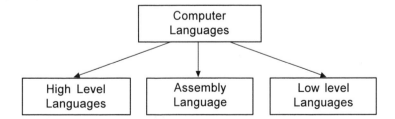

## 1.2.1  High Level Languages

High level languages are widely used by the people to communicate with the computer. They are called high level languages since they are of advanced form which are easier to learn and use. Many computer languages come under this category, e.g., BASIC, FORTRAN, COBOL, Pascal, C, C++, ALGOL, PL/1, Ada and so on.

In these languages, we use English like words as instructions to communicate with the computer.

## 1.2.2 Assembly Language

Before the high level languages came into existence, people used a language called Assembly Language to communicate with the computers. In Assembly language, the instructions would be in the form of Mnemonic Codes or Symbolic Codes.

Mnemonic or symbolic code contains the instructions in the form of abbreviations. For instance, we use the abbreviated codes like ADD, SUB or MULT and so on to Add, Subtract or Multiply.

But Assembly language is rarely used after the development of the high level languages as assembly language is difficult to use. In assembly language, the number of instructions is more compared to the high level languages. For example, to perform a simple operation of adding two numbers, the following single statement in high level language is enough

```
c = a + b
```

But, if the same thing is to be done in assembly language, it requires the following statements.

```
LOAD A
ADD B
STORE C
```

If you compare the number of instructions required for programming in a high level language and assembly language, you could really feel how difficult it would be for lengthier programs. The second difficulty in using assembly language is, we need to remember a lot of instructions which are in the abbreviated form.

Despite the disadvantages, using assembly language has an advantage. That is, the number of instructions is more than high level languages, but the object code produced is shorter in size compared to the object code produced by high level languages.

### What is Object Code?

Object code is the only language that is understood by the computer. It is otherwise called Machine Language. We can use any high level language to communicate with the computer, but the computer can understand only the instructions in the Machine Language.

Machine Language is a language in which the instructions are constructed only with 1s and 0s. In other words, we can say 1 and 0 are the only letters of the machine language. Different combinations of 1s and 0s form different words and thereby an instruction to the computer is generated. All instructions are generated by doing so.

But what happens when we use the high level languages? In the high level languages, we have the instructions similar to those of English words. But, the computer can understand the instructions in the machine language only. Then, how to make the computer understand the instructions in English like words?

A translator is the software which is used to convert the commands in the high level language into the machine language. Software is a program that can be run or executed on the computer. A program is a set of instructions to the computer to perform some action.

### 1.2.3 Low Level Language or Machine Language

As we saw, the computer can understand only the instructions in 1s and 0s. Using translators, the instructions in high level language are converted to machine language. But before the translators came into existence, machine language was the only means to communicate with the computer.

But just think of how difficult it will be if we use only 1s and 0s to construct instructions! Even a single change in 1s and 0s may mean a different thing and it may cause the program to perform an entirely different action. Pinpointing such errors is a tedious thing. Just imagine a page full of 1s and 0s. How could you trace the errors? It causes a lot of pain to the programmer (the person who writes the program or instructions).

Because of all these reasons, nowadays directly using low level languages is obsolete. But still they are used sparingly.

### 1.3 WHY C LANGUAGE?

C is one of the high level languages. It is a general-purpose language, which means it can be used to write programs of any sort.

It is the only language, which is in existence for more than four decades. There are so many advantages of this language over other languages, which were in existence. The following are some of the reasons, why the C language remains outstanding over other languages.

1. Easy to write
2. Rich set of operators and functions that are built-in
3. Support for bit-wise operation
4. Flexible use of pointers
5. Direct control over the hardware
6. Ability to access BIOS/DOS routines
7. Interacting using Interrupts
8. Ability to write TSR programs
9. Ability to create .COM files
10. Ability to create library files (.LIB)
11. Ability to write interface programs
12. Incorporating assembly language in C program, etc.

Because of the abovesaid merits, the C programming language is still surviving in the information and communication technology era.

### 1.4 HISTORY OF C LANGUAGE

The C language was developed from B by Dennis Ritchie at Bell Laboratories in the year 1972. C uses many important concepts of BPCL of B while adding data typing and other features. C initially became widely known as the development language of the UNIX operating system. Today, most of the operating systems are written in C and/or C++.

## 1.5   THE STRUCTURE OF C PROGRAM

The structure of C program is illustrated in the following:

```
Preprocessor/include, Header files
Global Variables declaration
main()
{
    Local variable declaration.
    Body of the program.
}
User-defined function
{
   Statements of function
}
```

*Example:*

```
#include <stdio.h>   /* Preprocessor or include file */
int a,b;             /* Global Variables declaration */
main()               /* main function              */
{
    int x;           /* Local variable declaration  */
    x=10;            /* Statement part of the program */
    printf("\nX = %d",x);
}
```

**Note & Quote:**
   ⇨ All the C programs must have the function main( ).
   ⇨ All the statements must be terminated with a semicolon ( ; ).
   ⇨ Other user-defined functions may be defined before or after the main( ) function.
   ⇨ Comments, if necessary, should be included between the '/*' and '*/'
   ⇨ Upper and lower characters are treated as distinct from each other,
      i.e. x and X are different since C is a case-sensitive language.
   ⇨ Compound statements must be enclosed by the braces {}.

## 1.6   WHAT IS CHARACTER SET?

Character set is the set of characters allowed and supported in the programming language. Generally a program is a collection of instructions, which contain groups of characters. Only a limited set of characters is allowed to write instructions in the program.

In C, the following is the character set.

| Alphabets | A–Z or a–z |
|---|---|
| Digits | 0–9 |
| Special Characters | + – * / % . , : ; ' " \| ! \ ~ > < = ( ) { } [ ] # & ^ _ ? |

## 1.7  IDENTIFIER

Identifier or word is a name to identify the particular information. For example, the following is a statement with the identifier and value.

```
Emp_Name = "Karthi"
Emp_Name = "Amir"
Emp_Name = "Mahesh"
```

Here *Emp_Name* is an identifier, common name, which is used to identify the employee names.

A program is a collection of statements and the statements are constructed using words. The words are of two types namely

1. Keywords (pre-defined word)
2. User-defined words.

Keywords are the words that have some pre-defined meaning. We cannot use these words as identifiers of a program. All such keywords are listed in the following table.

**KEYWORDS**

| | | | | |
|---|---|---|---|---|
| auto | break | case | char | const |
| continue | default | do | double | else |
| enum | extern | float | for | goto |
| if | int | long | register | return |
| short | signed | sizeof | static | struct |
| switch | typedef | union | unsigned | void |
| volatile | while | | | |

## 1.8  RULES FOR THE IDENTIFIER OR WORD

⇨ The first character must be an alphabet or underscore (_)
⇨ Digits may be included in the variable
⇨ The maximum number of characters in a word are 32
  (It may vary depending upon the platform)
⇨ No other special characters are allowed

The following are a few examples of valid and invalid identifiers based on the rules

| Valid | Invalid | |
|---|---|---|
| ab | ab+ | => + is not allowed |
| a12 | 1a2 | => number is not allowed as the first character |
| a_bc | a – b | => Operator is not allowed |
| _stu_rec | stu rec | => Blank space is not allowed |
| axyz123ab | 1.23 | => Floating point is also not allowed |

## 1.9  VARIABLE

An identifier is used to identify and store some value. If the value of the identifier is changed during the execution of the program, then the identifier is known as **variable**.

int a; /+ a is a variable */

When the variable holds numeric data, it is called **numeric variable** and when it holds character(s) it is called **Character/String variable**.

int a; /* Numeric variable_Integer */<br>float b; /* Numeric variable_Real */<br>char name[15]; /* character array_*/

## 1.10  CONSTANT

If the value of the identifier is not changed during the execution of the program, then the identifier is called constant.

For example, take a student's information in a class. Student-name is a variable, because it changes from student to student, but the class-name is a constant since it does not change for a particular class of students. The constants and their types are illustrated in the following diagram.

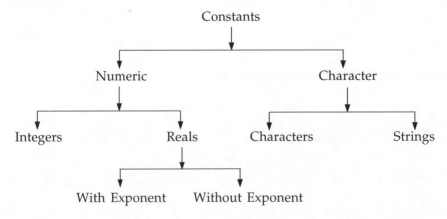

## 1.10.1  Integer Constant

An integer constant contains the numeric values without the fractional part. C also accepts the value as an octal and hexadecimal and they should appear with the characters '0' (zero) and '0x' respectively.

**Example:**

| Valid | Invalid |
|---|---|
| 1234 | 1.234  => Dot is not allowed |
| +421 | 1+2    => Operator is not allowed |
| –444 | 112–   => Sign must be placed in the front |
| 0725 (Octal) | |
| 0x12 (Hexadecimal) | |

## 1.10.2  Real Constant

This type of constants contain numerical values with the decimal part. Depending upon the necessity, any one of the two available types can be used.

1. Without exponent part, it is a single precision real constant, to maintain good accuracy (six decimal places).
2. With exponent, it is a double precision real constant, to maintain very good accuracy.

**Single Precision Constant**

| Valid | Invalid | |
|---|---|---|
| 11.23 | 123 | => There is no real part |
| +1.223 | 44.55.66 | => Two decimal points are not allowed |
| –0.001 | 1.2+3.4 | => Operator not allowed |

**Double Precision Constant**

If the user needs a very high accuracy, this option may be chosen. This real constant has two parts, a mantissa part and an exponent part.

The general format of a double precision constant is

$$\boxed{\textbf{Mantissa e Integer}}$$

⇨ Mantissa part contains real value
⇨ 'e' is the separator between mantissa and exponent
⇨ For both sides, the default sign is positive
⇨ After 'e' there must be an integer value

**Note:**
'e' represents 10 to the power

*Example:*

1. 1.23 e +5 equals to $1.23 * 10^5$
2. 0.01 e –2 equals to $0.01 * 10^{-2}$
3. 10.1 e 3 equals to $10.1 * 10^3$

## 1.10.3  Character Constant

The previous two types of constants are used to hold only the numeric values (numbers). But this is a character-based constant to hold a single character.

*Example:*

'a' , 'A' , '+' , '1'

## 1.10.4  String Constant

String is a collection of characters. The character may be any character, which is acceptable by C. The strings are **enclosed by double quotes (" ").**

*Example:*

| | | |
|---|---|---|
| "ABC" | "A1234" | "******" |
| "A+B+C" | "A B C" | "    " |

*Note:*

⇨ The character constant must be enclosed by single quotes (').
⇨ The string constant must be enclosed by double quotes (" ")
⇨ Empty character is treated as a blank space.

## 1.11  DATA TYPES

Before writing any program, we have to decide the variables that are going to be used in the program, the purpose of the variables and the type of data it should represent. The data may be of any one of the following four types.

1. **char** – to hold single character
2. **int** – to hold an integer value
3. **float** – to hold single precision real value
4. **double** – to hold double precision real value

In addition to the above data type, we can combine the word **signed, unsigned, long** and **short**. The following table gives all the other combinations of data types and the required memory size of the corresponding type.

| Data Type | Bytes | Range of values |
|-----------|-------|-----------------|
| char | 1 | −128 to 127 |
| unsigned char | 1 | 0 to 255 |
| signed char | 1 | −128 to 127 |
| int | 2 | −32768 to 32767 |
| unsigned int | 2 | 0 to 65,535 |
| signed int | 2 | −32768 to 32767 |
| short int | 2 | Same as **int** |
| long int | 4 | −2, 14, 74, 83, 648 to +2, 14, 74, 83, 647 |
| unsigned long | 4 | 0 to 4,294,967,295 |
| float | 4 | 3.4 e −38 to 3.4 e +38 |
| double | 8 | 1.7 e −308 to 1.7 e +308 |
| long double | 10 | Ten digits of precision |

**Note:**

⇨ The default type is signed.

⇨ The number of bytes required for the data type may vary depending upon the operating system used. (We have specified for the DOS).

## 1.12   WHAT IS SIGNED/UNSIGNED?

A numeric value, may have a positive or a negative sign. In the memory, for a variable, one bit is used exclusively to maintain the sign of the data. If we don't have sign, the sign bit also may be used for data. If the value is negative, the sign bit is **1**, and if it is positive, it will be **0**.

For example, the numeric value **−10** is stored as below. The binary equivalent of **10** is **1010,** and since it is a negative number, the leftmost bit is **1**.

This value is stored in the memory is as follows.

| 15 | 14 | 13 . . . . . . . | 3 | 2 | 1 | 0 |
|----|----|------------------|---|---|---|---|
| 1  | 0  | 0   . . . . .    | 1 | 0 | 1 | 0 |

(1 + 15 = 16 Bit)
⟶ Sign bit

If we declare a variable as **signed int**, we are allowed to use only **15** bits for data and **1** bit for sign value. So, the range of any variable of **signed int** is **32767** to **−32768,** that is all **0s** to all **1s**. The range is computed as follows:

$$1 * 2^0 + 1 * 2^1 + 1 * 2^2 + \ldots + 2^{14} = 32767$$

Suppose we have to declare a variable for age. Since there is no chance of negative age for any person, we need not use this bit. We have to declare the variable as **unsigned int**. In this variable, **65535** is the maximum value. Because all the 16 bits are used to hold data.

$$(1 * 2^0 + 1 * 2^1 + 2^2 + ... + 1 * 2^{15} = 65535)$$

## 1.13 HOW TO DECLARE A VARIABLE AND WHY?

Before using a variable in the program, we must declare it. The declaration of a variable tells the compiler about the type of data to be held by the variable and the memory to be reserved for it and to store the initial value in it. The following is the general format to declare variables.

```
Data-type   variable-name(s);
```

Look at the following declarative examples.

```
int  a;              // Integer variable declaration
char ch;             // Character variable declaration
float d;             // Real variable declaration
signed int a;
long unsigned int a;
```

If there are more than one variables with the same data type, the variables can be separated by comma (,) as below. For example, assume that the three variables **a, b, c** belong to the same data type and they are declared as

```
      int a;
      int b;
      int c;
```
or
```
      int a,b,c;
```

As mentioned above, memory will be allocated for each variable depending on the type of data. The memory allocation may be anywhere in the memory, and it is not compulsory that they should be in a consecutive order. The variable declarations and the memory allocation are illustrated below:

```
int a;
char ch;
float f;
```

| | | ch | | a | f | |
|---|---|---|---|---|---|---|

## 1.14 EXPRESSIONS

The algebraic expressions cannot be used directly in the C program. So we have to rewrite the algebraic equation clearly before using. Look at the following examples.

| Algebraic Form | Equivalent to C |
|---|---|
| pnr/100 | p*n*r/100 |
| $a^2 + b^2$ | a*a + b*b |

An expression is defined as a combination of operands and operator(s) to obtain some computation. Operands represent variables or values and the operator tells us what operation to be performed using that value. Examples for arithmetic expression:

1. c = a + b;
2. c = a + b * c / d

## 1.15  OPERATORS

C language has a plenty of operators to perform different operations. The following are some of the categories of operators of C.

1. Assignment Operator
2. Arithmetic Operator
3. Relational Operator
4. Logical Operator
5. Unary Operator (Inc / Dec)
6. Bitwise Operator

### 1.15.1  Assignment Operator

The Assignment Operator (=) is used to assign the value to the variable. The general format of assignment operator / statement is as follows:

```
Variable = value / variable / expression
```

The right hand side will be evaluated and assigned to the left hand side variable. The following are some examples of assignment and expressions.

1. a  =  10
   Here the value **10** is assigned to the variable **a**.
2. c  =  a + b
   The right hand side expression will be evaluated and assigned to the variable **c**.
3. x  =  a
   The value of the variable **a** is assigned to the variable **x**.

Sometimes, the initial value of the variable may also be assigned when we declare the variable.

1. int  a=0;
2. char  choice  =  'y';
3. float  sum=1.0;

We are allowed to assign one value to multiple variables at a time, and this is called multiple assignment.

$$a=b=c=d=e=0;$$

Here, all the variables such as **a, b, c, d** and **e** are initialized as **0**. Before performing any operation, the value of the variable should be defined clearly. Otherwise, garbage value will be taken and the operation will be performed which yields some other wrong result.

```
a=10;
s = s + a; // a may have some value
```

Here **s** is in the part of expression, which adds the values of **a** and **s**, stores the result into **s**. The value of **s** is not properly assigned and it may be any value. So, take care that the variables have the desired values assigned before performing any operation.

## 1.15.2   Arithmetic Operators

To perform the operations like addition, subtraction, etc., we have some operators given in the language itself. They are listed below.

| Operator | Description |
|----------|-------------|
| + | To add two numbers |
| − | To subtract two  numbers |
| * | To multiply two numbers |
| / | To divide two numbers |
| % | To obtain remainder after division |

**Note:**

In the expression, we should be clear about the operations and functions of each operator. Important things we should remember in the expression are

⇨ If both the operands are integers, the result will be an integer
⇨ If any one operand is real, the result will be a real
⇨ The integer division truncates the real part of the result.

**Examples:**

| Expression | Result | Expression | Result |
|------------|--------|------------|--------|
| 1+2 | 3 | 2/2 | 1 |
| 1*2 | 2 | −4%−2 | 0 |
| 2/4 | 0 | 2%4 | 2 |
| 2/3 | 0 | 1.0/2 | 0.5 |
| 4%2 | 0 | 3.0/4.0 | 0.75 |
| 4%3 | 1 | −5%2 | −1 |

In the above example, we may expect the result of 2/3 = 0.666. But the actual result we get is 0 since the **Int**eger part of 0.666 is 0. It happens so since both the operands are integers.

### 1.15.3  Relational Operators

Suppose if we want to compare the values like checking whether one value is greater than the other or not, we use another set of operators called relational operators. The following table shows the list of all the relational operators.

| Operator | Description |
|---|---|
| > | To check Greater than or not |
| < | To check Less than or not |
| >= | To check Greater than or Equal to |
| <= | To check Less than or Equal to |
| = = | To check Equal to |
| ! = | To check Not Equal to |

Assume that the values of **a** and **b** are 5 and 2. Then the following table shows the results of each comparison.

| Expression | Result |
|---|---|
| a > b | TRUE |
| a == b | FALSE |
| a != b | TRUE |

**Note:**
⇨ In C, any non-zero value is treated as TRUE and zero is treated as FALSE
⇨ Operator '=' is used for assigning the value.
⇨ Operator '==' is used to check whether the values are equal or not.

### 1.15.4  Logical Operators

When the number of relational expressions increases, the comparison becomes difficult. By using logical operators, we can combine more than one relational expression and evaluate the result. The expression may be relational or arithmetic. The following table gives the list of logical operators and their usage.

| Operator | Description |
|---|---|
| && | Logical AND |
| \| \|<br>(Pipe symbol) | Logical OR |
| ! | Logical NOT |

While executing the expression, the following table is used to decide the result of the logical expression and this table is called **truth table**.

**&& (AND)**

| Input | | Output |
|---|---|---|
| e1 | e2 | Result |
| F | F | F |
| F | T | F |
| T | F | F |
| T | T | T |

**|| (OR)**

| Input | | Output |
|---|---|---|
| e1 | e2 | Result |
| F | F | F |
| F | T | T |
| T | F | T |
| T | T | T |

**! (NOT)**

| Input | Output |
|---|---|
| T | F |
| F | T |

Here **T** represents **TRUE** and **F** represents **FALSE**, **e1** and **e2** are expressions.

⇨ The logical operator **&&** returns **TRUE** as result, only when both the inputs are **TRUE**.

⇨ The **||** Operator returns **TRUE** result, if any one input is **TRUE**.

For example, let us consider the values of **a=5**, **b=10** and **c=12**.

1. a>b && a<c
   => The result is **FALSE**. Because **a>b** is **FALSE**, **a<c** is **TRUE**.
   So, **FALSE && TRUE = FALSE**
2. a<b && a<c
   => The result is **TRUE**, because **TRUE&&TRUE**
3. a>b || b<c
   => It returns **TRUE** as a result (**FALSE || TRUE**)
4. ! a
   => It returns **FALSE** as a result (! **TRUE**)
5. a
   => It returns **TRUE**, because it has non-zero value.

## 1.15.5 More on Assignment Operators

The assignment operator (=) may be used to simplify or eliminate arithmetic expressions. The following are the assignment operators available.

```
+=, -=, *=, /=, %=, &= etc
```

For example, look at the following statement

```
s = s + a;
```

Here **s** appears on both sides. So, it can be simplified as

```
s + = a ;
```

Similarly, the following table shows the actual expression and its simplified form using the assignment operators.

| Actual expression | Simplified expression |
|---|---|
| a = a + b | a + = b |
| a = a − b | a − = b |
| a = a * b | a * = b |
| a = a / b | a / = b |
| a = a % b | a % = b |

## 1.15.6 Unary Operators

All the above operators require two operands on either side of the operator. But there is one more type of operators, which require only one operand (or variable). These operators are called unary operators. The following table shows the operators coming under this category.

| Operator | Meaning |
|---|---|
| ++ | Increment |
| − − | Decrement |
| − | Unary minus |
| sizeof | Size of operator |

++   => Increment Operator
− −   => Decrement Operator

The operators may be placed before or after the variable. If the operator is before the variable, it is called **pre-increment/decrement** and if it is after the variable, it is called **post-increment/decrement**.

    1. a = a + 1 will be replaced by the code a++ or ++a.
    2. a = a − 1 will be replaced by the code a− − or − −a
and
    1. ++a => Pre-increment
    2. a++ => Post-increment
    3. − −a => Pre-decrement
    4. a− − => Post-decrement

For example, assume that the value of the variable **a = 5,**

    1. c = ++a;
      ⇨ First the value of **a** is incremented to **6,** then it is assigned to c.
    2. c = a++;
      ⇨ First the value of **a**, that is 5, is assigned to c, then **a** is incremented to **6.**
    3. c = − −a;
      ⇨ First the value of **a** is decremented by **4,** then it is assigned to c.

The following is a complete example for testing these operators. The statements included in this program will be discussed in the latter chapters.

**Example:**

```
/* Simple example for Unary Operators */
main()
{
    int a=5, b;
    b=a;
    printf("\nActual value of b = %d ",b);
    b=++a; /* Pre increment */
    printf("\nAfter ++a value of b = %d ",b);
    b=a++; /* Post increment */
    printf("\nAfter a++ value of b = %d ",b);
    b= −a; /* Pre decrement */
    printf("\nAfter −a value of b = %d ",b);
}
```

**Output:**

```
Actual value of b = 5
After ++a value of b = 6
Actual a++ value of b = 6
Actual −a value of b = 6
```

## 1.15.7   Bitwise Operators

Compared to other programming languages, C has the facility to operate on bits (Individual bits of data, i.e., the binary information). Using the bitwise operators we can set/reset/ check any bit in the value of the variable. Also using this idea, we can find out the status of the devices or operations, etc. It is very useful while writing system-related programs. The following table gives us a brief idea of bitwise operators.

| Operator | Description |
|----------|-------------|
| &        | Bitwise AND |
| \|       | Bitwise OR  |
| ^        | Bitwise XOR |
| >>       | Right Shift |
| <<       | Left Shift  |
| ~        | 1's Complement |

The bitwise operator performs the operation on bits (i.e. bit by bit). For example, the shift operators are used to shift the bits to the left (or) right side. If one bit is right shifted from its value, a zero will be added to the left side and the remaining bits are shifted to the right by one position.

**Example:**

Assume a = 5; => 0000000101
         b = 1; => 0000000001

1. a & 1
   => Result of the expression is **TRUE** (00000001)

   > 0000000101
   > 0000000001

   > ―――――――――
   > 0000000001  => 1. So **TRUE**.

2. a>>2
   ⇨ After the two bits are right shifted **a** has the value 1.

   > 0000000101  >>1 will be right shifted as
   > **0000000010**

   Bolded **0** (Zero) is inserted at left side and right end **1** is shifted from the value. So, the result is **2**.

3. ~a
   ⇨ After the execution value of **a** is (11111010). Here all the **1s** are converted into **0s** and all the **0s** are converted to **1s**.

4. a ^ b
   ⇨ This expression produces the result as **TRUE**.

   > 000000101
   > 000000001

   > ――――――――
   > 000000100  => 4

   In **XOR** operation, the result is **TRUE** when one operand is **TRUE** and another is **FALSE**.

5. a | b
   ⇨ This expression produces the result as (00000101).

6. a & 0
   ⇨ Result is **0**.

## 1.16  HOW TO CHECK THE VALUE OF A PARTICULAR BIT?

As mentioned earlier, using the bitwise operator can check the individual bit of value. For example, if we want to check whether **2nd** bit is **ON** or **OFF**, we can make bitwise **AND** with the value 2 whose binary value is **10**. So if the second bit is **1**, the result of expression is **TRUE** and the bit is decided as **ON** otherwise **OFF** state.

For example, the variable **a** has some value and let us check whether the second bit is **ON** or **OFF**.

If **a = 10** then the execution takes place as follows:

00001010
00000010

―――――――
00000010  => 2.

So the result is **TRUE** and we can decide the **2nd** bit is ON

If a = 1

00000001

00000010

────────

00000000  => 0

So the result is **FALSE** and we can decide the 2nd bit is OFF

**Note:**

⇨ Right shift is equivalent to dividing the number by 2 and

⇨ Left shift is equivalent to multiplying the number by 2.

⇨ Bitwise operation is not possible in real data like float, double.

## 1.17  EVALUATION OF AN EXPRESSION AND PRECEDENCE OF OPERATORS

Expression is a combination of operators and operands. At the time of evaluation of the expression, the compiler gives more preference to some operators. If * and + appear in a single expression, the compiler gives first preference to the * operator to execute and then performs the + operation. The operators and their precedences are illustrated in the following table.

| Operators | Way of Execution |
|-----------|------------------|
| ( ) | Left to Right |
| ++  – – | Right to Left |
| *  /,  % | Left to Right |
| +  – | Left to Right |
| <<  >> | Left to Right |
| <  >  >=  <= | Left to Right |
| & | Left to Right |
| \| | Left to Right |
| && | Left to Right |
| \| \| | Left to Right |
| ?  : | Right to Left |
| =  +=  –=  *=  /=  %= | Right to Left |

## 1.18  WHY PRIORITY?

Priority should be given to the operators to avoid multiple results for the same expression. Giving priority to the operators must be followed in all the expressions. For example, if the priority is not given properly, the result of expression is

a = 5 * 2 + 3

=> 10 + 3 => 13

or

=> 5 + 5 => 10

Confusion arises if the priority is not followed while evaluating the expressions. The following are some examples of evaluation of an expression with proper priority followed:

1. a + b * c
   ⇨ b * c will be executed first
   ⇨ and the result of b * c is added to a.
2. a + b - c
   ⇨ first evaluate a + b
   ⇨ result of a + b will be used for subtraction with value of c
3. a * (b + c)
   ⇨ ( ) is the higher precedence than *. So evaluate (b + c) first.
   ⇨ Result (b + c) is used to multiply with a

## 1.19 `sizeof()` OPERATOR

Even though it looks like a keyword, **sizeof( )** is an operator which is used to know the memory size of the data types and variables. This operator returns the number of bytes allocated for the variable (or) data type. The format of the **sizeof( )** operator is as follows.

```
sizeof (v);
```

where **v** is a variable name / data type / value.

### *Example:*

1. sizeof(int);
   ⇨ It returns the number of bytes needed for the **int** data type. The result is **2**.
2. char a;
   sizeof(a);
   ⇨ It returns the number of bytes allocated for the **char** (character) variable **a**. (For single character **1** byte is allocated)
3. int a[5] ; /* Array Declaration */
   sizeof(a) ;
   ⇨ It returns **10**, the entire size of array variable **a**. The **int** data need **2** bytes. So for storing 5 **int** (integer) data, **10** bytes are necessary.

## 1.20 TYPE CASTING

The data type of variables should be dealt carefully while using expressions. Because sometimes we may expect one result, but our program may yield some other value. This happens due to data type conflicts.

For example, the expression **1 / 2** will produce the result as **0**. **Why?** Both the operands of expressions are of type **int** (integer) and the result of the integer expressions also integer, so its result is **0**.

## 1.20.1  How to Eliminate this Problem?

Using a method called type casting we can eliminate this problem. That is, the value can be converted into floating point type explicitly like

(float) 1/2

$\longrightarrow$ Explicit type conversion

Now, we can get the result **0.5** since the operand **1** is converted to **1.0.** When one of the operands is of type float, the result is also in float.

But be cautious when you are assigning the larger data type to smaller one! For example, when we assign the float value to an integer variable, the float will be converted into integer type and hence only the integer part will be maintained and the decimal part is discarded.

Small => Large → Ok!
Large => Small → Ok!

But be careful about the danger of losing the correct data.

```
int a;
a=1.234;
```

The value **1.234** is converted into **int** (integer) type and hence only the (integer) part, **1** will be stored into the variable **a**.

Another example with the character variable,

```
char ch;
ch = 500;
```

The value in the variable **ch** is not 500. Because in the character variable we cannot store more than 127.

## 1.21  A WORD—CONSTANT—VALUE CANNOT BE CHANGED

In some cases, the value of the variable is not going to be altered in the program. To keep the constant value like 3.14 (22/7), PI ($\pi$) value, instead of using the values directly, we can make use of identifier and keep the value. Sometimes unexpectedly, we may try to change the values in that variable. To avoid this problem, the identifier is going to be declared as **const** type. So the value in that identifier cannot be changed.

The format and the example are given below.

```
const variable = value;
const var PI = 3.14;
```

Here the value of PI is declared as constant type. So we cannot alter or change the value of the variable PI. The following program illustrates this concept clearly.

```
const int PI = 10;
PI = 30;
```

This statement will generate error. Because we cannot change the value of PI at any instance.

```
/* Example for constant declaration */
#include <stdio.h>
main()
{
  const int a=10;
  a = 20;
}
```

## REVIEW QUESTIONS ✍

1. What is the need of a language?
2. List out the three categories of computer languages.
3. Define mnemonic name and give examples.
4. What is object code and where it is being used?
5. _____ is a language that is understood by the computer directly.
6. Discuss the various advantages of C Programming language.
7. _____ and _____ developed C language at _____ in the year _____.
8. All the C programs should have main( ) function (True/False).
9. The statements in C language are terminated by _____.
10. C is a case sensitive language (True/False).
11. What do you mean by character set?
12. Define identifier and write the rules for identifier.
13. What is meant by keyword/reserved word? Give example.
14. What is meant by user-defined word? Give example.
15. What is a variable? Give examples.
16. What is a constant? Give examples for numeric and character constants.
17. What is a string? Give an example.
18. What are the data types in C?
19. What is the difference between float and double?
20. Differentiate between the signed and unsigned.
21. What is an expression? Give an example.
22. What is the difference between = and == operator?
23. What is pre-increment/post-increment? Explain with an example.
24. What is the use of bitwise operators?
25. Illustrate the use of **sizeof( )** operator with examples.
26. What is type casting?

# Chapter 2

# *Statements*

A program is a collection of statements and the statements may be any one of the following types. Based on the operation of the statement, they are grouped as:

1. Declarative statements
2. Assignment statements
3. Input/Output statements
4. Control statements
5. Looping statements

The first two types of statements are already discussed in the previous chapter and the remaining will be explained in the forthcoming chapters.

## 2.1  INPUT AND OUTPUT STATEMENTS

We had a nice introduction about C programming language, such as data types, variable declarations, operators, etc., in the previous chapter. In this chapter, we are going to study the Input and Output statements. There are two types of input and output statements available in C language, they are

1. Formatted I/O statement
2. Unformatted I/O statement

We will start the discussion with the formatted statements and then unformatted statements.

### 2.1.1  `scanf( )` (Input Statement)

This is a famous formatted input statement used to read all kinds of data from the user. It reads the data from standard input (normally keyboard), convert them into the specified format string and finally assign the value to the variable. The general format of this function is as follows:

```
scanf("format-string", Address of variable(s))
```

Here **format-string** indicates what type of data is going to be read for the variable. This statement provides the opportunity to include more than one variable in a single **scanf( )** statement. The format-strings always start with the character % (percentage) as below.

| Format String | Purpose |
|---|---|
| %d | To read an integer value |
| %c | To read a single character |
| %f | To read a float value |
| %lf | To read a double value |
| %s | To read a string |
| %0 | To read an octal number |
| %x | To read a hexadecimal number |
| %e | To read an exponent value |
| %u | To read an unsigned integer |
| %lu | To read a long unsigned integer |
| %Lf | To read a long double |
| %[ .. ] | To read only the specified character |
| %[^ ..] | To read other than the specified characters |

**Note:**

While reading values for the variables using the **scanf( )** statement, we must specify the address of the variable. For simple variable, the **&** (Address) operator should be present in front of the variable.

The number of format strings must match the number of variables in this statement. The general form of read statement, the **scanf( )** is

User Input == → Format string == → To variable

From Input stream                      scanf("%5d ",&a);
(From the keyboard or file)

The **scanf( )** statement first reads the data from the keyboard, converts them as per the format-string specifications and finally assigns the converted value to the variable.

How to read one integer value? First, the variable must be declared as an integer data type and then use **scanf( )** with %d as a format specifier as follows:

```
int a;
scanf("%d",&a)
```

By this way we can read a value for a variable. See the following example to know more about the **scanf( )** with provisions

1. `scanf("%d",&a)`
   ⇨ To read an integer data for the variable **a**

2. `scanf("%c",&c)`
   ⇨ To read the character data for the variable **c**.

3. `scanf("%lf",&i)`
   ⇨ To read the double value for the variable **i**.

4. `char  name[15];`
   `scanf("%s",name)`
   ⇨ Read a string, group of characters for the variable **name**

The **scanf( )** statement supports the reading of values for more than one variable. The format-string from left to right for the variables is in the same order. In the following example, the format string %d and %f are assigned to the variables **a** and **b** respectively.

5. `scanf("%d%f",&a,&b)`

   ⇨ To read **integer** and **float** values for **a** and **b**.

Specifying the format string as follows can restrict the number of characters of the input.

6. `scanf("%3d",&a)`
   ⇨ To read **integer** value, but **a** accepts only **3** digits

If we give **12345**, only the first **3** digits will be accepted and so the variable **a** will have the value **123**. The remaining digits will be omitted or may be assigned to the next variable.

7. `int  a,  b;`
   `scanf("%2d%d",&a,&b)`
   ⇨ While giving the inputs, the first two digits are assigned only to **a**, and the remaining will be assigned to **b**

For example, if we give the value **12345** as input, the first two digits **12** will be assigned for **a** and the remaining digits **345** are assigned to **b**.

8. `scanf("%x",  &n)`
   ⇨ To read the hexadecimal value for **n** and the given value is assigned as hexadecimal.

For example, if we give **10**, the value assigned to the variable **n** is **a**, which is a hexadecimal equivalent of **10**.

9. `scanf("%o",  &n)`
   ⇨ To read octal value to 'n', the given value is assigned as octal. For example, if we give **10**, the value assigned to **n** is **8** (octal equivalent of **10** is **8**).

Let us consider the declaration as **char str[25]** for the following examples.

## 2.1.2 Reading the Restricted Characters

By using the format string %[...], the character can be restricted while reading. Only the characters specified inside the brackets are accepted.

10. `scanf("%[a-f]",str)`
    ⇨ Accepts the characters from 'a' to 'f'. If we try to give other characters, they are not accepted.
11. `scanf("%[^a-f]  ",str)`
    ⇨ Accepts other than the characters from 'a' to 'f'.
12. `scanf("%[a,b,1,2]",str)`
    ⇨ Here 'str' accepts only the characters 'a','b','1' and '2'
13. `scanf("%[^\n]",str)`
    ⇨ Here str accepts all the characters except the '\n' character. So it can be used to read a higher number of characters.

## 2.1.3 `printf( )`—An Output Statement

The output statements are necessary for any programming language to produce the result of any calculation or process in different ways. Here C also supports a lot of output statements to print the result in different ways. Here, the **printf( )** is a formatted output statement used in different ways to display the result, messages, etc. Its formats are

1. `printf("format  string",variable(s)  );`
2. `printf("Message");`
3. `printf("Escape  sequence  character");`

We can use any one of the above output statements or combinations of **printf( )** depending on the need. The format strings are already discussed in the **scanf( )** function itself. The general form of output statement transaction

```
         From variable → Format-string → Output device

         printf("a=%d ", a) → Monitor / Printer
```

The value of any variable is first converted according to the format-string character and it will get printed in the corresponding output devices. The following is a function to print **int** (integer) value of the variable.

```
int a=100;
printf("%d",a);
```

## 2.2 ESCAPE SEQUENCE CHARACTERS

The escape sequence characters are some special functionality characters, which are used to transfer the control to the next line, leaving a number of blank spaces, etc. The escape sequence characters are listed in the following table.

| Character | Description |
|-----------|-------------|
| \n | New line character |
| \t | Horizontal Tab |
| \b | Back space |
| \f | Form feed |
| \a | Produce a beep sound |
| \0 | NULL Character used as an end of string |
| \' | Single quotes (') |
| \" | Double quotes (") |
| \\ | Back slash character |

Let us consider int a=10, b=20; and look at the following examples:

1. `printf("%d",a);`
   ⇨ It will display the result as **10** on the screen.

2. `printf("%d%d",a,b);`
   ⇨ It will display the result as **10 20**

3. `printf("%5d",a);`
   ⇨ Here the number of places for **a** is **5**. The result will be printed in the right justified format as **bbb10**. Here **b** represents a **blank space** character (or empty character).

4. `printf("%-6d"a);`
   ⇨ Now the value of **a** is printed in the left justified format because of the hyphen (-) in front of the character. So the result is displayed as **10bbbb**. Blank space can be viewed as empty space on the screen.

5. `printf("%05d",b);`
   ⇨ Instead of blank space, **zero** (0) will be filled. So the result of the above command is **00020**.

   **Note:**
   Zero will be filled only in the front side but not in back.

6. `float a=5.0`
   `printf("a = %f",a);`
   ⇨ Here the format-string %**f**, represents **float**. So, the result is **a=5.000000**. In default the number of decimal places is six.

7. `float a=12.345;`
   `printf("a = %5.2",f);`
   ⇨ Here the number of decimal places is only 2. So, the real part of the result is rounded to 2 decimal places. So, the result is **a = 12.35.**

8. `char name[10] ="KARTHI";`
   `printf("%s",name);`
   ⇨ It will display the value of the variable as **"KARTHI"**.

9. ```
   char name[ ] = "Karthi";
   printf("%10s",name);
   ```
   ⇨ Here the number of places allotted for **name** are **10**. But the string contains only **5** characters. The result is displayed as **bbbbbKarthi** (as a right justified result & **b** means blank)

10. ```
    char name[ ] = "Karthi";
    printf("%-10s",name);
    ```
    ⇨ Same as above but the result is left justified. So, the result is **Karthibbbb.** Blank spaces at the end.

11. ```
    char name[ ] = "Karthi";
    printf("%2s",name);
    ```
    ⇨ Here the no. of spaces are not taken into account. So the result is in normal, **Karthi.**

12. ```
    char ch='A';
    printf("Character = %c Ascii = %d",ch,ch);
    ```
    ⇨ Here the first format string is %c, so the corresponding character value will be displayed and the next is %d so it displays the ASCII value of that character. Finally the result is as follows:
    ```
                Character = A Ascii = 65
    ```

13. ```
    int a =10;
    printf("Decimal =%d \n Octal = %o \n Hexa = %x", a ,a ,a);
    ```
    ⇨ This statement produces the combinations of **octal**, **hexadecimal** and **decimal**. So, the result is
    ```
    Decimal = 10
    Octal = 12 /* Octal value of 10 is 12 */
    Hexa = a /* Hexa value of 10 is a or A */
    ```

    If the format string is % **X** the hexa result is **A** (uppercase).

14. ```
    printf("Welcome");
    ```
    ⇨ It will display the string with all the characters between double quotes as **Welcome**. We can include any acceptable character of C inside the double quotes.

15. ```
    printf(" *** GOOD ***");
    ```
    ⇨ It will produce the result as *** **GOOD** ***

The following are some examples with combinations of all the types of printf( ) statement.

16. ```
    a = 10, b = 20;
    c = a + b;
    printf("Result = %d",c);
    ```
    ⇨ It gives the output as **Result = 30**. The format string (**%d**) will be replaced by the value of the variable.

17. `printf("a = %d \n b = %d ",a,b);`
    ⇨ It produces the result as follows:
    **a = 10**
    **b = 20**
    Because **\n** character second part, i.e. **b=20** will be displayed in the next line. Transfer the control to the first column of the next line.

18. `printf("Sum = %d ",a+b);`
    ⇨ We are allowed to have a simple expression as above and the result is **Sum = 30.**
    How to print the message like **Hello "Sathya" sir**? Double quotes are treated as the end of the string. So this is going to be replaced by **\"**, equivalent to double quotes.

19. `printf("Hello \"Sathya\" sir ");`
    ⇨ The result of this statement is **Hello "Sathya" sir.**

20. `int a=8;`
    `printf("Octal = %o",a);`
    ⇨ The result of this statement is **10**. ( Octal equivalent of **8**)

21. `int age=25; char name[]="Karthi";`
    `printf("Age = %d \t Name = %s ",age,name);`
    ⇨ The result of this statement is

    Age=25   Name=Karthi

    (**\t** ( Tab ) can be used to give more spaces)

22. `int a=12345;`
    `printf("a = %d\b",a);`
    ⇨ The result of this statement is **12345**
    ⇨ The cursor will be at **5** not in the next location.
    ⇨ Because **\b** adjusts the cursor to the previous location

## 2.3   UNFORMATTED INPUT/OUTPUT STATEMENTS

The above inputs/outputs are formatted statements, because we have to specify the format for the variable. The unformatted statements are used to read/write the data without any specification of data format. These statements are mostly used for reading a character-based data. So all are character-based statements and they are:

| Input statements | Output statements |
|---|---|
| 1. getchar( ) | 1. purchar ( ) |
| 2. getch( ) | 2. putch( ) |
| 3. getche( ) | 3. puts( ) |
| 4. gets( ) | |

## 2.3.1  `getchar( )`  (To Read Single Character)

This is the simple input function to read a single character. But this function may be allowed to collect a number of characters until the **ENTER** key is pressed to complete the read operation. Even though a number of characters are accepted, only one character will be considered. The format and the example are given in the following passage.

```
int getchar ( );
```

```
/* Example for getchar() */
main()
{
  char ch;
  ch=getchar();
  printf("\nGiven character is: %c",ch);
}
```

For example, if we give the input characters like **abcdefg** and press the **ENTER** key, only the character **a** is assigned and all the other characters will be ignored.

## 2.3.2  `getch( )` and `getche( )`  (To Read a Single Character)

The drawback of the **getchar( )** function is that the user must press the **ENTER** key. This problem can be solved by using another function **getch( )**. This statement is waiting for just a key touch. Pressing the **ENTER** key is not compulsory, and any valid key can be pressed. The character that we have given will not be displayed on the screen.

We may use the **getch( )** function as **wait** statement on the programs.

Suppose the user who wishes to see the character which he has typed while using the **getch( )** statement, can use the **getche( )** function. The function **getche( )** is same as **getch( )**, but the first one echoes the character on the screen (echo) and it is not echoed in the latter case.

## 2.3.3  `gets( )` (To Read a String)

The three functions discussed above are used to read a character from the keyboard. The **gets( )** function is used to read the string, which is a group of characters.

## 2.3.4  Problems in `scanf( )`

The inputs for the **scanf( )** statement are identified by using delimiters such as blank space, comma, and new line character. When we use the **scanf( )** function to read the string, it does not accept a blank space. Suppose the user wishes to give an input like "**karthi keyan**", the **scanf( )** statement takes only the string "**karthi**" as input. Because, a blank space appeared after the string "**karthi**". By using the **gets( )** function, we can read the string including the blank spaces.

The **gets( )** function reads any number of and any type of characters until the new line (**\n**) character. The following program demonstrates the above idea.

**Example:**

```
/* Testing program to read space as an input */
main()
{
    char name[80];
    printf("Enter name : ");
    scanf("%s",name);
    printf("\nYour name is : %s ",name);
}
```

Output:

```
    Enter name : karthi keyan
    Your name is : karthi
```

We are expecting the result of the program to be **karthi keyan.** But it returns only the word **karthi**. Because when the space appears in the input data, the **scanf( )** function treats that space as the delimiter of data and the remaining will not be considered as input.

**Example:**

```
/* Example to read a string with space as input */
main()
{
    char name[80];
    printf("Enter name : ");
    gets(name);
    printf("\nYour name is : %s",name);
}
```

Output:

```
    Enter name: karthi keyan
    Your name is: karthi keyan
```

**Note:**

More than one argument is not possible in **gets( )** and **puts( )**.
For example, the statement **gets(s1, s2)** will generate an error.

### 2.3.5   How to Read More than one Line of Characters?

The **scanf( )** statement is used to read the characters until the delimiters and the gets( ) function is used to read the characters including the blank spaces until the new line character. Suppose we need more than one line of input characters, what is the solution? The format string %[...] can be used to read the specified characters only. Making small changes to it, like %[^.], we can read any character except the specified character. Using these ideas, we can read any number of characters including '\n' up to the specified character (termination character) occurs as in the input.

For example, the format specification %[^0] can be used to read any number of characters except the 0 (zero). Zero is the terminator from the input of the above format string.

### *Example:*

```
/* Example to read more characters */
main()
{
    char *a , i;
    printf("\nEnter a text (0-to terminate):");
    scanf("%[^0]",a);

    printf("\nYour text : %s",a);
    getch( );
}
```

Output:

```
    Enter a text ( 0 - to terminate ): Hard work never fails 0
    Your text: Hard work never fails
```

The above program reads the number of characters including blank spaces and the new line character. When reaching the character **0**, the **scanf( )** function terminates from reading. Zero is not included as part of the string.

## 2.3.6 `putchar( )` and `puts( )`

The abovesaid statements are used to read the data which may be a character (or) string. The **putchar( )**, **puts( )** functions are used to display the character and the string respectively.

There is no need of any format specification for these functions. The formats of these functions are:

```
int putchar( character );
int putch( character );
int puts( string variable );
```

### *Example:*

1. putchar ('a');
    ⇨ It just prints the character **a**.
2. putchar(65);
    ⇨ It prints the actual **ASCII** character of **65** as **A**.
3. puts("Good morning");
    ⇨ It displays entire string as **Good morning.**
4. char name[ ]="Karthi keyan";
    puts(name);
    ⇨ It produces the output as **Karthi keyan**, which is the actual value for the variable **name**.

*Note:*

Both **putch( )** and **putchar( )** are for displaying a character. The difference between them is, **putch( )** can be used only for the text windows, but **putchar( )** sends a character to any output stream.

The following declaration will clear the differences between the character, variable and string.

### Additional information

a => refers the value of variable **a**
'a' => refers the character '**a**'. (Single character)
"a" => refers the string "**a**", which includes the NULL string (\0).

## 2.4 LIBRARY FUNCTIONS

In general, the functions are used to reduce the program length. The functions can be classified as two types—**library functions** and **user-defined functions**. Some functions are pre-written by the C developers called **library functions**. These are used to do some specific operations, which are often used in programs. For example, if the user wants to find the square root of a number, no need to write a code for this operation. Because there is a pre-written program called **sqrt( )** available to find the square root of a number. C language has a lot of such library functions which are grouped under the header file based on its function.

The header file **math.h** contains mathematics related library functions, **string.h** contains strings related functions, etc. When we use these library functions, the corresponding header file must be included. Some library functions under the **math.h** header file are as follows:

| Function | Description |
|----------|-------------|
| abs(x) | To find the absolute value of x (x is integer) |
| ceil(x) | To find the smallest integer but not < x (x is float) |
| cos(x) | To find the cosine value of the radius x (x is float) |
| exp(x) | To find the "e" power of x (x is float) |
| floor(x) | To find the largest integer but not > x (x is float) |
| log(x) | To find the natural logarithm (x is float) |
| pow(x,y) | To find the value of x power y (x, y are double float) |
| sin(x) | To find the sine value of radius x (x is float) |
| sqrt(x) | To find the square root of x (x is float) |
| tan(x) | To find the tangent value of radius x (x is float) |

The following program illustrates some mathematically related library functions. For this, we must include the header file **math.h**.

**Example:**

```
/* Example for Math functions */
#include <math.h>
main()
{
   int a=-10,b=2,c=2,d=3;
   float e=1.99;
   printf("\nAbsolute value of a = %d",abs(a));
   printf("\n    Sqrt of b = %5.2f",sqrt(b));
   printf("\n    %d power %d is = %5.2f",c,d,pow(c,d));
   printf("\nCeil value of %5.2f = %5.2f",e,ceil(e));
   printf("\nFloor value of %5.2f=%5.2f",e,floor(e));
   getch( );
}
```

Output:
```
   Absolute value of a = 10
           Sqrt of b = 1.41
         2 power 3 is = 8.00
  Ceil value of 1.99 = 2.00
 Floor value of 1.99 = 1.00
```

In the above example, **abs( )** function returns always a positive value, even if the argument is negative. The function **ceil(e)** returns the result as 2.00, where e = 1.99. Because it returns next integer value (not rounds).

| | | |
|---|---|---|
| a=1.2 | ceil(a) → 2 | floor(a) → 1 |
| a=1.99 | ceil(a) → 2 | floor(a) → 1 |
| a=2.0 | ceil(a) → 2 | floor(a) → 2 |
| a=10 | abs(a) → 10 | |
| a=−10 | abs(a) → 10 | |

One more header file, **ctype.h,** checks to which type a character belongs—character, numeric, lowercase, etc. The relevent library function is listed in the following table.

These functions take one character as argument and return **TRUE** or **FALSE** as result.

**Note:**
The character is checked based on its ASCII value.

| Function | Description |
|---|---|
| isalpha(ch) | Returns TRUE if ch is a character (a–z or A–Z) |
| isdigit(ch) | Returns TRUE if ch is a numeric value ( 0–9) |
| isalnum(ch) | Returns TRUE if ch is alphanumeric |
| isspace(ch) | Returns TRUE if ch is a blank space |
| isupper(ch) | Returns TRUE if ch is upper case letter |
| islower(ch) | Returns TRUE if ch is lower case letter |

Other related functions are also available to check some control characters and we can make use of them when it is necessary.

The following is another program, which illustrates a few characters based the library function **ctype.h**.

**Example:**

```
/* Example for character-based functions */
#include <ctype.h>
main( )
{
   int a=65,b=55,c='A',d=' ',e=10;
   if (isalpha(a))
      printf("\n%d is alphabet",a);
   else
      printf("\n%d is not alphabet",a);
   if (isdigit(b))
      printf("\n%d is decimal",b);
   else
      printf("\n%d is not decimal",b);
   if (isspace(d))
      printf("\n%d is space",d);
   else
      printf("\n%d is not a space",d);
   if (islower(c))
      printf("\n%c is lower",c);
   else
      printf("\n%c is not lower",c);
   if (isalnum(e))
      printf("\n%d is alpha numeric",e);
   else
      printf("\n%d is not alpha numeric",e);
   getch( );
}
```

```
65 is alphabet
55 is decimal
32 is space
   A is not lower
   10 is not alpha numeric
```

The problem with the library functions is that they are programmed for specific purposes. Suppose the user wants to write a function for a purpose not defined by any of the library functions, he can write his own function and it is called **user-defined function**. The user-defined functions will be discussed in the latter chapters.

## REVIEW QUESTIONS

1. Explain the **scanf( )** function with necessary examples.
2. What is the use of format string character? Discuss.
3. Write the format string characters.
4. Discuss the various uses of **printf( )** function.
5. What are the escape sequence characters?
6. What is unformatted I/O statement?
7. What is the difference between **getch( )** and **getchar( )**?
8. What is the difference between **getch( )** and **getche( )**?
9. _____ is a function to read a string including blank spaces.
10. What is a library function? Give examples.
11. What is the use of format string in the input/output statement?
12. Discuss the impact of format string character
13. How to read octal value?
14. How to print hexadecimal value for a variable?
15. _____ is the format string character for double.

# hapter 3
# Control Statements

Normally the statements of a program will be executed sequentially, one-by-one from the **main( )** function. The control statements can alter the sequence of execution. These statements also can be used to take some decisions, repeat a process for certain number of times, etc. The control statement can be either of the following.

1. Unconditional control statement
2. Conditional control statement

## 3.1 UNCONDITIONAL CONTROL STATEMENT

The sequence of execution can be transferred unconditionally to other part of the program using the **unconditional control statements**. The **goto** statement is an unconditional control statement used for this purpose. The format of this statement is as follows

```
goto label;
```

Here **label** is the location where the control has to be transferred. The **label** looks like an identifier and it must be followed by a colon (:). The following is an example for the label declaration in a program.

```
main()
{
    /* Statements */
  start:
    /* Statements after label to be executed; */
}
```

Here **start** is a label and the transfer is made by the following statement.

```
goto start;
```

When it appears in the program, the control is transferred to the specified label **start** and continues the execution from that place.

Another advantage is that, the control can be transferred above or below the **goto** statement. If the control is transferred above, it is called **backward jump**. The example for this type is as follows:

```
read:

    _____

goto read;

    _____
```

If the control is transferred below the **goto** statement, it is called **forward jump**. The example is as follows:

```
goto read:

    _____

read;

    _____
```

### Example:

```
/* Example for goto (Backward and Forward) */
main( )
{
    int n,s=0;

read1: /* Label to read repeated values */

    printf("\nEnter the number ( 0 to Exit ) ");
    scanf("%d",&n);

    if (n==0)
       goto end; /* Transferred to end */
    else
    {  s=s+n;
       goto read1; /* Transferred to read1 */
    }
end:
    printf("\nSum : %d ",s);
    getch( );
}
```

Output:
```
        Enter the number ( 0 to Exit ) 5
        Enter the number ( 0 to Exit ) 7
        Enter the number ( 0 to Exit ) 0
        Sum : 12
```

In the above example, **read1** and **end** are labels. Here, label **read1** is used to jump backward and **end** is used to jump forward. When we enter the numbers other than 0 (zero), the value is summed and the control is transferred to the label **read1**. If the given value is 0, the control is transferred to the label **end**.

The following is another example for **goto** statement:

```
/* Example for goto statement */
main( )
{
   int a=10,b=20;
   if (a > b)
   {
      goto end; printf("Hello"); /*It will not be executed*/
   }
end:
   printf("Thanks");
}
```

In this program, whenever the condition is **TRUE**, the control enters inside **if** statement part and then reaches label **end**. In this program, the statement **printf("Hello ")** will never be executed.

## 3.2 CONDITIONAL CONTROL STATEMENTS

The **goto**, an unconditional control statement, is used to transfer the control without checking any condition. This is not always a preferable way. The conditional control statements are used to check some condition and then transfer the control based on the condition result. The following are the conditional control statements.

1. Simple `if`
2. `If-else`
3. Nested `if`
4. `Switch-Case`

### 3.2.1 Simple `if` (For Small Comparison)

This control statement is used to check a condition, and based on that result the order of execution will be changed. The general format and flow-chart for a simple **if** statement are as follows:

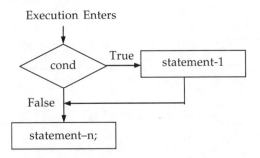

```
if (condition)
   {
       statement-1;
   }
statement-n;
```

First, the **condition** will be checked against the values of variables and sometimes it may be a simple expression. The result of the **condition** may be **TRUE (or) FALSE**.

- If the result of **condition** is **TRUE**, then the **statement-1** part will be executed.
- Otherwise, the control jumps to the **statement-n** part and continues the execution.
- The **statement-1** can be a simple statement or a compound statement.
- The compound statement must be enclosed by { }.

The following is an example that illustrates the functions of **if** statement.

### Example:

```
/* Example for a simple if statement */
main()
{
    int a;

    printf("\nEnter a number");
    scanf("%d",&a);

    if (a>0)
        printf("\nThe number is positive");
}
```

Output:

```
Enter a number 5
The number is positive
Enter a number -5
```

### Importance of the Compound Statement

When we use the compound statement (groups of statements to be executed) as the body of **if** statement, all the statements must be enclosed by { } which indicates the starting, {, and ending of the block ,}. The following is a simple example that illustrates the need of compound statement specification.

Assume that based on the result, a set of statements have to be executed, here compound statements can be used. Suppose we are going to write the statements like

```
if (bp > 5000)
    pf = bp * .12; // stmt - 1
    da = bp * 1.5; // stmt - 2
    hra = bp * .5; // stmt - 3
```

All the statements will not be executed followed by **if** statement. Only when the result of expression (bp > 5000) is **TRUE** all the statements are expected to be executed. The result of the expression may be **TRUE** or **FALSE**. But, here the statements **stmt-2** and **stmt-3** will be executed always, because they are not grouped. How to eliminate this problem? It is very simple. Look at the following code.

```
if ( bp >5000)
   {
      pf = bp * .12; // stmt - 1
      da = bp * 1.5; // stmt - 2
      hra = bp * .5; // stmt - 3
   }
```

## 3.2.2 `if-else`

The simple **if** statement is used to execute only one set of statement(s) depending upon the result of condition (**TRUE/FALSE**). What shall we do if there are two possible results (TRUE/FALSE). We have a solution with another type of control statement **if–else.** The general format of **if–else** is illustrated below with flowchart.

```
if (condition)
   stmt-1; // TRUE Part
else
   stmt-2; // FALSE Part

stmt-n;
```

First, the **condition** will be checked and if the result is **TRUE**, then the **stmt-1** part will be executed. Otherwise **stmt-2** will be executed. There is no scope to execute both the statements (**stmt-1** and **stmt-2**) simultaneously. After the execution of **stmt-1** (or) **stmt-2** the process continues till the **stmt-n**. The statements may be simple or compound statements.

### *Example:*

```
/* Example for if-else statement is here. */
main()
{
   int n;
   printf("\nEnter a number to check");
   scanf("%d", &n);
   if (n%2 = = 0)
      printf("\n%d is an even number",n);
   else
      printf("\n%d is an odd number",n);
}
```

Output:

```
Enter a number to check 5
5 is an odd number
Enter a number to check 6
6 is an even number
```

The following is another example for **if–else** to find the biggest of the two numbers.

**Example:**

```
/* Program to find the biggest among two numbers */
main()
{
   int a,b,big;

   printf("\nEnter two numbers");
   scanf("%d%d",&a,&b);
   if (a>b)
      big=a;
   else
      big=b;
   printf("\nBiggest number = %d ",big);
}
```

Output:

```
Enter two numbers 5   10
Biggest number is = 10

Enter two numbers 15   10
Biggest number is = 15
```

The values of **a** and **b** are compared using the relational operator >. When the result is **TRUE**, the value of **a** will be assigned to the variable **big,** otherwise the value of **b** will be assigned to **big**. Finally the value of the variable **big** will be printed which holds the biggest of two numbers.

## 3.2.3 Conditional Operator

The **if–else** statement can be simplified by using the conditional operator (**?:**), the format is

```
condition ? stmt-1 : stmt-2;
```

**How to Use?**

Here the **condition** is executed first and if the result is **TRUE**, then the **stmt-1** will be executed. Otherwise **stmt-2** will be executed. See the following example and how this operator is used

```
(a % 2 = =0)? printf("Even no"): printf("Odd no");
```

Let us assume that the value of **a** is **5**, the result of the expression **a%2** will be **1**, which is not equal to **zero**. So the result is treated as **FALSE** and the statement **printf("Odd no")** will be executed. Suppose the value of **a** is even then the statement **printf("Even no")** will be executed.

The conditional operator can also be used in another way for assigning the result to a variable. The following example illustrates this idea, to find the maximum of two numbers.

```
/* To find the biggest of two numbers using conditional operator */
   main()
   {
      int a=10,b=30,big;

      big = a>b ? a : b ;
         printf("\nBig = %d ",big);
   }
```

In the above program, the values of **a** and **b** are compared and if **TRUE,** the value of **a** will be assigned to the variable **big**. Otherwise the value of **b** will be assigned. Look at the next example: to find the biggest of the three given numbers using the **if** statement and conditional operator.

### Example:

```
/* Another way to find the biggest */
main()
   {
      int a,b,c,big;

      printf("\nEnter three numbers");
      scanf("%d%d%d",&a,&b,&c);
   if (a>b)
      big=a;
   else
      big=b;
   if (c>big)
      big=c;
   printf("\nBiggest number = %d ",big);
   }
```

Output:
```
   Enter three numbers   10 20 30
   Biggest number = 30
```

First, we have to find the biggest of the two, **a** and **b**, as in the previous example. From this result, we have to compare the **big** and c using same logic. If the value of **c** is greater than **big**, then the value of **c** is copied into **big**, otherwise **big** keeps the biggest value. So finally the variable **big** has the result.

```
/* To find the biggest of three numbers using ?: operator */
main( )
{
    int a, b, c, big;

    printf("\nEnter three numbers");
    scanf("%d%d%d",&a,&b,&c);

    big = a>b ? (a>c ? a : c) : (b>c ? b:c);

    printf("\nBiggest number = %d ",big);
}
```

First, we have to read three numbers for the variables **a, b** and **c**. In the expression, first we have to compare **a** and **b**. If the result is **TRUE**, then the comparison between **a** and **c** is enough and it will give the result as **a** or **c**. If the result is **FALSE**, then the comparison between **b** and **c** is enough and it will give the result **b** or **c**. Finally, the biggest of **a, b** and **c** will be stored in **big**.

The control statements are used in almost all the applications. The following is a program for solving quadratic equation with all the possible roots. The general formula to find the roots of the quadratic equation $(ax^2 + bx^1 + c = 0)$

$$-b \pm \sqrt{b^2 - 4 * a * c}/(2 * a)$$

This formula contains two portions + and −. The square root symbol will be replaced by the library function **sqrt( )**. The above formula, rewritten according to the C programming language, is given below.

```
    -b + sqrt(b * b - 4 * a * c ) / ( 2 * a) ← Root I
```
and
```
    -b - sqrt(b * b - 4 * a * c ) / ( 2 * a) ← Root II
```

Type of root is decided by the result of computation $b^2 - 4 * a * c$, and it may be any one of the following possible values.

| | |
|---|---|
| = 0, | Roots are equal |
| > 0, | Roots are real and unequal |
| < 0, | Roots are imaginary |

***Example:***

```
/* To find the roots of quadratic equation */
main( )
{
   float a,b,c,d,r1,r2,rr;

   printf("\nEnter the values of a, b & c");
   scanf("%f%f%f",&a,&b,&c);

   d = b * b - 4 * a * c;

   if (d>0)
   {
      printf("Roots are Real\n");
      r1 =-b+sqrt(d)/(2*a);
      r2 =-b-sqrt(d)/(2*a);

      printf("\Root 1 : %5.2f \t Root 2 : %5.2f",r1,r2);
   }
   if (d<0)
      {
         printf("\nRoots are Imaginary \n");
         d=abs(d);
         rr=-b/(2*a);
         r1=sqrt(d)/(2*a);
         r2=-r1;

         printf("\nReal Root : %5.2f ",rr);
         printf("\nImaginary Root 1 : %5.2f",r1);
         printf("\nImaginary Root 2 : %5.2f",r2);
      }
   if (d= =0)
      {
         printf("\nRoots are Equal \n");
         r1 = -b/(2*a);
         r2 = -b/(2*a);
   printf("\nRoot1 : %5.2f \t Root2 : %5.2f",r1,r2);
      }
}
```

```
Output:
   Enter the values of a , b & c 1 2 1
   Roots are Equal
   Root 1 : -1.00 Root 2 : -1.00
```

### 3.2.4  Nested `if` Statement—To Check More Conditions

Using the previous type of **if** statements, we can check the conditions at only one place. Alternatively, we can check more conditions using the logical operators. Suppose there is a situation to check the number of conditions in different parts of **if** statement, we can use the **nested if** statement. That is, the **if** statement contains another **if** statement as its body of the statement.

*Format–1*

```
if (cond-1)
   if (cond-2)
      statement-1;
   else
      statement-2;
```

*Format–2*

```
if (cond-1)
   if (cond-2)
      statement-1;
   else
      statement-2;
else
   statement-3;
```

The execution form of **Format-1**:

- First the **cond-1** is checked in both the formats
- If the result is **TRUE**, then **cond-2** will be checked. If **cond-2** returns **TRUE**, then **statement-1** will be executed.
- If the result of **cond-2** is **FALSE**, then **statement-2** will be executed.

The execution form of **Format-2**:

- As said above in **Format-1, cond-1** will be computer first
- If the **cond-1** and **cond-2** are **TRUE**, then **statement-1** will be executed.
- If the **cond-1** is **TRUE** and **cond-2** is **FALSE**, then **statement-2** will be executed.
- If the **cond-1** is **FALSE**, then **statement-3** will be evaluated.

### Note:
*Every else is closest to its if statement.*

The following program is an example for **nested if** to find the biggest among the three numbers.

### Example:

```
/* Example for nested if statement */
main( )
{
   int a,b,c;
   int big;

   printf("\nEnter three numbers : ");
   scanf("%d%d%d",&a,&b,&c);
   if (a>b)
      if (a>c)
         big=a;
      else
         big=c;
   else
```

```
        if (b>c)
           big=b;
        else
           big=c;
     printf("\nBiggest no. is : %d ",big);
     getch( );
  }
```

**Output:**

```
     Enter three numbers : 20 10 30
     Biggest no. is : 30
```

Another example to check whether the candidate is eligible to vote or not. The males are eligible to vote when the age>22 and the females are eligible to vote when the age>18. Here there are two conditions to be checked as sex and age.

***Example:***

```
   /* Checking the eligibility of voter */
main( )
{
int sex,age;
char name[15];
printf("\nEnter name,age,sex ");
   scanf("%s%d%d",name,&age,&sex);

if (sex==1)
{
   printf("\n %s is a male",name);
   if (age > 20)
     printf(" is eligible to vote ");
   else
     printf(" is not eligible to vote ");
}
else
{
   printf("\n%s is female ",name);
   if (age > 18)
     printf(" is eligible to vote");
   else
     printf(" is not eligible to vote");
}
   getch();
}
```

Output:

```
Enter name,age,sex : karthi 25 1
karthi is a male is eligible to vote

Enter name,age,sex : kavitha 15 0
kavitha is a female is not eligible to vote
```

### 3.2.5  What is the Difference between = and == Operators?

The two operators = and == are used for assignment and checking respectively. If not properly used, it causes many problems. The following program illustrates what will happen if we use = instead of = =.

```
/* Example for = and == operators */
   main()
   {
     int a =0;
     if (a=1)     /* Assign 1 to a */
       printf("\nGood morning");
     else
       printf("\nGood night");
   }
```

- First the value of **a** is initialized as **0** when it was declared.
- While checking condition, the value of **a** is initialized as **1** (no comparison is made, only an assignment operation is performed). So the expression gives the **TRUE** (non-Zero value, because a=1) and the result of this program is '**Good morning**'. But we may think '**Good night**' would be the result.
- To check the **TRUE** value of the expression, the following is an alternative way of programming.

```
if (a)       /*equals to (a!= 0) */
   statement-1;
else
   statement-2;
```

Here if the variable **a** holds non-zero value, which is equivalent to **TRUE**, then the **statement-1** will be executed. Otherwise **statement-2** will be executed. The following is an example for this approach.

```
/* Example for alternative approach */
main()
{
   int a=10;
   if (a)
     printf("\nGood");
   else
     printf("\nBad");
}
```

Result of the above program is **Good**. The statement **if (a)** returns **TRUE,** because the value of **a** is **10** (non-zero). If we change the value of variable **a** to **0**, what will happen? To see the result, execute the following program.

```
/*Example for new approach to if statement */
main()
{
    int a=0;
    if (a)
      printf("\nGood");
    else
      printf("\nBad");
}
```

### 3.2.6 `switch-case` Statement

Whenever we want to check more possible conditions for a single variable, a number of statements are necessary. For example, to check the 'category' of employee, the following code has to be used. Assume the categories 1-Managing Director, 2-Manager, 3-Asst. Manager and 4-Staff.

```
if ( category ==1)
   printf("\n Managing Director ");
if ( category ==2)
   printf("\n Manager ");
if ( category ==3)
   printf("\n Assistant Manager ");
if ( category ==4)
   printf("\n Staff ");
```

Is there any chance to reduce the repeated usage of `if` statements? Yes, we have the **switch–case** statement to check multiple conditions at a time, which reduces the number of repetitions of the statements. The general format of `switch-case` is as follows.

```
switch (expr)
{
   case c-1: statement-1;
   case c-2: statement-2;
   case c-3: statement-3;
   [default : statement-n;]
}
```

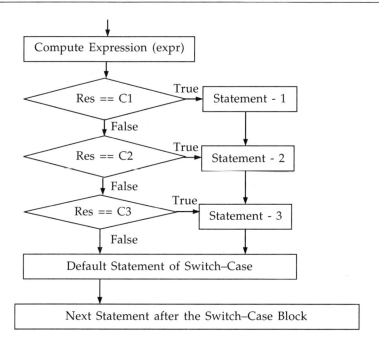

### How to Execute?

- First the **expr** will be evaluated and it must return a constant value. The constant can be numeric or character.
- The result of **expr** is checked against the constant values like **C1, C2,** etc., and if any value is matching, the execution starts from that corresponding statement. The execution will continue until the end of **switch** statement.
- To avoid this continuous execution problem, we can use the **break** statement. The **break** is used to terminate the process of blocks like switch, looping statements, etc.
- For example, if **res** matching with **C1** and then the corresponding statements in **stmt-1** will be executed. After this execution, the process continues the execution of **stmt-2**, and **stmt-3**, etc.
- Here the **default** is an optional statement in switch. If no matching occurrs, the **default** part of the statement will be executed and may occur anywhere in the switch statement.

### Example

```
/* Example for switch statement without break */
main()
{
    int a;
    printf("\nEnter any value for a : ");
    scanf("%d",&a);
    switch(a)
```

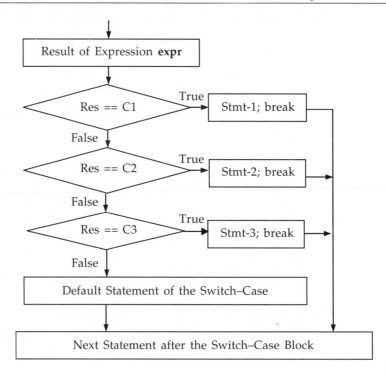

```
{
    case 1 : printf("\nGood");
    case 2 : printf("\nWell");
    case 3 : printf("\nExcellent");
    default : printf("\nBad Guy");
}
}
```

**Output:**

```
Enter any value for a : 2
Well
Excellent
Bad Guy
Enter any value for a : 5
Bad Guy
```

In the above program, check the value of **a** against the case values. Since **a=2**, case 2 is matching. So the corresponding statement part will be executed and all the remaining statements of switch-case block will be executed.

The flowchart for the **switch–case** with the **break** statement is shown above.

In the above flowchart, the result of expression is checked with the constant values like C1, C2, .... If any matching occurs, (i.e., TRUE), its corresponding statement will be executed. After completion of the statement, the control jumps to the next statement after switch–case block. Here the **break** statement is used to prevent the continuous execution of the block.

Below we have the previous example modified with **break** statement.

***Example:***

```
/* Example for Switch-Case with break statement */
main( )
{
    int a;
    printf("\nEnter any value for a : ");
    scanf("%d",&a);

    switch(a)
    {
       case 1 : printf("\nGood"); break;
       case 2 : printf("\nWell"); break
       case 3 : printf("\nExcellent"); break
       default : printf("\nBad Guy");
    }
}
```

Output:

```
    Enter any value for a : 1
    Good
    Enter any value for a : 5
    Bad Guy
```

***Note:***

Upon using the **break** statement, the statement corresponding to the matching **case** is only executed. **break** is not needed in the last statement or default statement, because there are no more statements for further execution in the **switch**.

The following program illustrates the choice of operation and performs the corresponding simple arithmetic expression.

***Example:***

```
/* Example of Switch Using Numeric Constant */
main()
{
    int a, b, c, ch;

    printf("\nEnter a, b values ");
    scanf("%d%d",&a,&b);
    printf("\n1.Add\t2.Sub\t3.Mul\t4.Div\n");
    printf("\nSelect a choice");
    scanf("%d",&ch);
```

```
switch(ch)
   {
      case 1 : c = a+b; break;
      case 2 : c = a-b; break;
      case 3 : c = a*b; break;
      case 4 : c = a/b;
   }
   printf("\nResult is = %d ",c);
}
```

**Output:**

```
Enter a, b values 5   2
1. Add       2. Sub       3. Mul     4. Div
Select a choice 1
Result is = 7

Enter a, b values 5   5
1. Add       2. Sub       3. Mul     4. Div
Select a choice 4
Result is = 1
```

Another example for **switch-case** statement using the character constant values is given below.

***Example:***

```
/* Example of Switch Using Character Constant */
main()
{
   int a, b, c;
   char ch;

   printf("\nEnter a, b values ");
   scanf("%d%d",&a,&b);
   printf("\n +.Add\t -.Sub\t *.Mul\t /.Div\n");
   printf("\nSelect a choice");
   scanf("%c",&ch);

switch(ch)
   {
      case '+' : c = a+b; break;
      case '-' : c = a-b; break;
      case '*' : c = a*b; break;
      case '/' : c = a/b; /*Integer division*/
   }
   printf("\nResult is = %d ",c);
}
```

**Output:**

```
Enter a, b values  2  2
+.Add    - .Sub  * .Mul /. Div

Select a choice *
Result is = 4
```

***Note:***
- case cannot have two equal values.
- Default may appear at any place and not compulsory.

***Example:***

```
/*Example for default in different places */
main()
{
   int a=10;
   switch(a)
   {
     case 1: printf("Good Morning");break;
     default: printf("Out of Choice");break;
     case 2: printf("Good Afternoon");break;
   }
}
```

**Output:**

```
Out of Choice
```

The following is a piece of code to execute some statements when the result of expression has the uppercase and lowercase letters.

```
switch(ch)
{
   case 'A':
   case 'a': Statements;
}
```

The switch–case does not allow the usage of string constant. So the following is an error statement.

```
switch(ch)
{
   case "Choice2": // Error Definition
      Statements;
}
```

There is no chance of duplication of the **constant** as shown below.

```
switch(ch)
{
   case 'A': Statements;
   case 'A': Statements;
      /* Re-Declaration not allowed. */
}
```

**Note:**
Result of the expression in **case** should be a numeric or character constant.

## 3.3  LOOPING STATEMENTS

The simple statements that we have discussed so far are used to execute the statements only once. Suppose a programmer needs to execute the specified statements multiple times. The looping statements overcome the problem of repeating statements multiple number of times. For example, to print the string **"Good morning"** five times, we have to use five individual **printf( )** statements. Imagine if the number to print increases to 1000 times or $N$ times. Using the looping statements, a statement or a set of statements can be executed repeatedly.

Here is a program without looping statement to print the string "**Good morning**" five times.

```
main()
{
   printf("\nGood morning");
   printf("\nGood morning");
   printf("\nGood morning");
   printf("\nGood morning");
   printf("\nGood morning");
}
```

When the number of repeated statements is low, we can write programs as above. But suppose to print the string 100 times or 1000 times or $N$ times, we have to write similar statements $N$ number of times as illustrated in the following simple program.

```
main()
{
   printf("\nGood morning"); /* First Time */
   printf("\nGood morning"); /* Second Time */
   .  .  .  .
   .  .  .  .
   printf("\nGood morning"); /* Hundredth Time */
}
```

In the above program, the purpose of each statement is same. We can reduce the size of the program using the looping statements as below to print 100 times.

```
main()
{
   for(i=1;i<=100;i++)
      printf("\nGood morning");
}
```

Just think about the number of statements in the above programs, with and without looping statement. From the above discussion, the importance of looping statement is realized. Different types of looping statements are

1. **while** statement
2. **do–while** statement
3. **for** statement

### 3.3.1 `while` **statement**

An **entry controlled** looping statement is used to execute the body of the statements any number of times until the condition becomes false. The general format of **while** statement and its flowchart are as follows:

```
while (condition)
   {
      Statements of while;
   }
next-statement;
```

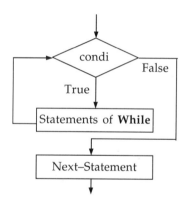

#### *How to Execute?*

- First the **condition** is checked, which will yield **TRUE** or **FALSE** result.
- If the condition is **TRUE,** the control enters inside the **statements of while** and after completion of these statements, once again the condition will be checked with new value for the next execution.
- Entry of the loop will be determined by condition. So it is also called **entry controlled looping** statement.
- So the statements of **while** are executed until the condition becomes **FALSE.**
- If the condition is **FALSE,** execution jumps to the **next-statement** after the **while** statement and continues the execution.

Just compare the following statements to understand the difference between **if** and **while** loops.

```
if (condition)                  while (condition)
   {                                {
      Statements;                      Statements;
   }                                }
next-statement;                 next-statement;
```

The first figure is for **if** statement and second one is for **while.** In case of **if,** the **statements** portion will be executed only once. But in **while,** the **statements** part will be executed until the condition becomes **FALSE.** Three basic things are required in any looping statement such as **initial value, condition** and **next value** for execution.

How to write a program to print the first 10 numbers using looping statements. Here, the initial value is **1,** the next values will be **2,3,4 ...** and the process will be repeated until **10.** The following is a pseudo code for this idea.

```
i=1;
while(i<=10)  /* Up to 10 numbers */
{
   printf("%d\n",i);
   i=i+1; /* Increment i by 1 */
}
```

Here the value of **i** is incremented by **1** to obtain the next value and the printing process will be continued until **i** reaches **10.** The next program is an example to print the numbers from **1** to **n** using **while** loop.

### Example:

```
/* Example for while loop */
main()
{
   int i=1,n;
   printf("\nHow many numbers");

   scanf("%d",&n);
   printf("\nThe numbers are ");

   while(i<=n)
   {
      printf("%5d",i);
      i++;
   }
}
```

**Output:**

```
How many numbers 5
The numbers are  1  2  3  4  5
```

The following program reads a number and prints its digits in the reverse order.

- First read a number
- Do the modulus operation (%) to obtain the last digit
- Do integer division (/) for truncation of the last digit
- Repeat this process until **n** becomes **0**.

*Example:*

```
/* Reverse the order of a given Integer number */
main()
{
    int n;
    printf("\nEnter a number :");
    scanf("%d",&n);
    printf("\nReverse of number :");

    while(n != 0)
      {
          printf("%d",n%10);
          n=n/10;
      }
}
```

```
Output:
    Enter a number : 123
    Reverse of number : 321
```

### 3.3.2  do-while  statement

It is also a looping statement to execute statements repeatedly for certain number of times or until some condition is satisfied. In **while** loop, the condition is checked first and its statement is executed only when the result is **TRUE**.

### 3.3.3   What is the difference between while and do-while?

**while** is an entry-controlled looping statement, because the statement of **while** will be executed only when the condition is **TRUE**. But in **do-while**, first the statements will be executed and then the condition will be checked. If the result of condition is **TRUE,** the statements will be executed next time. If the result is **FALSE,** the control will move to the next statement. So **do-while** will execute statements at least once. The general format and the flowchart are given below.

Entry

```
do
{
   Statements;
}
while(condition);

next-statement;
```

```
       ┌──────────────┐
       │  statements  │
       └──────────────┘
              │
      ┌───────▼───────┐
True  │     cond      │
      └───────┬───────┘
            False
              │
       ┌──────▼───────┐
       │ Next-Statement │
       └──────────────┘
```

Here, the **Statements** will be executed first and the **condition** will be checked. If the result is **TRUE** the control repeats the execution of **Statements** once again. This process will continue until the result of **condition** is **FALSE**. The following is a simple program to illustrate the do-while loop.

### Example:

```
/* Example for do-while looping statement */
main()
{
   int ch;
   do
   {
      printf("\n1. Add\n2. Sub");
      printf("\nSelect a choice");
      scanf("%d",&ch);
   }
   while(ch<3);
}
```

**Output:**

```
1. Add
2. Sub
Select a choice 1
1. Add
2. SubSelect a choice 3
```

The following is another example for do-while, which converts decimal to binary.

*Example:*

```
/* Converting Decimal number to binary */
main()
{
    int a,n,s=0,i=1;
    printf("\nDecimal No. :");
    scanf("%d",&n);
    printf("\nBinary No. :");

    while(n)
    {
        printf("%d",n%2);
        n=n/2;
    }
}
```

Output:

```
Decimal No. : 5
Binary No. : 101
```

### 3.3.4  `for`  statement—Flexible Looping statement

The **for** statement is also a looping statement used to execute the specified statements repeatedly in a simplified format than the previous loops. As we know, the looping statements discussed so far require the following:

1. Initialize the loop control variable
2. Check the condition whether TRUE/FALSE
3. Modify the value of the loop control variable for the next execution

In this type of looping statements, the statements are kept separately. But in case of **for** statement all the three parts are kept in one place. The general format and flowchart are given below:

```
      1      2      4

for(expr1;expr2;expr3)
{
    //stmts. of the for loop; 3
}
next-statement;
```

where,
- **expr1** is used to initialize the value for loop control variable
- **expr2** is used to check condition
- **expr3** is used to modify the value

The **expr1,** step 1 is the statement executed first and only once in the looping statement. The steps 2, 3 and 4 will be executed continuously until the condition becomes FALSE.

## How to Execute?

- First the value of loop control variable is initialized by **expr1.**
- Next the condition is checked by **expr2** and if it is **TRUE** then the **body of loop** will be executed, otherwise the control passes to the **next-statement** of the program.
- For every **Body of loop** execution, **expr3** will be executed to modify the value of the variable.
- The above process continues until the **expr2** becomes **FALSE.**

### *Examples:*

```
1. for(i=1;i<=100;i++) /* Increasing */
   {
      Body of loop
   }
```

Here **i** is initialized by **1** and for every execution, **i** value will be incremented by **1**. So, the body of loop will execute **100** times.

```
2. for(i=100;i>0;i=i-2) /* Decreasing */
   {
      Body of loop
   }
```

First the value of **i** is initialized to **100** and for every execution, **i** value is decremented by **2.** So the body of loop will execute **50** times.

The following is a pseudo code to print the numbers from **1** to **5** using for loop.

```
i=1;
for(i=1;i<=5;i++)
   printf("\n%d",i);
```

How to find the sum of the following (Sum of **n** Odd numbers)?

$$Sum = 1 + 3 + 5 + 7 + ... + N$$

Here the initial value is **1** and for every execution, the value of loop variable should be incremented by **2.** For every iteration, find the sum and this process continues until reaching **n.**

### *Example:*

```
/* To find the sum of N Odd numbers */
main()
{
   int n,i,sum=0;;

   printf("\nEnter a number");
   scanf("%d",&n);
```

```
    for(i=1;i<=n;i=i+2)
        sum=sum+i;

    printf("\nSum of %d Odd Nos. = %d ",n,sum);
}
```

**Output:**

```
    Enter a number 5
    Sum of 5 Odd Nos. = 9
```

The following program is used to calculate Factorial value for a given number, this is also similar to the above program. Instead of summation, multiplication has to be made.

General formula : n! = 1 * 2 * 3 * ... * n

### *Example:*

```
/* To find the factorial of a number */
main()
{
    int n, i, f=1;

    printf("\nEnter a number");
    scanf("%d",&n);
    for(i=1;i<=n;i++)
        f = f * i;

    printf("\nFactorial of %d = %d ",n,f);
}
```

**Output:**

```
Enter a number 5
Factorial of 5 = 120
```

Displaying the numbers from 1 to n (or) N Odd numbers (or) N Even number is simple and we can use the above ideas. Look at the following series, called **fibonacci series.**

0  1  1  2  3  5  8  13  . . .

How to generate this series? If we leave the first two elements in this series, the remaining elements are obtained by summing up previous two numbers. So, first initialize **0, 1** to **a, b** respectively, and find the next number as **c = a + b**. After that move the values of **b** and **c**, to **a** and **b** like **b → a, c → b**. Now **a** and **b** have the new set of values and do the sum again. This process will be continued until certain number of times or certain condition.

*Example:*

```
/* To Generate Fibonacci Sequence */
main( )
{
   int a=0,b=1,c,n,i;

   printf("\nHow many numbers :");
   scanf("%d",&n);

   printf("\nFibonacci Sequence \n");

   for(i=1;i<=n;i++)
      {
      c=a+b;
      printf("%d\t",c);
      a=b; b=c;
      }
}
```

Output:

```
How many numbers : 5
Fibonacci Sequence
1    2    3    5    8
```

## What is a prime number?

Prime number is a number, which is divisible only by **1 (one)** and **itself**. To check whether the given number is prime or not is very simple. If the number is not divisible by the numbers from **2** to **n–1**, then that number is prime number.

- Use modulo operator (%) and check the remainder from **2** to **n–1**
- Whenever the remainder is **0**, it is concluded that the number is divisible by some other number. So, the number is not a prime number.

The process is carried out as follows.

```
n % 2
n % 3
n % 4 etc until n % n-1.
```

These statements are simplified as

```
n % i,    where i = 2 to n-1.
```

*Example:*

```
/*To Check whether a number is prime(or)not*/
main()
{
   int n,i,prime=1;
```

```
    printf("\nEnter a number:");
    scanf("%d",&n);

    for(i=2;i<=n-1;i++)
       if (n%i = = 0)
          prime=0;
    if (prime= =1)
       printf("\n%d is a prime number",n);
    else
       printf("\n%d is not a prime number ",n);
}
```

**Output:**

```
Enter a number : 5
5  is a prime number

Enter a number : 6
6 is not a prime number
```

***Note:***
Instead of **n–1** in the above program, we can use **sqrt(n)**.

### 3.3.5  Additional Information about the `for` Loop

The **for** loop has three parts inside a set of parentheses and each is separated by the semicolon (;).

- The initialization portion may be before the **for** loop as follows.
  ```
  i=10;
  for( ; i <100 ; i++)
      {  }
  ```
- We can have more than one statement in the place of **expr1,** which are separated by commas (,). For example

  ```
  for(a=4,i=0;i<10;i++)
      {  }
  ```

- The **expr3** may also be placed in the body of the loop as

  ```
  for(i=10;i<100;)
      { i++; }
  ```

- If any part in the **for** is missing, the semicolon must be placed.

  ```
  for(i=0;i<100;)
      { i++; } /*expr3 is empty in loop*/
  ```

- The following loop is used to execute the statements indefinitely, because there is initialization, condition and modification.

  ```
  for( ; ; )
      {  }
  ```

- More than one condition statement can be used in the **expr2** place of **for** loop as

```
for(i=1;i<10&&j<20;i++)
  {  }
```

## 3.3.6  Nested `for` Loop

Just like a nested **if**, nested `for` loop is also possible. In the nested `for` loop, the statement part of the loop contains another `for` statement.

```
for(expr1;expr2;expr3)      <=  O
    for(expr4;expr5;expr6)  <=  I
    {
        Body of loop
    }
```

where **O** is an outer loop
**I** is an inner loop

### How to Execute?

For every value of outer loop, the inner loop will execute a number of times. In the nested loop, the body of loop will be executed until both the expressions **expr2** and **expr5** become **FALSE**.

For example,

```
for(i=1;i<=10;i++)   (1)
    for(j=1;j<=5;j++)   (2)
        printf("\nIndia");
```

Here for every value of **i** of **1**, the **j** of **2** loop executes the statement **5** times. So totally the string **India** will be printed **50** times **(10 * 5 = 50)**. The concept of nested loop is clearly illustrated in the following program.

### Example:

```
/* Example for "nested for" loop */
main()
{
    int i,j;
    for(i=1;i<=2;i++)
        for(j=1;j<=3;j++)
            printf("\ni = %d j = %d ",i,j);
}
```

Output:

```
i = 1    j = 1
i = 1    j = 2
i = 1    j = 3
i = 2    j = 1
i = 2    j = 2
i = 2    j = 3
```

For every value of **i** of the first loop, the **j** loop (the inner loop) executes **3** times. Generating multiplication table, a good example for nested loop is available in the following program. (It prints 20 Tables with 10 iterations).

```
/* Example for Nested loop - Multiplication Table */
main()
{
    int i,j;

    for(i=1;i<=20;i++)
       {
          for(j=1;j<=10;j++)
             printf("\n%d * %d = %d ",j,i,j*i);
          getch();   /* for waiting each table */
       }
}
```

The following is another program to find the **sine** value without using library function. The general formula for **sin(x)** is

$$\textbf{sin (x)} = x^1 / 1! - x^3 / 3! + x^5 / 5! \dots$$

Take the expression as **a / b**, where **a** is $x^i$ and **b** is **i** !. Find the sum of this expression and for every execution, sign has to be changed alternately. The given value should be converted into radius using the formula

$$rad = ( x * 3.14 )/180;$$

***Example:***

```
/* To find sin(x) value without using library fn */
#include <math.h>
main( )
    {
       int i,j,f,sign=1;
       float x,rad,s=0;

       printf("\nEnter the radius : ");
       scanf("%f",&x);
       rad = (x*3.14)/180; /*Converting radius value*/

       for(i=1;i<=10;i=i+2)
       {
          f=1;
          for(j=1;j<=i;j++) /* for i! value */
             f = f * j;
          s = s + pow(rad,i) / f * sign;
          sign = -sign; /* Alter the sign */
       }
       printf("\nSin(%3.0f) = %5.2f ",x,s);
    }
```

Output:

```
Enter the radius :  45
Sin(45) = 0.71
```

## 3.4  break STATEMENT—TO STOP THE PROCESS

The looping statement is used to execute a statement repeatedly for a specific number of times. There is no provision to stop the execution in the middle of the looping statement. The **break** statement provides the facility to exit from the loop when required. The **break** is mostly used in loops like **for, while, do–while** and **switch** statements. When it is used in the program it terminates the execution of the block or jumps from the current block to the next.

The following program sums up the positive numbers only and when user gives a negative number, the program breaks the process.

### *Example:*

```
/* Example for calculating the sum of positive numbers using break
statement */
main( )
{
   int n,s=0;
   printf("\nEnter numbers one by one -ve to stop\n");
   do
   {
      scanf("%d",&n);
      if (n>0)
         s=s +n;
      else
         break;
   }while(1);
   printf("\nSum = %d ",s);
}
```

Output:

```
Enter numbers one by one and -ve to stop
3
5
1
-4
Sum = 9
```

The **break** statement is used to terminate the execution process from the block where it is specified.

*Example:*

```
/* Example for break statement */
#include <math.h>
main( )
{
    int i,j;

    for(i=1;i<=5;i++)
        for(j=1;j<=5;j++)
            if (j%2= =0)
                break;
            else
                printf("\ni= %d - j=%d",i,j);
}
```

Output:
```
    i = 1 - j=1
    i = 2 - j=1
    i = 3 - j=1
    i = 4 - j=1
    i = 5 - j=1
```

Here, when the value of **j** is **2**, the expression **j** %2 is **0**. So the control will exit from the inner loop (i.e. **j**th loop) and not from both. So, the **j** loop will never execute more than once.

Check the following pseudo codes for understanding more about the break statement.

```
(1)  main()
     {
         printf("\nHello");
         {
            printf("\nWelcome");
            break;
            printf("\nTo India");
         }
     }

(2)  main()
     {
     Statement
     {
     Statement
             {
                  Statement
                  Break;
                  Statement
             }
     Statement
         }
     }
```

## 3.5 continue STATEMENT

Normally, the body of the loop will be executed for every iteration. Suppose if we wish to skip the body of the loop at a particular time or condition or some other situation, the **continue** statement is used.

Let us consider that there is a program for processing the data of *N* students. If a few students of the class had left (for example, rollno's 10, 15 and 30), how can we get details except numbers 10, 15 and 30? The solution is using the **continue** statement as follows:

```
for(i = 1; i <= 60; i++) // Assume 60 Students
   if (( rollno = =10)||( rollno = =15)||(rollno= =30))
      continue; // Continue with next student
   else
      {
         // Read the details of students
      }
```

Another example is printing all the numbers from **1** to **n** except the numbers which are divisible by **3**. For this program, when **(i%3 == 0)** the number must not be printed and the execution must continue with the next **i** value.

### *Example:*

```
/* Example for continue statement */
main()
{
   int n,i;

   printf("\nHow many no.");
   scanf("%d",&n);

   for(i=1;i<=n;i++)
      if (i%3= =0)
         continue;
      else
         printf("%d\t",i);
}
```

Output:
```
How many no. 10
     1   2   4   5   7   8   10
```

Here for every value of **i**, the condition is checked. If the value of **i** is divisible by **3**, the print statement is skipped and the execution continues with the next number.

### *Note:*
**continue** cannot be used for other than the looping statements.

# REVIEW QUESTIONS ✍

1. What is the necessity of control statements.
2. Explain the unconditional control statement with example.
3. Explain the forward and backward jump with necessary example.
4. What are the conditional control statements?
5. Explain **if-else** with an example.
6. How to use conditional operator?
7. Discuss the **nested-if** statement with an example.
8. Write a program to find the maximum of three numbers using conditional operator.
9. Explain the **switch-case** statement with example.
10. Whether default is mandatory in all the switch-case. (True/False)
11. Strings are allowed as a case values in switch-case. (True/False)
12. What is role of looping statement?
13. Explain the entry controlled (**while**) looping statement.
14. Explain the exit controlled (**do-while**) looping statement.
15. Write a program to find the Max of N numbers using loop.
16. Explain the nested loop.
17. What is the difference between **break** and **continue**?
18. **continue** can be used in control statement. (True/False)

# Arrays

## 4.1 INTRODUCTION

What is the use of a variable? Generally a variable is used to store a value, which may be used for further reference. In a simple variable, only one value can be stored at a time. For example

```
a=10; /* Now the value of a is 10 */
a=20; /* Now the value of a is 20 */
```

In the first statement, value **10** is assigned to the variable **a** and in the next it is replaced by a new value **20**. Can we refer the previous value of **a**, i.e., **10**? No, we cannot. Then how to preserve the previous value? One solution is, using more variables to store each value.

For example, to store **5** values, we can use the variables like **a, b, c, d** and **e**. It is very difficult to maintain when there are **n** variables and **n** values in a program. It may cause the program to look like:

```
/* Example to illustrate the need of array */
main()
{
    int a=1,b=2,c=3,d=4,e=5,...,z=26;
    int sum;
    sum = a+b+c+d+e+...+z;
    printf("\nSum : %d ",sum);
}
```

In this example, there are **26** variables, from **a** to **z** are of the same data type. It is very difficult to write large programs with 26 variables repeated in many parts of the program. So, the final solution for these kind of problem is an **array** and the definition is

- Array is a collection of data items
- All the data items must be of same data type and
- They are stored in consecutive memory locations

## 4.2  HOW TO DECLARE ARRAY VARIABLES?

The elementary variables are declared as follows:

```
int a,b,c;   /* Simple variable Declaration */
```

Similarly, an array variable can also be as follows:

```
Data-type  Array-variable  [size];
```

where
- **Data-type** refers to the type of data such as int, char, etc.,
- **Array-variable** refers to the name of the array variable
- **Size** refers to the maximum number of elements that can be stored in the array and the size must be an integer value.

Example for array declaration is

```
int a [ 5 ] ;
```

- **a** is the name of the array variable of type **int**eger
- In the variable **a,** we can store **5** integer values.
- All these elements are stored in consecutive memory locations

Let us consider that the starting address of the array is **1000** and the remaining elements are stored as follows. Each element of the array occupies **two** bytes because of **int**eger data type.

| Element Location | 1 | 2 | 3 | 4 | 5 |
|---|---|---|---|---|---|
| Memory Address | 1000 | 1002 | 1004 | 1006 | 1008 |

## 4.3  HOW TO REFER THE VALUES OF THE ARRAY VARIABLE?

The above diagram illustrates how the elements of an array are stored. In **C** the first element of the array is stored at the location **0** not from **1.** So the total numbers of elements are **5,** but the elements are stored in the locations **0,1,2,3,4 and 5.** These elements are accessed as follows:

- First element is referred as **a[0]** and its address is **1000**
- Second element is referred as **a[1]** and its address is **1002**
- Third element is referred as **a[2]** and its address is **1004** etc.
- Here **0, 1, 2, ...** are called subscripts (or) index. So array is also called **subscripted variable**

The above type of array is called **one-dimensional array,** because the information in the index is enough to refer to any data item in the array.

## 4.4  ASSIGNING DATA FOR ARRAY

We are allowed to assign some values to the variables at the time of declaring variables. Like a simple variable assignment, the values can also be assigned to the array variable as given in the following example.

`int a[5] = {10,20,30,40,50};`

Here,

    1st element 10 is stored at location a[0]
    2nd element 20 is stored at location a[1]
    3rd element 30 is stored at location a[2]
    4th element 40 is stored at location a[3] and
    5th element 50 is stored at location a[4]

The following are some of the ways to assign values to array variables.

- `int a[10] = {20,30};`
  Here **20 (10 * 2 = 20)** memory locations are reserved for variable **a,** because of **10** integers. But we use only **4** and the remaining **16** locations are unused.
- `int a[ ] = {10,20,30};`
  In this declaration, the above problem has been solved. The size of array is decided automatically depending on the number of values in the assignment.
- Suppose if we wish to initialize the value **0** to the whole array, the following declaration can be used.
  `int a[100] = {0};`
- The default values of variable elements are **garbage value.**

## 4.5  RELATIONSHIP BETWEEN THE LOOP AND ARRAYS

The elements of the array are referred by specifying the array variable name followed by the index as `a[0]`, `a[1]`, `a[2]`, `a[3]`, etc. If the number of elements is less, we can use the indices to refer the individual elements. But if we have to refer 100 elements sequentially what can we do? We can have 100 statements to refer to the individual elements, but it requires a lot of typing like:

```
printf("%d",a[ 0 ] );
printf("%d",a[ 1 ] );
printf("%d",a[ 2 ] );
printf("%d",a[ 3 ] );
   .  .  .
printf("%d",a[ 9 ] );
```

The alternative way is to use a looping in which the index can be varied is shown below.

```
for (i=0;i<=9;i++)
   printf("%d",a[ i ] );
```

The following is a simple example, which illustrates how to use arrays in the program. The number of steps involved in referring the elements of array using looping statement is also illustrated.

### Example:

```
/*Example for Reading and Displaying the elements */
main()
{
   int i, a[5];

   printf("\nEnter 5 Elements for array \n");
   for(i=0;i<5;i++)
      scanf("%d",&a[i]);

   printf("\nYour Given values are\n");
   for(i=0;i<5;i++)
      printf("%d\t",a[i]);
}
```

Output:

```
Enter 5 Elements for array
10   20   30   40   50
Your Given values are
10   20   30   40   50
```

Let us see some examples using arrays, how it is used in applications. The following is a program to finding the biggest of **N** numbers, the algorithm is:

1. Read **N** numbers into the array
2. Assign the first element of array to the variable **MAX** and assume this is the biggest one
3. Compare this element with the remaining elements of the array
4. If any element is bigger than the value in **MAX**, assign this value as new value of **MAX**
5. If not, do not change the existing value of **MAX**
6. Repeat the steps from 3 to 5 till the last element is compared
7. Finally the value in **MAX** is the biggest element in the array

### Example:

```
/* To find the maximum of N values */
main()
{
   int i, n, max, a[5];
```

```
    printf("\nHow many values :");
    scanf("%d",&n);
    printf("\nEnter %d values \n",n);
    for(i=0;i<n;i++)
        scanf("%d",&a[i]);

    printf("\nYour Given values are\n");

    for(i=0;i<n;i++)
        printf("%d\t",a[i]);

    max=a[0]; /* Assume a[0] is a maximum */

    for(i=1;i<n;i++)
        if ( max<a[i] )
            max=a[i];

    printf("\nMaximum Number : %d ",max);
}
```

**Output:**

```
How many values: 5

Enter 5 values
66 11 22 55 33

Your Given values are
66 11 22 55 33

Maximum Number: 66
```

The following is another example to find the mean value for the set of numbers.

1. Read the set of values one by one
2. Add those values one by one keep its sum
3. Finally divide the sum by the number of elements
4. The result of the above is called mean value of the set

***Example:***

```
/* To find the mean for a set of values  */
main()
{
    int i,n,a[10];
    float s=0,mean;

    printf("\nHow many values :");
    scanf("%d",&n);

    printf("\nEnter %d  values \n",n);

    for(i=0;i<n;i++)
```

```
    {
      scanf("%d",&a[i]);
      s = s + a[i];
    }

    mean = s / n;
    printf("\nSum   = %5.2f  ",s);
    printf("\nMean value : %5.2f ",mean);
}
```

**Output:**

```
How many values : 3
Enter 3 values
11  22  33
Sum  = 66.00
Mean value : 22.00
```

Arrays are used in many applications and almost in all kinds of programs. The following is an idea for inserting a new element in the array. The array is

```
        a[1]=10; a[2]=20; a3]=30; a[4]=40; and a[5]=50;
```

To insert a new element in this array, we require two kinds of information: the location where the new element is going to be inserted and the value in that location.

The insertion at the end of the array is made very simple. Suppose we want to insert a new element in the 3rd location. The 3rd element should be moved to 4th and like this 4th moved to 5th etc. Finally the 3rd location is empty and so we can assign the new value to this location directly. The movement will be made from the end and not from the first. Otherwise the values will be overwritten. In general **i**th element will be at **(i+1)**th location.

### *Example:*

```
/* To insert a new item in the specified location */
main()
{
    int i,n,p,value,a[10];

    printf("\nHow many values :");
    scanf("%d",&n);
    printf("\nEnter %d  values \n",n);
    for(i=0;i<n;i++)
        scanf("%d",&a[i]);

    printf("\nWhere toinsert a new value :");
    scanf("%d",&p);

    printf("\nValue of that location :");
    scanf("%d",&value);
```

```
printf("\nData Before Inserting\n");
for(i=0;i<n;i++)
  printf("%d\t",a[i]);

for(i=n-1;i>=p;i--)
  a[i+1] = a[i];
     /* Moving ith element to (i+1)th location */

  a[p] = value;

  printf("\nData  After Inserting\n");

  for(i=0;i<=n;i++)
     printf("%d\t",a[i]);
}
```

**Output:**

```
How many values :5
Enter 5   values
10   20   30   40   50
Where to insert a new value :3
Value of that location :100
Data Before Inserting
10      20      30      40      50
Data  After  Inserting
10      20      30      100     40      50
```

## 4.6  MORE DIMENSIONS—MULTI-DIMENSIONAL ARRAY

We discussed one-dimensional array and some simple applications in the previous section. There are new problems like how to store the **5** marks of **N** students in the class. For one student, we can declare the arrays as follows.

```
int marks[5];
```

How to store the same for **N** students? Here comes the **two-dimensional array**. By making a simple modification to the one-dimensional array declaration, two-dimensional array can be created.

A very good example of a two-dimensional array is a **matrix** represented by the number of rows and columns. To refer any element of a matrix, we need two kinds of information—row number and the column number. Suppose there is a matrix with 3 rows and 3 columns, the representation is as follows.

Columns (3 Columns)

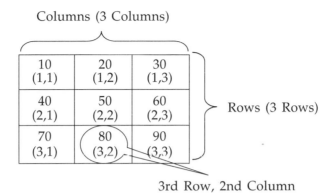

Rows (3 Rows)

3rd Row, 2nd Column

## 4.7 HOW TO DECLARE A TWO-DIMENSIONAL ARRAY?

Similar to one-dimensional array and simple variable declaration, the two-dimensional array is declared as

```
Data-type Array-variable [size1] [size2];
```

In two-dimensional array, we can store the maximum of **(size1 * size2)** number of elements. For example:

```
int a[20][10];
```

Here **a** is the two-dimensional array variable and we can store **200** elements (because **20 * 10 = 200**). The index of the array in this array also starts from **0**. Total memory allocation for this array is **200 * 2 = 400** bytes.

## 4.8 HOW TO PROCESS THE ELEMENTS IN A TWO-DIMENSIONAL ARRAY

As stated above, for any reference we need two kinds of information. In case of matrix, the row and the column of the element must be specified. For example, the above array is accessed as follows.

a [ 0 ] [0 ] => First row First Column value
a [ 0 ] [1 ] => First row Second Column value
a [ 0 ] [2 ] => First row Third Column value
a [ 1 ] [ 0] => Second row First Column value
a [ 1 ] [ 1] => Second row Second Column value
. . .

The indexes of arrays are in a sequence. In a matrix (with rows & columns) each row contains a number of columns. Can we simplify the above statements? Think about the nested loops, in which, for every value of the first loop, second loop will execute a number of times. Apply this approach here. Assume there are two loops (nested) namely **i** and **j,** for rows and columns respectively. So, every value of **i, j** will execute N times.

```
for ( i=1 ; i < n; i++ )
   for ( j=1 ; j < n; j++ )
      // Statement of nested loop
```

Here, statements are executed **n * n** times. That is for every value of **i**, the **j** will be executed **n** times. The individual statements are simplified by using nested loop as shown below

```
for ( i=0 ; i < 3 ; i++ )
   for ( j=0 ; j < 3 ; j++ )
      printf( "%d", a [i][j] );
```

Think about the relationship between the two-dimensional arrays and the nested looping statements.

## 4.9  ASSIGNING VALUES

Once again, the elements of two-dimensional array can also be assigned at the time of declaration as follows.

```
int a[2][3] = {
                {1,2,3},       First row
                {4,5,6}        Second row
              };
```

- Each row is separated by braces { } and each element by commas.
- Here there are two rows and three columns.
- The values like **1, 2, 3** are assigned to the first row and the elements **4, 5, 6** are assigned to the second row.

The following is an example program of a two-dimensional array illustration for reading and displaying the elements of the matrix.

**Example:**

```
/* Example for reading and displaying a matrix */
main()
{
   int i,j,r,c,a[5][5];   /*Declared as 5 x 5 matrix*/

   printf("\nNumber of rows : ");
   scanf("%d",&r);

   printf("\nNumber of columns : ");
   scanf("%d",&c);

   printf("\nEnter %d x %d matrix\n",r,c);

   for(i=0;i<r;i++)
      for(j=0;j<c;j++)
         scanf("%d",&a[i][j]);
```

```
    printf("\nYour matrix is \n");

    for(i=0;i<r;i++)
      {
         for(j=0;j<c;j++)
            printf("%d\t",a[i][j]);
         printf("\n");
      }
}
```

**Output:**
```
Number of rows : 2
Number of columns : 2
Enter 2 × 2 matrix
10   20   30   40

Your matrix is
10   20
30   40
```

Another application of two-dimensional array is Matrix multiplication. The important condition for matrix multiplication is that the number of columns in the first matrix and the number of rows in the second matrix must be equal.

***Example:***
```
/* Matrix Multiplication with equal rows & columns  */
   main()
   {
      int i,j,k,row,col,a[5][5],b[5][5],c[5][5];

      printf("\nNumber of Rows    : ");
      scanf("%d",&row);

      printf("\nNumber of Columns : ");
      scanf("%d",&col);

      printf("\nEnter first matrix values\n");
      for(i=0;i<row;i++)
         for(j=0;j<col;j++)
            scanf("%d",&a[i][j]);

      printf("\nEnter Second matrix values\n");

      for(i=0;i<row;i++)
         for(j=0;j<col;j++)
            scanf("%d",&b[i][j]);

      for(i=0;i<row;i++)
```

```
        for(j=0;j<col;j++)
        {
          c[i][j] = 0;
          for(k=0;k<col;k++)
            c[i][j] = c[i][j] + a[i][k] * b[k][j];
        }
      printf("\nResult matrix\n");
      for(i=0;i<row;i++)
        {
          for(j=0;j<col;j++)
            printf("\t%d",c[i][j]);

          printf("\n");
        }
  }
```

**Output:**

```
Number of Rows     : 2
Number of Columns : 2
Enter first matrix values
1 2 3 4
Enter Second matrix values
1 2 3 4
Result matrix
    7    10
    15   22
```

Another example is the transpose of a matrix. Here, the elements in the row are transferred to the elements of columns and vice versa.

***Example:***

```
/* Transpose of Matrix */
main()
{
  int i, j, row, col, a[5][5],b[5][5];

  printf("\nNumber of rows    : ");
  scanf("%d",&row);
  printf("\nNumber of Columns : ");
  scanf("%d",&col);
  printf("\nEnter the matrix values\n");

  for(i=0;i<row;i++)
    for(j=0;j<col;j++)
      scanf("%d",&a[i][j]);
```

```
        printf("\nTransposed matrix is \n");
        for(i=0;i<row;i++)
           {
               for(j=0;j<col;j++)
                  {
                      b[i][j] = a[j][i];
                      printf("%5d ",b[i][j]);
                  }
                  printf("\n");
           }
   }
```

**Output:**

```
Number of rows    : 2
Number of Columns : 2
Enter the matrix values
1 2 3 4
Transposed matrix is
1      3
2      4
```

The next example is entirely different from matrix and one of the applications of a two-dimensional array called preparation of Electricity Bill for N customers.

***Example:***

```
/* Electricity Bill preparation for N customers  */
main()
{
   char name[50][15];
   int i,n,cusno[50];
   float oldr[50],newr[50],units,amt;

   clrscr( );
   printf("\nHow many customers : ");
   scanf("%d",&n);

   for(i=0;i<n;i++)
      {
          fflush(stdin);
          printf("\nDetails of  %d   customer : ",i+1);
          printf("\nEnter the name :");
          gets(name[i]);
          printf("\nConsumer Number : ");
          scanf("%d",&cusno[i]);
          printf("\nOld Units :");
          scanf("%f",&oldr[i]);
          printf("\nNew Units :");
          scanf("%f",&newr[i]);
```

```
          }
    /* Calculation Part  */
    for(i=0;i<n;i++)
         {
         units = newr[i] - oldr[i];
         amt   = units * 0.75;
         printf("\n\t ELECTRICITY BILL \n");
         printf("\nName:%s\t Number:%d",name[i],cusno[i]);
         printf("\n\nOld Reading\tNew Reading\tUnits\tAmount");
         printf("\n%5.2f \t %5.2f \t %5.2f \t
              %5.2f",oldr[i],newr[i],units,amt);

         printf("\nPress a key to next bill ...");
         getch( );
         }
      getch( );
    }
```

**Output:**

```
How many customers : 2
Details of  1  customer :
Enter the name : Karthikeyan
Consumer Number : 1000
Old Units : 235
New Units : 400
Details of  2  customer :
Enter the name: Sanjay
Consumer Number: 1001
Old Units: 5678
New Units: 7500
```

```
          ELECTRICITY BILL
Name:Karthikeyan          Number:1000
Old Reading  New Reading    Units    Amount
235.00          400.00      165.00   123.75
Press a key to next bill...

          ELECTRICITY BILL
Name:Sanjay          Number:1001
Old Reading  New Reading    Units    Amount
5678.00         7500.00     1822.00  1366.50
Press a key to next bill...
```

## 4.10  MULTI-DIMENSIONAL ARRAY

We have seen a two-dimensional array and how it has been used in some applications like matrix and Electricity Bill preparation. Suppose there is a need to design software in the University to maintain all the information about all the students. There are many colleges, each college has many students and each student has many subjects. In this case, we require three kinds of information to access the particulars of one student. That is the college to which the student belongs to, class name and roll number of the student. Now we have to use multi-dimensional array or three-dimensional array and it can be declared as follows:

```
int student[75][30][60];
```

This refers to **75** colleges in the university, **30** classes in a college and **60** students each class. For example, **student [3][10][6]**, refers 3rd College, **10**th Class and 6th Student. This way we can extend the arrays for any kind of applications.

## 4.11   ARRAY INDEX OUT OF BOUNDS

The reference of any array should be very clear, that is the range of array. Suppose if we refer the index of an array without proper specification, we may get garbage value. Look at the following example.

```
#include <stdio.h>
main()
{
   int a[2]={10,20},i;
   for(i=0;i<10;i++)
      printf("%d\t",a[i]);
}
```

Only two values were assigned to the array variable **a,** but in the program we refer **10** elements. First two elements will be retrieved properly, the remaining elements will be a garbage value.

## REVIEW QUESTIONS ✍

1. Define array.
2. What is the necessity of arrays?
3. What is one-dimensional array? Give example.
4. What is two-dimensional array? Give example.
5. Write a program to illustrate how to read/write array.
6. The elements of array must of same type. (True/False)
7. The elements of array are stored in consecutive memory locations. (True/False)
8. Why the elements of an array index starts with 0?
9. Write a program to perform all kind of array operations.
10. What is the maximum size of array?
11. Write a program to delete an element in an array.
12. Write a program to prepare a mark list using two dimensional array.

# Chapter 5

# *Strings*

## 5.1 INTRODUCTION

What is a string? *A string is a collection of characters that are enclosed within double quotes* (" "). A string can also be also called a **character array**. Inside the double quotes, any acceptable character from the character set can be present. To store a single character, we have to use the **char** data type. But there is no specific data type to store a string of characters. This problem is overcome by declaring the group of characters in an array, using **char** data type. Therefore a simple string is declared in one-dimensional character array. The format for declaring the string variable is as follows.

```
char variable [size];
```

- **char** is the data type of the variable
- **variable** of a character array represents the name given to the array
- **size** represents the maximum number of characters that can be stored in the array

There is no difference between the one-dimensional array and the string. So the declaration is

```
char str[15];
```

Here **str** is the name of the array variable, which is also called as string variable. The variable **str** can have a maximum of 15 characters.

## 5.2 WHAT IS THE END OF A STRING?

In case of numeric array, there is no special character to indicate the end of any array. Only we have to use limit to travel in the numeric array. But in character array or string, the **NULL** character '\0', is indicate the end of string. All the strings in C are ended by this character. The ASCII value of this character is **0** (zero). Usually this **NULL** character will be appended automatically at the end of string by the complier. The programmer is also allowed to insert this one explicitly in some cases.

## 5.3 ASSIGNING VALUES TO THE STRING VARIABLE

The values to the string can be assigned in any one of the formats shown below:

1. `char str[10]={'K','A','R','T','H','I'};`
   - In this one-dimensional array, values are assigned character by character to the string variable **str**.
2. `char str[10]="KARTHI";`
   - In contrast to the above mentioned character-by-character assignment, the entire string can also be assigned to the string variable **str**.
3. `char str[ ]="Coimbatore";`
   - Here, the size of the variable **str** is decided automatically depending on the number of characters. Memory allocation is done automatically based on the number of characters assigned to the variable.

The following diagram shows the values and their memory locations

`char name[ ]="KARTHI";`

| Location → | 0 | 1 | 2 | 3 | 4 | 5 | 6 | |
|---|---|---|---|---|---|---|---|---|
| Character → | K | A | R | T | H | I | \0 | |

From this figure, we may conclude

The character **K** is stored at name[0]
The character **A** is stored at name[1]
The character **R** is stored at name[2]
The character **T** is stored at name[3]
The character **H** is stored at name[4]
The character **I** is stored at name[5] and
The end of string **\0** is at name[6].

## 5.4 HOW TO READ A STRING?

Input for the string can be read character by character using %c format string or the whole string using the format string %s. Reading a single character at a time is not entertained. The following code can be used for reading the string.

```
char name[25];
scanf("%s",s);
```

Normally when we read a value for any variable, we have to specify the address of that variable like **&a**, to read a value. But here there is no need of & operator.

```
/* Simple example to read and display a string */
#include <string.h>
main( )
{
   char str[15];
   scanf("%s",str);
   printf("\nString : %s ",str);
}
```

Unfortunately **scanf( )** function does not allow a blank space in the input. For example, we are not allowed to enter the values like "**My India**", because there is a space between the two. But, we can use **gets( )** function to read string with blank spaces. Otherwise, we can use [...] and [^ ...] options in **scanf( )**.

The whole string can be read or displayed using the **%s** format string, this provision is not available in numeric array. The following is a program illustrating how the characters of the array are processed.

```
/* To read Characters of a string */
main( )
{
   char s[15];
   int i=0;

   scanf("%s",s);
   printf("\nString : ");

   while(s[i] != '\0')
      printf("%c",s[i++] );
}
```

The **while** loop will execute until the end of the string (i.e. '\0') and it is checked by the condition **s[i] != '\0'**. If the character present in the **i**th location is equal to '\0', then the loop will stop its assigned function.

The following program counts the occurrence of a particular character in a string. For this, the particular character that we desire to count has to be compared with the other characters present in the string. If there is a matching, the counter value is incremented by one.

*Example:*

```
/* Counting the occurrence of character */
#include <string.h>
main()
{
   int i=0,count=0;
   char s[25],ch;
```

```
printf("\nEnter a string : ");
gets(s);
printf("\nCharacter to check : ");
scanf("%c",&ch);

while( s[i] ! = '\0')
     if ( ch= =s[i++])
         count++;

     printf("\n%c occurs %d times ",ch,count);
}
```

**Output:**

```
Enter a string : india
Character to check : i
i occurs 2 times
```

## 5.5  LIBRARY FUNCTIONS FOR STRINGS

The operations such as copying a string, joining two strings, extracting a portion of the string, determining the length of a string, etc., cannot be done using arithmetic operators. The string-based library functions are used to perform this type of operations and they are located in the header file **<string.h>**

Four important string-based library functions are

1. strlen( ) – To find the length of a string
2. strcpy( ) – To copy one string into another
3. strcat( ) – To join strings
4. strcmp( ) – To compare two strings.

### 5.5.1  strlen( )  (Finding the Length of the String)

The function, **strlen( )** is used to find the length of the given string. The general format is as follows.

```
int strlen ( str );
```

Here **str** is a string variable and it returns the number of characters present in the given string. Look at the following examples.

1. char  str[10]  =  "Karthi";
   len  =  strlen(str);
   ⇨ It returns length of the string as **6** and it is stored in the variable **len**.
2. len  =  strlen("God");
   ⇨ Instead of declaring a variable to the character array, it can also be passed directly as in this example. The value **3** will be returned as a result.

3. `char s[10] = "Welcome\0";`
   `len = strlen(s);`
   ⇨ This example returns the length as **7,** because it will not count the NULL character ('\0') as a character of the string.
4. `len=strlen("ABbbbCD ");`
   ⇨ where **b** is a blank space. In this case, the blank space is also treated as a character. So, the length of this string is **7.** (Including the blank space)
5. `len = strlen("AB+*/CD");`
   ⇨ In this case, we have a combination of alphabets and special characters. So, the result of **len** is 7.

**Note:**
The NULL character (\0) is not a countable character in the string.

### 5.5.2 `strcpy( )` (Assigning the String)

The function **strcpy( )** is used to copy the content of one string into another. We cannot use the **assignment operator** ( = ) to assign a string to the variable.

```
char s[15];
s = "Man"; /* This is not possible in C */
```

The general format is

$$\boxed{\texttt{strcpy( s1, s2);}}$$

where **s1** and **s2** are string variables.
    Here **s2** is the source string and **s1** is the destination string. After the execution of this function, the content of **s2** is copied into **s1** and finally both the **s1** and **s2** contains the same values.

**Example:**

1. `char s1[ ] = "Karthi";`
   `char s2[ ] = "Good";`
   `strcpy(s1,s2);`
   ⇨ After the execution, the content of the string **s2** is copied into string **s1**. Therefore the string **"Karthi"** is replaced with the string **"Good".** Finally both **s1** and **s2** will have the string **"Good".**
2. `char s1[10];`
   `char s2[10] = "Karthi";`
   `strcpy(s1,s2);`
   ⇨ Here also the content of **s2** is copied into **s1** and both contain the string as **Karthi.**

### 5.5.3 `strcat( )` (Joining Strings)

We are not able to use + operator to join two strings. The function **strcat( )** is used for joining two strings. The general format is as follows

```
strcat(s1 , s2);
```

Here **s1** and **s2** are the string variables. Here the content of **s2** is appended (or) joined to the contents of **s1**. Look at the following examples:

1. `char s1[10] = "Good" , s2 [10] = "Morning";`
   `strcat (s1,s2);`
   ⇨ After the execution of this function, **s1** contains **"GoodMorning"** and **s2** contains **"Morning"**.
2. `char s1[10] = " " , s2 [10] = "Welcome";`
   `strcat (s1,s2);`
   ⇨ After execution, both **s1** and **s2** have **"Welcome"**, because the first variable **s1** does not have any character in it.

## 5.5.4 `strcmp( )` (To Compare)

This function is used to compare two strings. To compare any numeric values we use relational operators. By using these operators we cannot compare strings. The **strcmp( )** performs the function of comparison. The general format is as follows.

```
int strcmp(s1, s2);
```

where **s1** and **s2** are string variables. This function returns any one of the three possible results.

- Result is **0** when both the strings are equal. (s1 = s2)
- Result is **Positive** value, if **s1** is greater than **s2**. (s1>s2)
- Result is **Negative** if **s1** is less than **s2**. (s1<s2)

### Note:

The result of comparison is obtained by calculating the difference between the ASCII values of the corresponding characters. For example, if we compare the characters '**a**' and '**b**', the compiler uses its ASCII value.

### How the actual comparison is made?

The first character of **s1** is compared with the first character of **s2**. If they are equal, the process passes on to the next character on the string until they meet with mismatch or no more character to process. The process of comparison is terminated if any mismatching occurs or the end of the string is reached.

### Example:

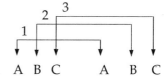

1. `char s1[ 5 ] = "ABC";`
   `char s2[ 5 ] = "ABC";`
   `strcmp(s1,s2);`
   ⇨ This function returns **0** as a result, because both **s1** and **s2** contain the same characters. The character of **s1** equals to the character of **s2**. So, the result is **0** (the ASCII difference of these characters).

2. ```c
   char  s1[ 5 ]  =  "ABC";
   char  s2[ 5 ]  =  "abc";
   strcmp(s1,s2);
   ```
   ⇨ This function returns **–32** as a result, as ASCII difference between **A** and **a** is **–32** (65 – 97). The ASCII value of '**A**' is **65** and '**a**' is **97**.
3. ```c
   char  s1[ 5 ]  =  "ABz";
   char  s2[ 5 ]  =  "ABC";
   strcmp(s1,s2);
   ```
   ⇨ This function returns **55** as result. Because ASCII difference between **z** and **C** is **55** (122 – 67). The ASCII value of '**z**' is **122** and '**c**' is **67**.

Here is a program to illustrate how to read a string and find out its length without using the library function.

***Example:***

```c
/* Implementing strlen( ) function */
#include <string.h>
main( )
{
   int i= 0;
   char str[25];
   printf("\nEnter a string    : ");
   gets(str);
   printf("\nYour given string : ");
   while(str[i])
      printf("%c",str[i++]);
   printf("\nLength of string  : %d ",i);
}
```

**Output:**
```
Enter a string    : karthi
Your given string : karthi
Length of string  : 6
```

Here the statement **while(str[i])** will return **TRUE** until the **NULL** character. Finally, the variable **i** contains the number of characters in the string, which gives the string length.

### How to check whether the given string is palindrome or not?

Whenever the given string and its reverse are equal, that string is called **palindrome**. For example, the string **"liril"**, both the original string and its reverse are equal. So **liril** is one of the palindromes. The character comparison is illustrated below.

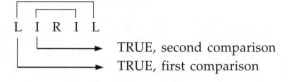

If the result of all the comparisons is **TRUE**, then we can decide that the string is a **palindrome**. The comparison starts from the first character and last character, then 2nd character from the first and 2nd character from the last and continue the same up to the half of the string. If any one character is not matched, we can decide that the given string is not a palindrome.

Here, first the given string is assumed as palindrome and set value of **poly** as **1**. Whenever whenever there is mismatch **poly** changes to **poly=0**.

### Example:

```
/*Check whether the given string is palindrome or not*/
#include <string.h>
main()
{
    int i,l,poly=1;
    char s[50];

    printf("\nEnter a string    : ");
    gets(s);
    printf("\nGiven string  is  : %s",s);
    l=strlen(s);
    printf("\nLength of string  :  %d\n",l);
    l = l-1;
    for(i=0;i<=l/2;i++)
       if (s[i]!=s[l-i])
       poly=0;

    if (poly = =1)
       printf("\n'%s'  is polindrome",s);
    else
       printf("\n'%s'  is not polindrome",s);
}
```

Output:
```
Enter a string    : karthi
Given string  is  : karthi
Length of string  :  6
'karthi' is not polindrome

Enter a string    : malayalam
Given string  is  : malayalam
Length of string  :  9
'malayalam' is polindrome
```

The condition **if (s[i]!= s[l–i])** is used to check the characters. The length of the string is in the variable **l**. The characters are stored from **0th** location and so the last character is at **l–1**. Here the value of **l** is decremented by 1. So, for every iteration of loop, **i** value is used to travel in the right side and the value of **l–i** is used to travel in the opposite side.

The following is another interesting example frequently used in many programs, called sorting of N names using string functions.

**Example:**

```c
/* Sorting of N names */
#include <string.h>
main()
{
   int i,j,n;
   char str[15][20],temp[20];
   printf("\nHow many names :");
   scanf("%d",&n);
   fflush(stdin);  /* To clear the buffer  */
   for(i=0;i<n;i++)
   {
      printf("\nEnter %2d name :",i+1);
      gets(str[i]);
   }
  printf("\nNames Before Sorting\n----------------");
  for(i=0;i<n;i++)
     printf("\n%s",str[i]);

  for(i=0;i<n-1;i++)
  for(j=i+1;j<n;j++)
     if (strcmp(str[i],str[j])>0)
                    /* Comparing String */
     {
        strcpy(temp,str[i]);
        strcpy(str[i],str[j]);
        strcpy(str[j],temp);
     }
  printf("\nNames After Sorting\n-----------------");
  for(i=0;i<n;i++)
     printf("\n%s",str[i]);

     getch( );
   }
```

**Output:**
```
How many names :3
Enter  1 name :peter england
Enter  2 name :zodiac
Enter  3 name :raymonds
```

```
Names Before Sorting
--------------------
peter england
zodiac
raymonds

Names After Sorting
-------------------
peter england
raymonds
zodiac
```

The names are compared using the **strcmp( )** function. If the result of comparison is positive, we can decide that the first string is greater and the second string is smaller. If so the strings are swapped. The swapping is performed using the **strcpy()** function.

Another program, which is going to count the number of characters, words and lines in the text. In this program, the input is the number of lines.

## 5.6  HOW TO READ A TEXT INPUT?

Using the advantage of **scanf( )** function it can be achieved. The following is a statement for reading a text

```
char s[250] ; /*String declaration */
scanf ( "%[^z]",s);
```

This function reads the characters until the character '**z**'. When we give this character, the process terminates from the process of getting input.

Alphabets in lower- and upper-cases are counted by checking whether the character is between alphabet values (a–z/A–Z). If so it is treated as an alphabet (Checking by its ASCII value). The following is the condition to check alphabet

```
if ((s[i]>='A')&&(s[i]<='Z')||(s[i]>='a')&&(s[i] <='z' ))
    /* Count Alphabets */
```

In general, the words are identified by blank space. Sometimes the word is counted when new line starts. So using the value ' ' and '\n' the words are counted. The statement has checked it

```
if ((s[i]= =' ') || (s[i] = = '\n'))
    words++;
```

Number of lines are counted by using the new line character '\n' and the statement is

```
if (s[i]= ='\n')
    lines++;
```

A complete program to count characters, words and lines is given below.

**Example:**

```
/*Counting characters words and lines from the text */
main()
{
   char s[250];

   int lines=0,words=0,alpha=0,i=0;

   printf("Enter a text 'z'  to terminate :\n");
   scanf("%[^z]",s);

   while (s[i] != '\0')
   {
   if ((s[i]>='A')&&(s[i]<='Z')||(s[i]>='a')&&(s[i]<='z'))
      alpha++;

   if ((s[i]==' ') || (s[i]== '\n'))
      words++;

   if (s[i]=='\n')
      lines++;

   i++;
   }
   printf("\nCharacters : %d ",i);
   printf("\nAlphabets  : %d ",alpha);
   printf("\nWords      : %d ",words);
   printf("\nLines      : %d ",lines);
}
```

**Output:**

```
Enter a text 'z'  to terminate :
India is our
country
z

Characters : 19
Alphabets  : 17
Words      : 4
Lines      : 2
```

**Other String Related Library functions are listed below**

1. strrev( ) => This function is used to reverse the string
   char s[ ] ="Hello";
   strrev(s);
   ⇨ Now the content of the string **s** is reversed.

A program to find out whether the given string is palindrome or not using the library function.

```
/* Palindrome checking using library functions */
main()
{
   char s1[15],s2[15];

   clrscr();
   printf("\nEnter a string:");
   scanf("%s",s1);
   strcpy(s2,s1);
   strrev(s2);
   if (strcmp(s1,s2)==0)
      printf("\nGiven strnig is palindrome");
   else
      printf("\nGiven string is not palindrome");

      getch();
}
```

Here the **strrev(s2)** is used to reverse the content and the **strcmp(s1,s2)** is used to compare the two strings. If the result is **0**, string and its reverse are equal. Therefore, the given string are palindrome.

## REVIEW QUESTIONS ✍

1. How to find the end of the string?
2. What is the difference between three representations **a**, **'a'** and **"a"**?
3. How do we read string including blank space?
4. Can we use **scanf()** to read string with blank spaces? If so How?
5. Write a program to find the occurrence of a character?
6. Explain the string based library functions with necessary examples
7. NULL character (end of string) is also counted when we find the length. (True/False)
8. Implement a **strlen( )** function to find the length of string.
9. Characters of string is compared according to the ASCII values (True/False)
10. How to read a text (more than one line)?

# Chapter 6
# *Functions*

## 6.1 INTRODUCTION

A Program is a collection of instructions and in some cases, with repeated statements. If the number of repeated statements in a program is one or two, then it is not a problem. Suppose the number of repeated statements is more, it will automatically increase the size of the program. We can reduce the size of the program by writing these repeated instructions in a separate program. These programs can be utilized whenever needed. That separate code/program is called as a **function**. Function may also be named as procedure. The functions are of two types

1. Library functions.
2. User-defined functions.

## 6.2 READYMADE LIBRARY FUNCTION

This is a special type of function, which is pre-written and present along with the compiler itself. For example, **abs( ), sqrt ( )**, etc. are library functions and we have discussed about them in the second chapter. The drawback of library function is that, it has restricted operations and it is not allowed to alter the existing functionality.

The library functions are just like our readymade dresses. The drawback of ready made is that it will not match everyone's needs, but can be used on suitable occasions.

## 6.3 DESIGN YOUR OWN KIND USER-DEFINED FUNCTIONS

The user can write a function according to his requirements and this type of function is called user-defined function. It is just like designing a dress depending according to a person's taste. So if you are not satisfied with the readymade, design your own.

The purpose of having a function in a program is to reduce the size of the program and in some cases this can also be achieved by using the looping statements. The following is a program. The same program is rewritten next in a reduced format.

```
main()
{
    printf("\nHello");
    printf("\nGood morning");  ⎱  Set 1
    printf("\nHello");         ⎰
    printf("\nGood morning");  ⎱  Set 2
    printf("\nHello");         ⎰
    printf("\nGood morning");
    printf("\nHello");
    printf("\nGood morning");
    printf("\nHello");
    printf("\nGood morning");
            printf("\nHello");
    printf("\nGood morning");
}
```

Can we reduce the size of the above program? Yes, we can. The following is a revised version of the program using **for** looping statement.

```
/* Minimized program using for loop */
main()
{
    int i;
    for(i=1;i<=3;i++)
    {   printf("\nHello");
        printf("\nGood morning");
    }
}
```

Suppose the repetition occurs in different parts of the program instead of a continuous one, looping is not a solution. This can be solved by keeping the repeated set of statements in a separate part of the program (sometimes called sub-program). Whenever these repeated statements are required, the sub-program can be invoked and utilized.

Figure 6.1(a) is a program with repeated code in three places and the aim of all the 10 lines is same. Can we reduce the program size of **Figure 6.1(a)**? Yes, we can, by using subprogram. In **Figure 6.1(b),** the repeated statements are available as a sub-program/ function. This function can be invoked/called wherever the repeated code is necessary.

In **Figure 6.1(a)**, the repeated code is **10** lines, totally it occupies 30 lines, because it is in 3 places (3 * 10 = 30). But in **Figure 6.1(b)**, instead of **10** lines, only one instruction **(CALL)** is used to invoke the sub-program. The 30 lines of **Figure 6.1(a)** are reduced to **3** lines and **10** lines in the function. This function can be invoked any number of times at any place.

The following pseudo code gives an idea as to how the function is defined and invoked.

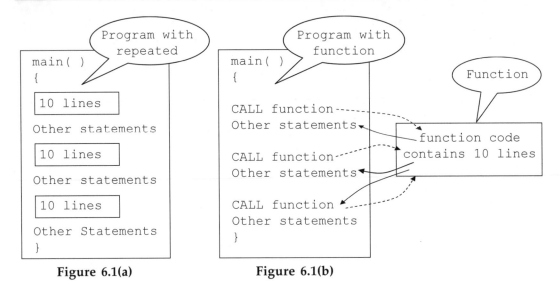

Figure 6.1(a)                    Figure 6.1(b)

```
/* Example for function definition and calling */
main( )
{
   //Statements;
    test( );   /* User-defined function calling */
 }

test( )    /* User-defined function definition */
{
    //Body of the function;
}
```

Here the **main( )** program invokes a user-defined function named **test( )**. As I mentioned earlier, execution of the C program always begins from **main( )** function. Whenever a function like **test( )** appears in the program, the control is transferred to the user-defined function and the execution continues in **test( )**. Before transferring control to **test( )**, the status of **main ( )** program is pushed into a stack. If the process completed in **test( )**, control returns to the **main( )** program and pops the status of the **main( )** which is available in the stack. The purpose of the stack and its operation are explained in the data structure section.

The following diagram illustrates how the functions are being invoked and processed with multiple functions.

- In the above diagram there are two subprograms namely **test1** and **test2**.
- First we know that the **main( )** function starts its execution and it calls the user-defined function **test1( )**
- Before starting the process, the status of **main( )** is stored into stack and execution continues in **test1( )**

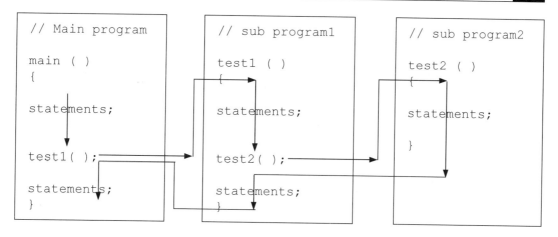

- The function **test1( )**, in turn calls another function **test2( )**
- As in the previous case, status of **test1( )** is pushed into the stack.
- Now the stack contains status both the **test1( )** function and **main( )**
- The execution continues in **test2( )**
- After completion of **test2( )**, the control is returned to the **test1( )** and continues the execution until the end of the function
- When **test1( )** is completed, the control returns to **main( )** program and once again the process is resumed.

The formula to compute the binomial coefficient **(nCr)** value is

$$nCr = n! \ / \ (n–r) \ ! \ * \ r \ !$$

To finish the above expression, we have to calculate three factorial values such as **n! , (n–r)!** and **r!** Here we are calculating the factorial value three times with different values like **n, n–r** and **r**. For this, we have to write the same piece of code (factorial program) three times to calculate each factorial value.

To avoid this repetition, we can write a separate function to calculate the factorial value exclusively. To calculate the factorial value at any time, this function can be invoked with the necessary number as a parameter and the factorial value will be obtained. This is the way we can reduce the program size.

## 6.4 GENERAL FORMAT FOR FUNCTION DECLARATION

```
Return-type Function-name(arg1, arg2...)
   {
       Local variable declaration

       Body of the function

       [ return; ]

   }
```

Here

> ⇨ **Return-type** is the type of data returned by the function
> ⇨ **Function-name** is the name of the function
> ⇨ **arg1, arg2, ...** are parameters of the function

Look the example for a function declaration

```
int swap(int a, int b)
{
    // Body of the function;
}
```

The first **int** is the type of data to be returned by the function **swap( )** and **a, b** are the arguments to the function.


## 6.5  WHAT IS A PARAMETER/ARGUMENT?

A variable, that is used to carry the data to the function, is called **parameter** or **argument**. The parameter may be either a **value parameter**, carrying value directly or a **variable parameter** carrying values using the variable.

In the example, the arguments **a** and **b** belong to the same data type. The function declaration with the parameter is as follows:

```
int swap(int a, int b);
    /* a & b must be declared individually */
```

The arguments of the function can also be declared as shown below:

```
int swap(a, b)
int a, int b;
{
    /* Body of the function; */
    return (5); /* Returns Integer Value */
}
```

This type of declaration is called **K-R declaration.** (**K**–Kerninghan and **R**–Ritchie, who are the authors of C programming language).

In case of a normal variable declaration, the number of variables of the same type may be declared by a single declarative statement. Even though the variables are of the same type, we cannot declare them as shown above in a function.

```
int swap(int a, b); /* Error */
```

**Note:**
The arguments must be declared individually even if they belong to the same data type.

## 6.6 HOW TO CALL THE FUNCTION?

We used to call persons by their names. Here too the function is invoked by specifying the **function-name** with the **required parameters**. The following is an example program for function call with parameters.

```
/* Simple example for function definition and calling the same */
main()
{
    display(10);
}

display (int a)
{
    printf("a=%d ",a);
}
```

Function calls with **10**

The **main( )** function calls the user-defined function namely **display( )** with the value **10** and it is an argument to the function. Now the value **10** is carried and assigned to the variable **a**. It is actually an assignment statement like **a=10**.

## 6.7 `return` STATEMENT

This is a simple statement used to return the control to the calling function from the called function and this is required in some cases. The **return** statement can be used to return a value from the called function to the calling function. The format of return statement is

```
return (expression);
```

⇨ It is an optional statement in the function
⇨ It may occur more than once in the function
⇨ It may appear anywhere in the function

Let us see some of the possible uses of the return statement

1. **return (5)**    => Return value **5** to the calling function
2. **return (a+b)** => Result of expression **a+b** will be returned
3. **return ('a')**  => Returns the character **'a'** to the calling function
4. **return (&a)**   => Returns address of **'a'**
5. **return**        => Returns the control to the called function.
                       (It is used to stop and return explicitly)

Look at the following program, which is a complete program illustrating the function and how it has been invoked.

```
/* Complete example for a function */
main()
{
    int   a=10,  b=20,c;

    c=sum(a,b);
    printf("\nSum=%d",c);
}

int   sum(int   x,  int y)
{
    return (x+y);
}
```

Here we are passing the values of **a** and **b** to the user-defined function **sum( )** and this function computes the sum of these two numbers and returns the result to the calling function.

## 6.8   TYPES OF FUNCTIONS

The functions are of four types, classified based on the parameter passed to the function and the value returned by the function. They are functions with

1. No argument and No Return
2. No argument and Return
3. Argument and No Return
4. Argument and Return value

### 6.8.1   No Argument and No Return

In this type of function, nothing is passed to the called function from the calling function and also nothing is returned from the called function to the calling function. The following is an example for this

```
//Main program

main()
{

    line();
    printf("Welcome to all");
    line();
}
```

```
//User-defined function

void line()
{
    int i;

    for(i=1;i<50;i++)
        printf("-");
}
```

In the above example, we are not passing any value to the function **line( )** and it does not return any value to the called function. The aim of the function is very simple that it prints a line. The **void** is a data type, which represents returning **NULL** data and here the function returns nothing.

### Note:

Default return type of the function is **integer**.

## 6.8.2 No Argument and Return Value

In this type of function, the user may define a function to return some value without passing anything. This type of function does not take any argument to the called function, but it returns value to the calling function.

```
main()
{
    int a, b, c;

    a=input( );
    b=input( );
    c=a+b;
    printf("Sum=%d",c);

}
```

```
int input()
{
    int x;

    printf("Enter a value");

    scanf("%d",&x);

    return (x);
}
```

Here the function **input( )** is used to read an integer value without the **scanf( )** statement in the calling program. We can use it when we are in need of any integer value. This function does not take any argument but it returns an integer value to the calling function.

## 6.8.3 Argument and No Return Value

This type of function receives an argument but it does not return any value to the calling function.

```
// Main program
main( )
{
    line();

    printf("Welcome to all");

    line(15 );

}
```

```
//User defined function

void line(int n)
{
    int i;

    for(i=1;i<n;i++)
        printf("-");
}
```

The **line( )** function receives an argument as no. of characters (–) to print, here **15** times and they are printed as line. But this function does not return anything to the **main ( )** function.

### 6.8.4 With Argument and a Return Value

This type of function receives an argument and also returns a value to the calling function.

```
main()
{
    int a=10,  b=20,c;

    c=sum(a,b);
    printf("Sum=%d",c);


}
```

```
int sum(int x,  int y)
{

    return (x+y);

}
```

The function **sum( )** takes two integer values as arguments and returns the sum to the calling function.

The passed values are only the copies of **a** and **b**. If any modification is made to this value inside the function **sum( )**, it does not affect the **main( )** function's **a** and **b** values, as the modifications in the photocopy do not affect the original documents.

***Note:***
Normally a function cannot return more than one value.

In the functions, the changes in the local variable do not affect the arguments of the calling function value. The following example will illustrate this.

***Example:***

```
/* Example for passing values to the function and result of changes */
main( )
{
   int   a=10;
   printf("\nBefore passing: %d",a);

   disp(a);
   printf("\nAfter  passing: %d",a);
}
void disp(int   x)
{
   printf("\nValue inside the function: %d",x);
   x=100 ;
   printf("\nValue inside the function: %d",x);
}
```

Output:

```
Before passing: 10
Value inside the function: 10
Value inside the function: 100
After passing: 10
```

In the **main( )** program the variable **a** contains the value **10**. The function **disp(a)** is called with the value of **a**. Now the copy of **a** is passed (assigned as **x=a**) to the function **disp( )**. Inside the function **disp( )**, **x** contains the value of **a**. In the function the value of **x** is changed to **100**. This change affects only the local variable **x** and note that the value of **a** in the **main( )** program remains the same.

### 6.8.5 Same Variable Name—No Problem

Name of the variable is an identifier and it is only for the user's reference. System uses its own way to access the values and to identify it. So the variable name in one function may occur in any other function or in the block also with the same name.

```
/* Illustration of same variable in the program */
main()
{
    int   a=10;
    disp(a);        /* a is local  to  main( )   */
}

void disp(int   a)
{
    a=100;          /*  a  is  local  to disp( )  */
    printf("\na = %d",a);
}
```

In the above program, the variable **a** occurs in both the **main( )** function and the user-defined function **disp( )**. Though the variable names seem to be identical, their memory allocations are different. The variables are individual components of each of the function and it will not confuse the compiler.

The following program illustrates the above discussion, about the different addresses and it solves the problem of the same variable.

### *Example:*

```
/* To prove the memory allocation can vary even when the
   names of the variable are same */
main()
{
    int a;
    printf("\n%Address of a in main   : ",&a);
    test();
}
```

```
void test()
{
   int a;
   printf("\nAddress of a in function  : %u",&a);
}
```

**Output:**

```
Address of a in main        : 23344
Address of a in function    : 24444
```

The output of this program is the memory address of two variables, which are equal. But the memory address is not same. So this is not a problem in a program.

The following is a program to find a maximum of the two numbers using the function

**Example:**

```
/* To find the maximum of two using function */
main()
{
   int a, b, big;

      printf("\nEnter two numbers : ");
   scanf("%d%d",&a,&b);
   big = max(a,b);
   printf("\nBiggest no is = %d ",big);
}
int    max(int x, int y)
{
   int temp;
   temp = x>y ? x : y;
   return (temp);
}
```

**Output:**

```
Enter two numbers : 10 30
Biggest no is = 30
```

The calculation of **nCr** value is a very good example of using function. We have already discussed it theoretically. In this program, the function **fact( )** is used to calculate the factorial value of a given number.

**Example:**

```
/* To find nCr program using function */
main()
{
   int n, r;
   float ncr;
```

```
        printf("\nEnter the value of N  &  R : ");
        scanf("%d%d",&n,&r);

        ncr =(float)fact(n)/(fact(n-r)  *  fact(r));
        printf("\nnCr  value  =   %5.2f  ",ncr);
    }
    int fact(int m)
    {
        int i,f=1;
        for(i=1;i<=m;i++)
            f =f * i;
        return f;
    }
```

**Output:**

```
Enter the value of N & R : 5     2
nCr value   =   10.00
```

If **function** is not used in the above program, we should write separate set of statements to calculate the 3 different factorial values, as we did in the starting of this chapter.

While using function, to calculate **n!** value, just the statement **fact(n)** is enough. So **fact(n)** gives **n!** , **fact(n–r)** give **(n–r)!** and **fact(r)** gives the **r!** It reduces the number of instructions and memory automatically.

The following is another example to implement the **pow( )** function.

***Example:***

```
    /* To compute x^n without using library function */
    /* or Implementation of power() function  */
    main()
    {
        int n;
        float x, s;

        printf("\nEnter the values of X & N ");
        scanf("%f%d",&x,&n);

        s = power(x, n);

        printf("\nPower(%5.2f , %d ) = %5.2f",x,n,s);
    }

    float power(float x, int n)
    {
        int i,s=1;

        for(i=1;i<=n;i++)
        s = s * x;

        return (s);
    }
```

**Output:**

```
Enter the values of X & N 10 3
Power(10.00 , 3 ) = 1000.00
```

## 6.9  PROBLEMS IN RETURN TYPE—TAKE CARE

The return type of the function should be specified carefully. If it is not proper, the value may be converted into some other format and the result may go wrong. We should be careful while returning a real value. The following program tells the importance of the return type specification.

```
/* Program without specifying return type */
main()
{
    float a;                    No return type is specified,
                                by default it is an integer
    a=test();
    printf("\nResult of function calling : %f",a);
}
test()
{
    return(2.5);
}
```

**Output:**
```
    Result of function calling: 2.000000
```

The return type of the function is not properly defined here. In C, the **default return type is integer**. Here the function returns the value 2.5, using the return statement, which is actually a float value. But the return type is not matching with it and the float value is converted into an integer value. Finally we are getting the unexpected result as **2.000000**. If we add the correct return type in the function declaration, the modified program is as follows:

```
/* Program with correct return type */
main()
{
    float a;                    Return type is specified
                                properly as float
    a=test();

    printf("\nResult of function calling : %f",a);
}
float test()
{
    return( 2.5);
}
```

`Output`:
```
    Result of function calling: 2.500000
```

Now we got the correct result from the function. So the return type of the data from the function should be considered important.

## 6.10  CALLING WITH EXPRESSION

The parameter to the function may be a value or variable or it may be an expression. The function can be called by value by directly giving the value as a parameter to the function. The following is a program to illustrate the function call by giving the values directly.

```
/* Calling a function by value */
main()
{
   display( 10 );                   Function calling with value 10
}                                    10 is assigned to the variable a

display ( int a)
{
   printf("a = %d ",a);
}
```

Here the function **disp( )** is called directly with value as **10.** The other way to call the function is by using a variable. In this case, instead of value, a variable is used as a carrier of the value.

```
/ * Calling a function by variable */
main()
{
   int a =10;
   display( a );
}
                                     Function calling with a
display (int b)
{
   printf("b = %d ",b);
}
```

Another way to call the function is by passing an expression. In this case, the result of the expression will be passed as argument to the function. The example below illustrates the function call made using an expression.

```
/* Calling by Expression */
main()
{
   int a=5 , b=10;
   display( a + b );
}

display (int c)
{
   printf("c = %d ",c);
}
```

Function with result of **a+b**

In this program, the result of expression 'a+b' is passed as argument to the function **display( )**. The value of **a** is **5** and **b** is **10** and therefore **a+b** is **15**. The result **15** is passed to the function **display( )** and received by the function argument c. (i.e., c = a + b).

## 6.11  PASSING ARRAY TO THE FUNCTION

What we have discussed so far is passing and returning one or more simple values. This is not enough for us in all the applications and we may require passing the arrays to the function. Now let us learn, how to pass the array value to the function. The following is the simple example for passing array values to the function.

**Example:**

```
/* Example for passing array to the function */
main()
{
   int i, n, a[15];
   printf("\nNumber of elements :");
   scanf("%d",&n);
   printf("\nEnter %d values\n",n);

   for(i=0;i<n;i++)
      scanf("%d",&a[i]);

   printf("\nYour values are \n");
      for(i=0;i<n;i++)
         display(a[i]);
}
display(int m)
{
   printf("%d\t",m);
}
```

**Output:**
```
Number of elements :3
Enter 3 values
10   20   30
Your values are
10      20      30
```

The above program simply passes the values one by one just like passing ordinary values. A better way of passing the array values is by using pointers and reference.

Before discussing about the pointers, let us see the following simple example for passing array to the function.

***Example:***
```
/* Passing array by using reference and pointers */
main( )
{
   int i, n, a[15];

   printf("\nNumber of elements :");
   scanf("%d",&n);
   printf("\nEnter %d values\n",n);
      for(i-0;i<n;i++)
   scanf("%d",&a[i]);

   display(a,n);
}

display(int x[],int m)
{
   int i;

printf("\nPassed array values are \n");
   for(i=0;i<m;i++)
      printf("%d\t",x[i]);
}
```

**Output:**
```
Number of elements :5

Enter 5 values
10   20   30   40   50

Passed array values are
10      20      30      40      50
```

The aim of the program is to read array of data in the **main( )** program and the read data is displayed using the function **display( )**. In the above program, we are passing the entire array to the function by reference method. In this method of passing by reference, the modification of the values in the called program, will affect the values in the calling function. In the function, **a** is an ordinary variable, but it passes the base address (starting address) of the array **a** to the function.

## 6.12  RECURSIVE FUNCTION

A function can be called by any number of functions, any number of times. The following example illustrates the calling of a function from different functions.

*Example:*

```
/* Calling function from other function */
main( )
{
   printf("\nInside main( ) ");
   function1( );
}
function1( )
{
   printf("\nInside function1 ");
   function2( );
}
function2( )
{
   printf("\nInside function2 ");
}
```

Output:
```
Inside main( )
Inside function1
Inside function2
```

Here the **main( )** function calls the function **function1( )**. The **function1( )** turn calls another function, namely **function2( )**. Function calling starts from the **main( )** and **function1( )**. Order of completion is in reverse, first **function2( )** will be completed and then **function1( )**, finally control will come back to function **main( )**.

In some cases, the function invokes itself, whenever the function calls itself, this special type of function is called **recursive function**. The following example is the simple recursive function calling.

```
/* Function calling itself or recursive call */
display( )
{
   printf("\nWelcome");
   display();    /*function calls itself or recursive */
}
```

The calling of function **display( )**, will execute the instructions within it and one of the instruction is **display( )** (i.e., statement for invoking itself). If the function is somewhere else, the control will be transferred as usual, but here the function **display( )** calls itself. Therefore, for every execution, the function is called indefinitely. The result of the above program is

```
Welcome
Welcome
Welcome
. . . . .
```

Here, there is no chance of terminating the function from execution. To avoid this indefinite execution, we have to use conditional statements to stop the recursion.

A very good example for recursive function is finding factorial of a number. The factorial value of a number is calculated by any one of the two methods given below.

```
(i)  n! = 1 * 2 * 3 * ...... * n
        (or)
(ii) n! = n * ( n-1 )!
```

First method of calculation has been discussed already and the second method needs a different approach.

As a part of this expression, we have to calculate **(n–1)!** which is again similar to calculating **n!** value. This process will continue until the value of **n** becomes **1**. If the value of **n** is **1**, the function returns to the calling function.

$$n! = n * (n-1)!$$
$$(n-1)! = (n-1) * (n-1-1)!$$
$$(n-1-1)! = (n-1-1) * (n-1-1-1)!$$

---

process continues until n=1.

---

$$n! = n* \qquad n-1 * \qquad n-1-1 * \;....$$

***Example:***

$$3! = 3 * (3-1)!$$
$$2! = 2 * (2-1)!$$
$$1!$$

Now **n** is 1. So it returns the value 1.

$$3! = 3 * \qquad 2 * \qquad 1$$

$$= 6$$

Another example for recursive function here is generating Fibonacci sequence.

***Example:***

```
/* Program for fibonacci sequence using recursion */
main()
{
    int a=0,b=1,n;
    printf("\nEnter the number of terms : ");
    scanf("%d",&n);
    printf("\nFibonacci sequence\n");
    fib(a,b,n);
}

void fib(int a, int b, int n)
{
    int c;

    if (n<1)
       return ;

    c = a+b;

    printf("%d\t",c);
    a=b;        b=c;

    fib(a,b,--n);      /* recursive call  */
}
```

**Output:**
```
Enter the number of terms : 5
Fibonacci sequence
1    2   3   5   8
```

In the above program, for every iteration of recursive calls, the value of **n** will be decremented. When the value of **n** reaches **1,** the process will be stopped and control returns back to the calling program.

***Note:***
Recursive function is just like a looping statement and the termination from the recursion is achieved using conditions.

## 6.13  FUNCTION CALLING CONVENTION

The calling convention specifies how machine code is generated to place the function call arguments on the stack. Most of the applications are C Calling conventions, which push the argument in the right to left order. The following program makes a confusion for us.

*Example:*

```
/* Calling Convention Example */
main()
{
    int a=5;
    printf("\n%d    %d",a++,++a);
    printf("\n%d ",a);
}
```

Output:

```
6    6
7
```

Why the output is surprising? This is because of the calling convention. In the first printf( ) statement, the arguments **a++**, **++a** are pushed into the stack from left to right order. So, first **a++** and **++a** are pushed into the stack. Operations on the stack are executed in LIFO (Last In First Out) order. While evaluation of expression **++a** will be executed first and followed by **a++**. Finally, the result of the program is **6,6** and at last the variable **a** holds value **7**.

## 6.14 STORAGE CLASSES

What is the use of the variable declaration? The variable declaration instructs the system about the type of data that can be stored in that variable, memory allocation including the number of bytes, default value or initial value, life of the variable, etc. We have discussed so many programs and their characteristics and they are mostly local variables and they have so many drawbacks while using large applications.

For example, there is a variable that is going to be referred in all the functions. What to do then? We may pass it as argument. Suppose, we want to return more than one value or process more values like array. In that case, we can use pointers.

The variable can be declared with additional functionality by using storage classes. When we add these features, the variable may be with different qualifications like scope, default value, etc., are different to compare with ordinary variable declaration.

## 6.15 WHY PROPER INITIALIZATION IS NEEDED?

While using the variables in the calculation, the initial value of the variable should be given. Otherwise, it makes a problem. For example, the following is a program for finding the factorial value of a given number.

```
/*Illustrating the need of variable initialization */
main()
{
   int f, n, i;
   scanf("%d",&n);
   for(i=1;i<n;i++)
      f = f* i;

   /*Initial Value of 'f' is not properly mentioned and it may be any */

   printf("\nResult is :  %d",f);
}
```

The result of this program may be any value. Because, while executing the expression **f= f*i**, value of **f** is not properly initialized, so any garbage value may be taken into calculation.

## 6.16  HOW TO DECLARE THE VARIABLE WITH STORAGE CLASS?

Normally a variable is declared in the following format.

**Datatype Variable(s);**

The variable declaration with storage class is

**StorageClass Datatype Variable(s);**

There are four storage classes available in C and they are

1. Automatic variable
2. Static variable
3. External variable
4. Register variable

### 6.16.1  Automatic variable

⇨ The variable of automatic storage class can be declared using the key word **auto**.
⇨ In default all the variables are **auto**matic variable. So, it is optional.
⇨ Automatic variable contains a **garbage value** by default.
⇨ **Life** of the variable is **local** or inside the **block**

The variable declaration with **auto**matic storage class is as follows:

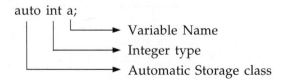

Automatic is optional, so the above declaration can be replaced by the traditional statement

```
int a; /* Default automatic variable */
```

Look at the following example for automatic variable and its default value.

```
/* Example for automatic storage class */
main()
{
    auto    int   a;
    printf("a = %d ",a);
}
```

### 6.16.2  What is Garbage Value?

Result of the above program may be any value, positive or negative or zero. This unexpected value is called **garbage value**. While declaring the variable, memory is reserved and if we initialize some value to the variable, that memory location is filled by new value. Suppose we do not initialize, what will happen while referring? The previously assigned value will be returned.

For example, the following diagram shows the memory allocation and its default value. From the following declaration, 'a' is an **int**eger variable (So **two** bytes of memory allocation) and its initial value is **10**, its memory representation is in the diagram.

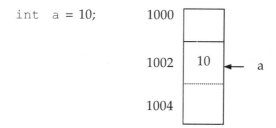

For the variable **a**, the location **1002** is reserved and its initial value is '**10**'. Suppose the same memory location is going to be allocated for the variable of another program without initial value, what will happen? That location retains the same value, which is assigned in the previous program. This value is called **garbage value**. We cannot expect the correct value. Sometimes it is **0** (zero).

Variable declaration without proper initialization

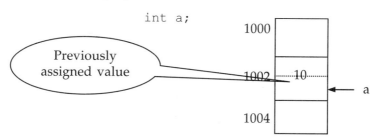

The value of the variable **a**, may or may not be **10**, because the memory address **1002** is not initialized by the new value until the reference.

The address is not always the same for the variables. For example, here I referred the same address for both the programs. Another functionality of automatic variable is scope; its scope is in block or in local.

**Example:**

```
/* Example for scope with in the block  */
main()
{                       'a' belongs to this block
     int  a = 10;

     printf (" a = %d ",a);

     {                  'a' is local to this block
        int   a= 20;
        printf("\n a = %d ",a);
     }
     printf("\n a = %d ",a);
}
```

Output:
```
a = 10
a = 20
a = 10
```

Are you surprised about the result? In this program there is a variable 'a', which is declared two times and in different blocks. So, only the variable name is same but the memory locations are different. If both the variables refer to the same memory location, then the changes will automatically affect.

```
/* Without automatic storage class */

main()

{
    int   a;

    printf(" a = %d ",a);

}
```

```
/* With automatic storage
   class    */

   main()
   {
       auto   int   a;
       printf(" a = %d ",a);
   }
```

The values from both the programs may be same. So, **auto**matic is not necessary. Even if we include, there is no change in the result.

## 6.16.3  Static Storage Class

Sometimes we are in a position to retain the last value of evaluation in a program or initialization should be only once for many function calls. To obtain this feature, **static** storage class is used. The following list gives some additional information about it

⇨ It is used to keep the variables static
⇨ Default value of static variable is **0** (zero)
⇨ Life is until the program termination
⇨ Initialization of a variable is only once
⇨ Scope is local only

When the variable is declared as static, its default value is assigned as 0 (zero). Look the following example and you may clear the above.

**Example:**
```
main()
{
    static   int   a ;

    printf("Value of a = %d ",a);
}
```
Output:
```
Value of a = 0
```

Another characteristic is one time initialization. This is illustrated in the following program.

**Example:**
```
/* Example for static storage class */
main()
{
    int i;
    for(i=1;i<=3;i++)
        {
            static int a=10;        Only one time
            printf("\na = %d ",a);   execution
            a++;
        }
}
```
Output:
```
a = 10
a = 11
a = 12
```

Here the variable **a** is declared inside the **for** block. So, for every execution, there is a variable declaration. But here with the additional keyword **static**. So the initialization is only once and not for every execution. You check the same program without **static** storage class. For every execution, the result is same.

Another characteristic is the scope of the variable. The scope of the variable is only inside the block, not everywhere.

**Example:**

```
/* Example for static storage class with block */
main()
{
   int a=10;

   printf("\nValue of  a = %d ",a);
   {
      static int a=100;
      printf("\nValue of  a = %d ",a);
   }
   printf("\nValue of  a = %d ",a);
}
```

Output:
```
Value of a = 10
Value of a = 100
Value of a = 10
```

Here the scope is local, so while exiting from the block, the variable is not taken into account and removed from the memory.

One more characteristic is it is local. That is, the variable could not be accessed outside the function.

**Example:**

```
/* Using static   */

main ()
{
   int i;

   for(i=1;i<=5;i++)
      test();
}
test( )
{
   static int a=5;

   printf("\na = %d ",a);
   a++;
}
Output:
   a = 5
   a = 6
   a = 7
```

**Example:**

```
/* Without using static   */
main ()
{
   int i;

   for(i=1;i<=5;i++)
      test();
}

test()
{
   int a=5;

   printf("\na = %d ",a);
   a++;
}
Output:
   a = 5
   a = 5
   a = 5
```

## 6.16.4 External Variable

We have discussed so many programs and all of them are based on the local variable. Suppose if any variable is going to be referred all the places of the program, we can declare that variable as **extern**al variable. This type of declaration is also called **global variable** declaration and can be declared using the keyword **extern.**

The external variable should be declared outside the **main( )** function or before the **main( )** function. If it is declared outside the **main( )** there is no need of the keyword **extern**. The following is a piece of code with external variable declaration.

```
int a = 10; /* Global declaration */
main()
{
    // Statements of main function
}
void test()
{
    // Statements of user defined function
}
```

The visibility of the global variable **a** is illustrated in the following diagram. Here the variable **a** is visible not only to main( ) function but also all the sub-programs.

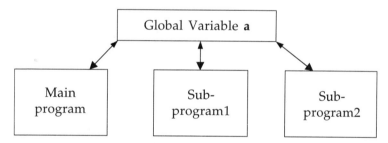

The usage of external variable is explained in the following program:

***Example:***

```
/* External storage Class   */

extern int a=10;      /* Global variable */
main()
{
    printf("\nIn main a = %d ",a);
    test();
}

void test()
{
    printf("\nIn function  a = %d ",a);
}
```

**Output:**

```
In main a = 10
In function a = 10
```

From the result, we can conclude that the variable **a** can be accessed anywhere in the program. The following program illustrates that any changes will affect the global variable value.

**Example:**

```
/* Example for external variable */
int a=10;
main()
{
   printf("\nBefore Call  a = %d ",a);
   a=a+10;
   test( );
   printf("\nAfter  Call  a = %d ",a);
}

void  test()
{
printf("\nValue of  a in function  = %d ",a);
a=a+10;
}
```

**Output:**

```
Before Call a = 10
Value of a in function = 20
After Call a = 30
```

Below is a program to find the biggest number from the array using global variable.

**Example:**

```
/* To find the maximum of Array using external variable */

int a[10],n,i,bigs,big;
main()
{
   printf("\nHow many elements : ");
   scanf("%d",&n);

   for(i=0;i<n;i++)
      scanf("%d",&a[i]);

      maximum();
      printf("\nBiggest number =  %d ",maximum());
}
```

```
int maximum()
{
   big=a[0];

   for(i=1;i<n;i++)
      if (big<a[i])
         big=a[i];

   return (big);
}
```

**Output:**

```
How many elements : 5
20   50   10   70   10
Biggest number = 70
```

## 6.16.5  `register`  Storage Class

What is a register? Register is a small area, which is used to store the data temporarily while doing calculation. A few such important registers are AX, BX, Count Register, Status register. Primary uses of these registers are to reduce the time to perform calculations. In general, the value is stored in memory (RAM) and it will move to the register for the process. But it takes time if the process is to be performed very often. In this situation, we can keep the values in the register itself. So the memory movement will be reduced.

register int i;

Here the value of **i** is stored in the register instead of memory. If it is going to be used frequently, as in the looping statement, it is very useful.

```
/* Example for register storage class */
main( )
{
   register int i;

   for( i = 1;i < =100; i++)
      printf("\n%d ",i);
}
```

**Note:**
Generally the register size is 16 bits. So there is no possibility to store the float or double value.

## 6.17  VARIABLE NUMBER OF ARGUMENTS

The library functions are predefined functions which accept mostly fixed number of arguments such as **sqrt( )**, **abs( )**, **strcmp( )**, etc. We wrote many functions in the earlier chapter. The restrictions in the functions are we cannot pass a variable number of arguments to the function. The functions like **printf( )** and **scanf( )** accept any number of arguments. That is there is no fixed number of arguments that are passed always. For example, look at the following examples:

```
1. printf("%d",a)              // One argument
2. printf("%d %d %d %d",a,b,c,d) // Four arguments
3. printf("%d%f%s",a,f,s)       // Three different type of arguments
```

One function receives different arguments. Can we write a function that receives a variable number of arguments? Yes.

The function declaration is similar to the normal function, but we need some redefinition as follows:

$$int\ test(char\ *s,\ ...)$$

Here the three dots (...) indicate that the function will be able to receive a variable number of arguments. The first argument may be of any type and we should specify this argument. The remaining arguments are not necessary to specify because we are going to pass a variable number of arguments.

In order to access the arguments of the function, the header file **<stdarg.h>** must be included. The following are the functions used to access the arguments

1. `va_list`
   ⇨ The list of variables to be accessed should be declared of this type first.

   Example                  `va_list a;`

2. `void va_start( va_list list, Type)`
   ⇨ This function sets up the pointer to the first argument of the function being processed via **va_arg** and **va_end**. Once it is initialized, the subsequent access is very simple

3. `va_arg(va_list list, type)`
   ⇨ Each call of this function will extract the next argument from the argument list of the specified type

4. `void va_end(va_list list)`
   ⇨ After completion of process all the arguments, the **va_end ( )** should be called.

**Note:**
First the **va_list** should be used to declare the variable of this type. After that call **va_start( )** to start the read operation and **va_arg( )** will be used in further for accessing the arguments.

The following is an example program that illustrates the variable number of arguments in a function.

**Example:**

```
/* Variable number of arguments
   Printing numbers—various sizes */

#include <stdarg.h>
#include <stdio.h>
#include <conio.h>
```

```
void print(int c, ...)
{
    va_list ap;
    int arg;
    va_start(ap, c);
    printf("\n%5d",c);
    while ((arg = va_arg(ap,int)) != 0)
      printf("%5d",arg);

    va_end(ap);
}
int main(void)
{
    clrscr();
    printf("\nCalling with three arguments");
    print(1,2,3);
    printf("\nCalling with five arguments");
    print(10,20,30,40,50);
    return 0;
}
```

Output:

```
Calling with three arguments
   1    2    3
Calling with five arguments
  10   20   30   40   50
```

The following is another program, which is used to find the biggest of different set of numbers using function with a variable number of arguments.

**Example:**

```
// To find the maximum of different set
#include <stdarg.h>
#include <stdio.h>
#include <conio.h>

int maxi(int c, ...)
{
    va_list ap;
    int arg,max;
    va_start(ap, c);
    max=c;
    while ((arg = va_arg(ap,int)) != 0)
      if (max<arg)
    max=arg;

    va_end(ap);
    return max;
}
```

```
int main(void)
{
    clrscr();
    printf("\nBiggest number is : %d ",maxi(1,12,3));
    printf("\nBiggest Number is : %d "
            ",maxi(312,43,657,123,222));
    return 0;
}
```

**Output:**
```
Biggest number is : 12
Biggest Number is : 657
```

The above kind of programs can be extended for strings and other possible types.


## REVIEW QUESTIONS ✍

1. What is the need of function in a program?
2. What are the two general types of functions?
3. Write some examples for library functions.
4. Write the general format of function definition.
5. What is a parameter?
6. Write short notes on return statement.
7. Discuss the various types of functions with necessary examples.
8. Can we pass the whole array to the function. (True/False)
9. What is the use of void type?
10. Default return type of the function is _____.
11. Define recursive function. Discuss with example.
12. Write a program to find the sum of N numbers using recursive function.
13. What is calling convention?
14. What is the role of storage classes? Discuss.
15. Explain the static storage class with an example.
16. What is garbage value?
17. By default all the variables are _____ storage class.
18. Register storage class can also be used for float/double. (True/False)
19. Discuss about variable number of arguments.
20. Write a program to print the Fibonacci sequence using recursive function.

# Chapter 7

## Pointers

### 7.1 INTRODUCTION

People always have some wrong opinions about pointers, and think this concept is difficult to understand and hard to use. Pointers have a lot of advantages. This chapter will relieve you from such misconceptions about pointers and their applications.

### 7.2 WHAT IS POINTER?

- It is a powerful feature of C Language
- It is a new kind of data type
- It stores the addresses, not values
- It allows indirect access of data
- It allows to carry whole array to the function
- It will help in returning more than one value from function
- It helps for dynamic memory allocation

Pointer is an indicator, that helps to reach a particular place, like a symbol, marker, etc. For example, the finger pointer in the following is directing the people towards **Coimbatore,** using the **Hand** symbol.

☞ Way to Coimbatore

We know some basics regarding the variable declaration and how the memories are being allotted for them. Memory is divided into small pieces called **bytes** (8 bits). Our program and data will be stored somewhere in the memory where the free area is available. The variables are the names used for reference but everything is internally referred by the memory address. Let us see the following diagrams and how the memory is allocated for the variables.

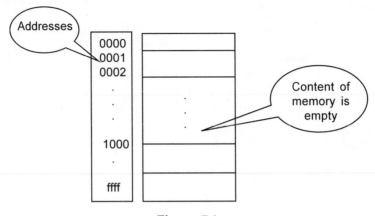

**Figure 7.1**

There is a declarative statement

```
char ch = 'A' ;
```

At the time of execution, the compiler will make the following process.

⇨ **One byte** memory is reserved for the character variable **ch**
⇨ and store the character value **'A'** in that memory location

The memory allocation may be as follows:

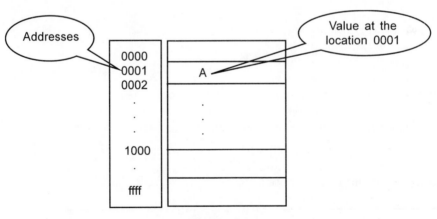

**Figure 7.2**

The character variable **ch** is stored in address **0001** and the value of that location is **'A'**. The address of the variable is not constant and it may vary for the next execution.

**Note:**
The address of **ch** is not a constant for every execution and for any user-defined variable, the address is not constant.

## 7.3 OPERATORS IN POINTERS

The pointers will help us in doing variety of operations and applications. The two essential operators are given below.

1. *
   ⇨ Indirection operator, which is used to retrieve the value from the memory location
2. &
   ⇨ Address operator, which is used to obtain the address of the variable

We discussed many times about reading the variable and how it is stored in a memory location. Theoretically you may be satisfied, but in practice, no one can see the memory address of any variable or where it is stored. It is not visible to the user easily. Now the above two operators will help you all in viewing the address and the values. Consider the declarative statements

`int a =10;`

⇨ If we refer **a**, it returns the value of **a** as 10
⇨ If we refer **&a**, it returns the address of **a**, that is, where the memory is allocated for this variable and
⇨ ***(&a)** refers to the value of **a**. Because **&a** refers to the address of **a** and ***(&a)** means the value at address of **a**

If we test the previous idea via a program, it will be more clear. Execute the following program and realize that the address is retrievable.

### Example:

```
/* Program to collect the address of variable */
main()
{
   int  a=10;

   printf("\n Value of a = %d ",a);
   printf("\n Memory address of  a = %u",&a);
}
```

Output:
```
   Value of a = 10
   Memory address of  a = 8716
```

### Note:
Memory address is always a positive value. So we can use format string character **%u** for printing the address.

## 7.4 HOW TO DECLARE THE POINTER VARIABLE?

No need to worry about the declaration of a pointer variable. It can be declared as simple variable declaration with small change as follows.

```
Data-type *pointer-variable;
```

Here, the character '*' indicates that the variable is a pointer variable. For example, the declarative statement:

```
int *ptr;
```

⇨ Here **ptr** is a pointer variable and
⇨ It will point to one integer memory location (or) hold the address of integer variable.

How to use pointer variables? Before any operations on the pointer variable, we must store the address, because the pointer variables will have addresses and not values.

```
int *ptr;
ptr = 10;
```

The compiler will show an error, because we cannot store the value in a variable in this manner. We can assign the direct address or address of the variable to the pointer variable as follows:

```
int a=10;
int *ptr;
ptr = &a;   /* Address of a is assigned to ptr */
```

Now the address of **a** is assigned to the pointer variable **ptr**. So, **ptr** will point the same memory location where **a** points to.

```
ptr = 0x41700000; /* Direct Address, Hexadecimal */
```

This assignment statement is direct address assignment and **0x41700000** is an address not a value. So we can assign the address to the pointer variables in any one of the ways.

How to retrieve the values from the memory? We know that the * operator will help here. If we know the address of **a**, then without the assistance of variable **a** we can access the values of **a**, and its illustration as shown below.

```
int a=10;
int *ptr;
```

The following is a pictorial representation of the above declarative statements. Before processing the assignment statement, the memory representation is as follows.

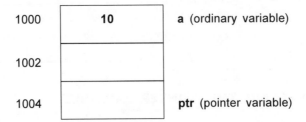

**Figure 7.3**

From this diagram, we can conclude the following:

⇨ Address of **a** is **1000**.
⇨ Value at memory location **1000** is **10**.
⇨ Address of pointer variable **ptr** is **1004**.

After the assignment statement **ptr = &a**, the diagram is as follows:

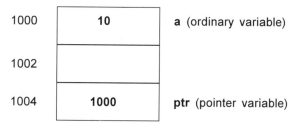

| 1000 | **10** | a (ordinary variable) |
| 1002 | | |
| 1004 | **1000** | ptr (pointer variable) |

**Figure 7.4**

From this diagram, we can get the following information

⇨ Address of **a** is **1000** and the value at memory location **1000** is **10**
⇨ **ptr** holds the address of **a** (i.e. **1000**)
⇨ So, **ptr** points to **a** indirectly and
⇨ memory address of **ptr** is **1004**

If we refer the value stored at **ptr** by ***ptr**, we may expect the result as **1000**. But **1000** is not a value and it is an address of variable **a**. So, ***ptr** returns the value stored at location **1000,** that is the value **10**, which is a value of **a**. The following program illustrates the previous theoretical discussions.

***Example:***

```
/* Accessing values indirectly using pointers */
main()
{
  int  a=10;
  int *ptr;

ptr = &a;
/*Address of a is assigned to pointer variable ptr*/
printf("\n Value of a = %d ",a);
printf("\n Value of a = %d ",*ptr);
printf("\n\nMemory address of variable a = %d ",&a);
printf("\nMemory address of variable a = %d ",ptr);
printf("\nMemory address of variable ptr = %d ",&ptr);
}
```

Output:
```
    Value of a = 10
    Value of a = 10
    Memory address of variable a    = 1000
    Memory address of variable a    = 1000
    Memory address of variable ptr = 5000
```

From the above program, we come to the conclusion that the value of **a** can be accessed by referring **a** and using the pointer variable by **\*ptr**.


## 7.5 OPERATIONS ON POINTER—INDIRECT MODIFICATION

What we have discussed so far is about the fundamental idea of pointers. Now we are clear about how to use pointer variable and access the value of any variable indirectly. In addition to these operations, pointers are also used change the value of the specified memory locations indirectly.

```
int a=10;
int *ptr=&a;  /* Address of 'a' is assigned to 'ptr' */
*ptr =100;    /* Value of 'a' is changed indirectly */
```

We are able to refer the value of any variable indirectly without the help of that variable. The changes on a variable can also be made without using that variable. The following program illustrates change of variable value indirectly.

***Example:***
```
/* Program for changing values indirectly */
main( )
{
    int  a=10;
    int *ptr;

    ptr=&a;
    printf("\nOld Value of a = %d ",a);

      *ptr=100;
      printf("\nNew Value of a = %d ",a);
}
```

Output:
```
    Old Value of a = 10
    New Value of a = 100
```

In the above program, we have not made any change in the value of **a** directly. But the statement **\*ptr=100** changes the value of **a** as **100**. Because the variable **ptr** is pointing to the memory address of **a**, we changed the value of **a** indirectly.

## 7.6 POINTERS AND EXPRESSIONS

With the help of simple arithmetic operations, a pointer variable can travel to any location in the memory. Consider the following as a memory structure for our discussion.

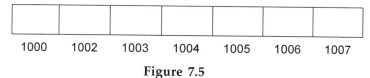

Figure 7.5

The declaration

```
int *ptr;
```

Assume that the starting address of integer pointer variable **ptr** is pointing to the first memory address **1000**. If we increment the pointer variable **ptr** by **1**, we may expect **ptr** to become **1001**. But it is not correct? The variable **ptr** is an integer pointer variable. Each integer requires two memory locations. So every increment in **ptr** will point to the **next integer memory location**—here it is **1002**. Suppose **ptr** is a **char**acter pointer variable, for every increment of **ptr**, it will be pointing to the adjacent memory location, because **char** need **1** byte memory. Look at the following examples:

```
int *ptr;
```
⇨ Assume **ptr** is now pointed to the location **1000**.
```
ptr++;
```
⇨ After this statement **ptr** is pointed to the location **1002**
```
ptr–;
```
⇨ Now ptr is adjusted to the previous location **1000**.
```
ptr=ptr+3;
```
⇨ **ptr** is now at the location **1006**

**Note:**
⇨ The pointer variables are always adjusted to the next memory location depending on their data type.
⇨ Operations other than addition and subtraction are not possible.

## 7.7 POINTERS AND ARRAYS—ONE-DIMENSIONAL

Array is a collection of the same class of elements stored in continuous memory locations. How to prove that the elements are stored in continuous memory locations? You can prove this statement when you execute the following program. Assume that the following array elements are stored in memory as below:

```
int a[5]={10,20,30,40,50};
```

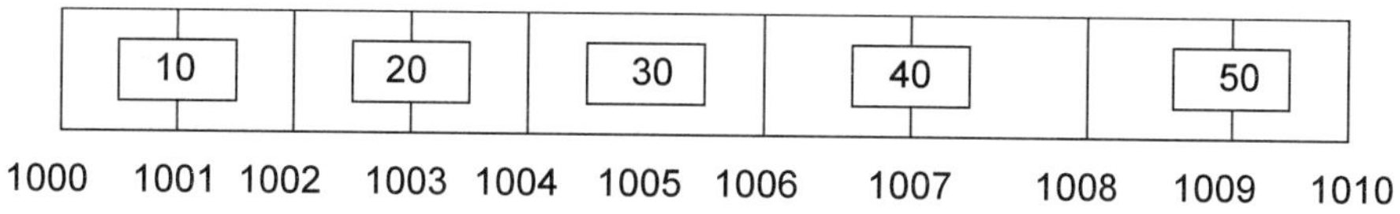

|  10  |  |  20  |  |  30  |  |  40  |  |  50  |
|------|--|------|--|------|--|------|--|------|

1000   1001   1002   1003   1004   1005   1006   1007   1008   1009   1010

Figure 7.6

**Example:**

```
/* Program to check the definition of array    */
   main()
   {
      int  a[5] ={10,20,30,40,50};
      int i;

      clrscr( );
      for(i=0;i<5;i++)
        printf("\n%d is stored at location %d ",a[i],&a[i]);


   }
```

Output:

```
   10 is stored at location 1000
   20 is stored at location 1002
   30 is stored at location 1004
   40 is stored at location 1006
   50 is stored at location 1008
```

It is an interesting result. Using this idea, we are going to access the elements of an array using pointers, without the array variable.

What is the base address of array? How to obtain the same? Consider the following declaration and see how the base address or starting address of the array will be obtained.

$$int\ a[5]\ =\ \{10,20,30,40,50\};$$

The first element of an array is referred by **a[0]** and its address by **&a[0]**. Here **&a[0]** refers to the starting address or base address of the array **a**. Otherwise, the name of the array itself refers to the base address, i.e. **a**. Once we know the starting address of array, we can travel through all the elements of the array easily by making simple arithmetic operations.

```
int *ptr;
ptr = &a[0]; /* &a[0] refers to the starting address of array */
       (or)
ptr = a;     /* a also refers to the starting address */
```

The first element is referred by **\*ptr** (or) **\*(ptr+0)**.
The second element is referred by **\*(ptr+1)**.
The third element is referred by **\*(ptr+2)**.
The fourth element is referred by **\*(ptr+3)** and in common, the element is referred by **\*(ptr+i)**.

The following program is an example for processing the array elements using the pointer variable.

**Example:**

```
/* Program to process the array using pointers */
main()
{
    int   a[5] ={10,20,30,40,50};
    int i, *ptr;

    /*Starting address of array is assigned*/
    ptr=&a[0];

    for(i=0;i<5;i++)
       printf("\n%d is stored at location:%d",*(ptr+i),(ptr+i));
}
```

Output:

```
10 is stored at location : 1000
20 is stored at location : 1002
30 is stored at location : 1004
40 is stored at location : 1006
50 is stored at location : 1008
```

The following is a famous and traditional program used to sort the numbers using pointers. We are also finding the maximum and minimum from the set of numbers after sorting.

**Example:**

```
/* Program to sort numbers using pointers  */
main()
{
   int   a[15],n,i,j,temp,*ptr;

   printf("\nHow many numbers ");
   scanf("%d",&n);

   printf("\nEnter %d values\n",n);
   for(i=0;i<n;i++)
        scanf("%d",&a[i]);

      /* Starting address of a is assigned to ptr*/
   ptr = a;

   printf("\nValues before sorting\n");
   for(i=0;i<n;i++)
      printf("%d\t",*(ptr+i));

   for( i = 0 ;  i<n-1 ;i++)
      for(j =i+1 ; j<n; j++)
```

```
        if (*(ptr+i) > *(ptr+j))
          {
              temp  = *(ptr+i);
             *(ptr+i) = *(ptr+j);   /* Swapping   */
             *(ptr+j) =  temp;
          }

    printf("\nValues after sorting\n");
    for(i=0; i<n; i++)
       printf("%d\t", * (ptr + i));
 }
```

**Output:**

```
How many numbers 5
Enter 5 values
22 55 11 44 33

Values before sorting
22 55 11 44 33

Values after sorting
11 22 33 44 55
```

## 7.8  WHY AN ARRAY STARTS FROM ZERO (0)?

Let us consider the following declaration of array for our discussion.

$$int\ a[5]=\{10,20,30,40,50\};$$

First element **10** is stored at **a[0]**
Second element **20** is stored at **a[1]**
Third element **30** is stored at **a[2]**, etc.

As you know, array elements start from **0th** location in C language. The first element of the array is referred by **a[0]**. Are you confused about this kind of reference? It actually creates a problem to the user, like where is the first element, and why it is stored at **0th** location, etc. Most of the programming languages use **a[1]** to refer to the first element of array.
The pointer variable declaration statement is

```
int *ptr ;
ptr=a;   /* Base address of array */
```

Here **ptr** points to starting address of array **a**. The elements of the array are referred as follows using the pointer variable **ptr**.

The first element by **\*(ptr+0)**
The second element by **\*(ptr+1)**
The third element by **\*(ptr+2) etc.**

When we use the notation **a[0]** to refer to the first element of array, the compiler converts the notation **a[0]** into *(a+0) internally. If we use **a[1]** to refer to the first element of the array, the equivalent expression is internally converted as *(a+1) and the result of this reference is the second element not the first element. **Why?**

At the time of evaluation of expression, the problem will occur. Assume that the base address of array is **1000** and the remaining values are stored in consecutive memory locations. Our reference **a[1]** will be converted to *(a+1). The value of **a** is **1000** and **1000+1** is **1002**. That is *(a+1) will be replaced by *(1000+1) and the reference becomes *(1002), will return the value stored in second location not the value from the first location. This is the reason why the array index starts from **0** instead of **1**.

**Alternative reference?** The reference of **a[0]** will be replaced by *(a+0). This reference may also be changed as *(0+a) because **0+a** or **a+0** give the same result. So instead of traditional reference **a[1]**, we can use **1[a]**, to refer the same.

```
/*Referring array elements-alternative method */
#include <stdio.h>
main()
{
int a[3]={10,20,30},i;

clrscr();

printf("\nThe elements of array are : ");
for(i=0;i<3;i++)
    printf("%5d",i[a]);

getch();

}
```

## 7.9  POINTERS AND STRINGS

String is a collection of characters and it can be also be called **character array.** In the previous topic, we discussed many programs using numbers. The pointers are beneficial in character-based applications also. The character pointer variable is declared as follows

```
char *ptr;
```

Here **\*ptr** is a pointer variable, which points to the array of characters. The string value can be assigned to the variable as below

```
char name[ ]="Karthikeyan";
```

The starting address (base address) of the string is taken from any one of the following ways with the help of the above declaration

**name** (or) **&name[0]**

/* Both are points to the starting address of the string */

The statements

```
char *ptr;
char name[ ] ="Karthi";
```

are declarative statements and the assignment statement is

```
ptr = name;
```

Here the starting address of the character array variable or string variable **name** is assigned to the pointer variable **ptr.** Now both **name** and **ptr** point to the same memory location. The following diagram illustrates the above.

| K | a | r | t | h | i | \0 | |
|---|---|---|---|---|---|---|---|
| 1000 | 1001 | 1002 | 1003 | 1004 | 1005 | 1006 | 1007 |

**Note:**

'\0' is the NULL character, which indicates the end of string.

Now we are going to see how to access the characters of the string variable using pointers.

**Example:**

```
/* Accessing string values using pointers */
main( )
{
   char   *ptr, name[]="Karthi";
   int   i , l;

   ptr = name;
      /*Starting address is assigned to ptr*/
   l=strlen(name);

   for(i=0;i<l;i++)
      printf("%c",*(ptr+i));
}
```

Output:

```
Karthi
```

How to use pointer variable to read a string value? Test the following simple program.

**Example:**

```
#include <stdio.h>
main()
{
   char *s;
   printf("\nEnter a string : ");
```

```
    gets(s);
    printf("\nYour given string is : ");
    while(*s)
        printf("%c",*s++);
    getch();
}
```

Output:

```
    Enter a string : You are welcome
    Your given string is : You are welcome
```

In the above simple program one character pointer variable is **\*s**. It is also used to read a string using **gets()** function. Finally the characters of this variable are referred by **\*s++**. What is this? Here **\*s,** refers the value of the string variable in every iteration. The pointer will be moved to the next location **s++**.

The program given below implements the **strcpy( )** function and it is used to copy the content of one string to another string variable.

### *Example:*

```
/* Implementation of strcpy command */
main()
{
    char s1[15],s2[15],*ptr;
    int i,j,l;

    printf("\nEnter a source string  : ");
    gets(s1);

    ptr = s1;
    l=strlen(s1);

    for(i=0;i<l;i++)
        s2[i] = *(ptr+i);

    s2[i]='\0';
    printf("\nCopied string  :%s",s2);

}
```

Output:

```
    Enter a source string : karthi
    Copied string : karthi
```

## 7.10  POINTERS AND FUNCTIONS

We discussed the importance of **function** in a program and how the same is used in various applications in the previous chapter. The drawback of **simple function** is that, we

**cannot return more than one value from it**. The change made in the called function does not reflect in the calling function. (Calling function—A function from which the new function is invoked and the Called function—A function to which the control has to be transferred). One more problem is that we cannot pass the entire array to the function. The first problem of a **function** is explained by using the following program.

**Example:**

```
/* Testing the values of changes */
main( )
{
   int a=10;

   printf("\nBefore change   : %d ",a);
   change(a);
printf("\nAfter    change  : %d ",a);
   getch( );
}

void change( int b )
{
   b=100;
   printf("\nInside the function : %d ",b);
}
```

Output:

```
Before change : 10
Inside the function : 100
After change : 10
```

In this program **change( )** the value of a in **main()** is **10** and it is passed to the user defined function. The function receives the value of **a** via **b.** Inside the function, the value of **b** has been changed to **100.** But this change will affect only in **b** not in the value of **a,** because **b** is local to the function. The value of **a** has been copied to **b**. This is equivalent to the statement **b=a;** So any changes in **b** will never affect the value of **a** here. Go ahead and read the next topic to solve these problems.

## 7.11   HOW TO CHANGE THE VALUE USING FUNCTION?

Are you able to change the value of argument in the called function? If so, how? Using pointers, you can achieve this. You can pass the address of a variable to the calling function and so the changes made in the called function will be reflected in the calling function. The following program example illustrates this idea.

*Example:*

```
/* To changes the values of variables using pointers */
main()
{
   int a=10;
   printf("\nValue before change = %d ",a);
   change(&a);    /* Passing address of a*/
   printf("\nValue After   change = %d ",a);
}

void change (int *b)
{
   *b=100;       /* Changing values indirectly */
}
```

**Output:**

```
Value before change = 10
Value After   change = 100
```

How the value of **a** has been changed here? From the **main()** we are passing the address of **a** to the function by the statement

```
change(&a); /* Address of a is passing */
```

Now we are passing the address of **a**, not the value of **a**. So the address must be received by the pointer variable only and the function definition will be

```
void change(int *b)
```

At the time of execution, the address of **a** has been assigned to the pointer variable **b**, which is equivalent to the following statement

```
int *b;
b = &a;
```

Now both **a** and **b** are pointing to the same memory location and any change made in **b** will automatically affect the value of **a**.

**Same variable name appearing in many parts of the program leads to confusion.** The name of the variable in one function may be same in another function. The variable name is only for the user reference not for the system. This problem is clearly presented in the following program.

*Example:*

```
/* Getting the address of the variable */
main( )
{
   int a=10;

   printf("\nAddress of 'a' in main : %d ",&a);
```

```
   change() ;
}

void  change()
{
   int a=100;
   printf("\nAddress of 'a' in function: %d ",&a);
}
```

**Output:**

```
Address of  'a'  in  main    : 5000
Address of  'a'  in  function  : 7000
```

In this program, there are two variables with same name as **a**. One is in **main( )** and the other is in the user-defined function **change( )**. For every declaration, the memory allocation for each variable is different from others. So that the result of the above program is **5000** and **7000**, two different addresses even though names are same.

## 7.12  CALL BY VALUE AND CALL BY REFERENCE

A function can be invoked in so many ways as we discussed in the previous chapters. The methods of calling a function can be classified into two,

1. Call by value
2. Call by reference

Here is a program, to find the sum of two numbers that illustrate the above ways.

### Call by value

This can be done in two ways, either by using a variable or directly passing a value.

```
/* Passing values to the function */
main()
{
   int a=10,b=20,c;

   c=sum(a,b);    /* Passing the values of a,b */
   printf("\nSum = %d ",c);
}

int sum(int x, int y)
{
   return (x + y);
}
```

In this program, the values of **a** and **b** have been passed to the function to find the sum. It is just like the following simple assignment statement

$$x = a \quad \text{and} \quad y = b;$$

We can pass the value to the function by giving direct value also.

```
sum (10, b);
sum (10,20)
```

### Call by reference

What is reference? Here the variables indirectly use the reference instead of direct involvement. So the function can also be invoked by using the reference, that is addresses (using pointers). The previous program with a simple modification of using reference.

```
/* Example for Call by Reference */
main()
{
   int a=10,b=20,c;

   c = sum( &a, &b);     /* Passing the addresses of a, b */
   printf("\nSum  = %d ",c);
}

   int sum (int   *x,   int *y)
   {
      return (*x+*y);
   }
```

What is the difference between the previous two programs? In the first one values are passed to the function in a simple manner. But in the second one, addresses (i.e. references) of those variables are passed.

## 7.13 PASSING ARRAY TO THE FUNCTION

In general, we are not allowed to carry the whole array to the function. We can pass the elements one-by-one. If we need to process the whole array at the same time, this provision will not help. Now the hidden features of the pointer will be used to carry the entire array without more risks.

Array elements are always in the continuous memory locations. First you obtain the base address of the array. If we get the starting address of the array, we can reach any element in the array by making simple arithmetic operations. For the function side, just we have to pass the base address of array to the function. This idea is illustrated in the following program.

***Example:***

```
/* Passing array to the function using pointers  */
main()
{
   int a[ ]={10,20,30,40,50};

   display(a);
      /* Passing the base address of array */
}

display (int  *x)
{
   int i;

   printf("\n Array elements are   : ");
   for(i=0;i<5;i++)
      printf("%5d",*(x+i));
}
```

**Output:**

Array elements are:   10    20    30    40    50

In the above program, the starting address of the array is passed to the function by the statement

```
                    display(a);
```

The function will receive the starting address of array by defining the function argument as follows.

```
                    display(int *x)
```

This is equivalent to the assignment as **x=a;** The following is a program to test the previous idea by sending an array element to the function and the elements are doubled in the function. Finally, the changes are ensured by displaying the values in **main( )** function.

***Example:***

```
/* Program to pass the whole array to the function */

#include <stdio.h>
main()
{
   int i, a[5]={10,20,30,40,50};

   clrscr();
   printf("\nElements before invoking function:");
   for(i=0;i<5;i++)
      printf("%5d",a[i]);
```

```
      test(a);
      printf("\nElements after invoking function:");
      for(i=0;i<5;i++)
         printf("%5d",a[i]);
      getch();
   }
   test(int *x)
   {
      int i;
      for(i=0;i<5;i++)
         *(x+i) = *(x+i) * *(x+i);
   }
```

**Output:**

```
   Elements before invoking function: 10   20 30   40   50
   Elements before invoking function: 100 400 900 1600 2500
```

I hope now you have an idea about how the array elements are carried to the function. Here is a program to find the mean, variance and standard deviation of **N** floating point numbers. Formula to calculate the standard deviation is

$$\text{Standard deviation} = \sqrt{\text{variance}}$$

where
variance = $1/n \sum (X_i - \text{Mean})^2$ and $i = 1$ to $n$
mean = $1/n \sum X_i$

So, to find standard deviation, the following are the general steps.

1. Find the sum and mean
2. Find the variance and
3. Finally calculate the standard deviation.

***Example:***

```
/*Program to find the standard deviation using pointers */
#include <math.h>
main()
{
   float a [ ]={1.1,2.2,3.3,4.4,5.5};
   sd(a);
}

void sd (float *x)
{
   int i;
   float s1=0,s2=0,s3=0,sddev,mean,var,temp;
```

```
    printf("\nValues : ");
    for(i=0;i<5;i++)
    {
        s1 += (*(x+i));    /* Finding  summation */
        printf("%5.2f\t",*(x+i));
    }
    mean = s1/5;      /* Calculation of   Mean   */

    for (i=0;i<5;i++)
    {
        temp=*(x+i)-mean;
        s2+=pow(temp,2);
    }

    var   = s2/5; /* Calculation of variance */
    sddev = sqrt(var);   /* Calculation of S D */

    printf("\nMean          = %5.2f",mean);
    printf("\nVariance      = %5.2f",var);
    printf("\nStd.Deviation = %5.2f",sddev);
}
```

**Output:**

```
    Values:  1.10    2.20    3.30    4.40    5.50
    Mean            =   3.30
    Variance        =   2.42
    Std. Deviation =   1.56
```

You can try for the sorting program in the above manner.

## 7.14  PASSING STRING TO THE FUNCTION

As we know, the string is a collection of characters and it is also called character array. How to pass string to the function? It can be passed to the function as we did in the previous section.

How the **strlen( )** function works and how it returns the length of a given string. The following program is to find the length of a string and illustrate how to pass the string (character array) to the function.

*Example:*

```
/*Implementation of strlen() function, passing string to the function */
#include <string.h>
main()
{
    char str[ ] ="Karthikeyan";
    int l;
    l = len(str);
```

```
printf("\nLength of string is  : %d ",l);
    }

    int len(char *s)
    {
    int i=0;
    printf("\nGiven string is  : ");
    while(*s)
    {
       printf("%c",*(s++));
       i++;
    }
    return (i);
}
```

**Output:**
```
Given string is      : Karthikeyan
Length of string is : 11
```

Here the user-defined function is invoked by the statement **len(s).** It passes the starting address of the string and it is received by the function. The **while** loop is used to travel up to the end of character. Whenever there is a NULL character ('\0'), the loop terminates.

The statement **\*(s++)** is used to adjust the next character of the string. First the character is processed and incremented (post-increment). Finally, the function returns the length of string.

### Note:
Base address of array cannot be changed at any time

The address can be changed only in the temporary pointer variables. Suppose we would like to change the base address of any array, what would happen? We cannot recall the starting address of array and we are not able to process the first element of array. So, the starting address of the array should not be changed.

```
/* Example to change the base address */
main( )
{
   int a[ ]={10,20,30,40,50};
   int i;
   for(i=0;i<5;i++)
      printf("%d",*(a++));  /* ERROR */
}
```

Here, **a** refers to the base address of the array. **a++** indicates that the starting address of array will be incremented by **1,** and now **a** points to the second element. After some increments, how can we obtain the base address? For this, we are not allowed to modify the base address of the array.

## 7.15   2D ARRAY AND POINTERS

We understood that the pointer gives a very good support to arrays including two-dimensional arrays. Matrix is a traditional and famous example for a two-dimensional array. Consider the following declarative statement

```
int a[2] [3] ;
```

This declaration tells

⇨ **a** is a two-dimensional array
⇨ The maximum number of elements are 6 (2 x 3 = 6)
⇨ and all are **int**eger type of data
⇨ So, each element occupies **2** bytes (Totally **12** bytes)

The values for the above two-dimensional array are initialized as below and its corresponding memory allocation is illustrated.

```
int a[2][3] = {
              {10,20,30},◄────── First row
              {40,50,60},◄────── Second row
          };
```

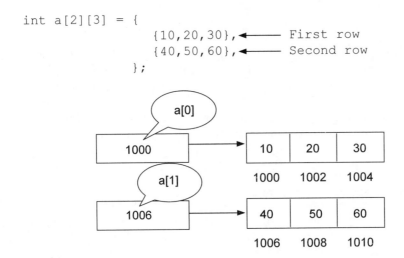

Two-dimensional array is a collection of one-dimensional arrays and each single array is pointed by the pointer variable. Here **a[0]** points to the first one-dimensional array, **a[1]** points to the second one-dimensional array, etc.

a [0] can be rewritten as *(a+0) and
a [1] can be rewritten as *(a+1) etc.

So, **a[0]** refers to the starting address of first array, and its values are referred as,

a[0][0] => First row first column
a[0][1] => First row second column, etc.

How to refer the element **a[0][0]** using pointer variable? The reference of two-dimensional value, using pointer, is as follows. Here **a[0][0]** can be referred as *(*(a+0)+0)).

```
  *(a+0)     => Starting address of first array, i.e. a[0]
 (*(a+0)+0)  => address of the first row's first element, i.e. &a[0][0]
*(*(a+0)+0)  => Value of the first row's first element, i.e. a[0][0]
                (* is the value at the location operator )
```

The above discussion is general and we are going to discuss with the array which has been declared as above.

Value returned by a[0] is 1000
Value returned by a[1] is 1006

Value returned by &a[0][0] is 1000
Value returned by &a[0][1] is 1002, etc.

The following is an example program to check the starting address of each array.

**Example:**

```
/* To get the base addresses of 2D Array  */
main()
{
   int a[2][3]={
                 {10,20,30},
                 {40,50,60},
               };
   int i;

   for(i=0;i<2;i++)
      printf("\nBase address of %d array:%u",i+1,a[i]);
}
```

Output:
```
Base address of 1 array: 1000
Base address of 2 array: 1006
```

One more program is here to give a better idea about two-dimensional array and pointers.

**Example:**

```
/* Accessing the elements of array */
main()
{
   int a[2][3]={
                 {10,20,30},
                 {40,50,60},
               };
   int i, j;
```

```
for(i=0;i<2;i++)
   for(j=0;j<3;j++)
      printf("\na[%d][%d]= %d is stored at:
         %u", i,j, a[i][j], &a[i][j]);
   getch();
}
```

**Output:**

```
a[0][0] = 10   is stored at : 1000
a[0][1] = 20   is stored at : 1002
a[0][2] = 30   is stored at : 1004
a[1][0] = 40   is stored at : 1006
a[1][1] = 50   is stored at : 1008
a[1][2] = 60   is stored at : 1010
```

Referring the elements of a two-dimensional array is a little bit difficult than a one-dimensional array. The following is an example for this reference, which is based on the previous declaration and its addresses. We are going to refer the element at **a[1][2]**, the pointer notation is as follows. Here **i** is **1** and **j** is **2**.

$$*(*(a+1)+2)$$

1. `*(a+1)`
   ⇨ It returns the starting address of the second array equal to **a[1]** and it returns **1006**.
2. `(*(a+1)+2)`
   ⇨ The value returned by **\*(a+1)** will be incremented by **2**. So it returns the address **1010**.
3. `*(*(a+1)+2)`
   ⇨ It returns the value of that location, i.e. value at location **1010** is **60**.

The next program illustrates how to access the elements of a two-dimensional array using pointers.

**Example:**

```
/* Accessing the elements of 2D using pointers */
main()
   {
      int a[2][3]= {
                     {10,20,30},
                     {40,50,60},
                  };
      int i, j;

      for(i=0;i<2;i++)
         for(j=0;j<3;j++)
            printf("\n%d is stored at : %u",
               *(*(a+i)+j),(*(a+i)+j));
      getch( );
   }
```

Output:

```
10 is stored at : 1245032
20 is stored at : 1245036
30 is stored at : 1245040
40 is stored at : 1245044
50 is stored at : 1245048
60 is stored at : 1245052
```

Traditional program for two-dimensional array is matrix operations. So the following program is an example for matrix multiplication using pointers.

***Example:***

```
/* Matrix multiplication using pointers */
main()
{
   int a[3][3],b[3][3],c[3][3],i,j,k,n;

   printf("\nNo. of rows and columns : ");
   scanf("%d",&n);

   printf("\nEnter the value of matrix A");
   for(i=0;i<n;i++)
      for(j=0;j<n;j++)
         scanf("%d",(*(a+i)+j));

   printf("\nEnter the value of matrix B");
   for(i=0;i<n;i++)
      for(j=0;j<n;j++)
         scanf("%d",(*(b+i)+j));

   /* Matrix multiplication */

   for(i=0;i<n;i++)
      for(j=0;j<n;j++)
         for(k=0;k<n;k++)
         {
            *(*(c+i)+j)=0;
            *(*(c+i)+j) += *(*(a+i)+k) * *(*(b+k)+j);
         }

   printf("\nResult  matrix C \n");

   for(i=0;i<n;i++)
      {
         for(j=0;j<n;j++)
            printf("%6d",*(*(c+i)+j));

         printf("\n");
      }
   getch();
}
```

Output:

```
No. of rows and columns : 2

Enter the value of matrix A
1 2 3 4

Enter the value of matrix B
1 2 3 4

Result matrix C
6      8
12     16
```

## 7.16 ARRAY OF POINTERS

What is the use of an array? Array is used to store a number of elements in a single variable. The elements may be of any type. But all of them must be of the same type. We have discussed many programs using arrays with different types of values like integer, real and character, etc.

Can we store addresses as array elements? Yes. Instead of simple data, the addresses can be stored. The way of declaring array of pointer is explained in the following:

```
int *ptr;
```

Here **ptr** is a pointer variable, which points to one integer memory location. With a small change in the above declaration, the statement is

```
int *ptr[5];
```

Here **ptr** is a variable and it is allowed to have addresses of **5** variables (not values). In this case, we can store **5** different integer addresses to this array variable. Elements of the array may contain different addresses.

```
int a,b,c;
ptr[0] = &a;
        /* Address of a is assigned to first element of array */
ptr[1] = &b;
        /* Address of b is assigned to second element of array */
ptr[2] = &c;
```

The value of **a** can be referred as **\*ptr[0]**. The following is a program which gives an idea of our discussion.

**Example:**

```
/* Example for array of pointers */
main( )
{
    int a=10,b=20,c=30;
    int *ptr[5];            /* Array of pointers */

    clrscr( );
    ptr[0]=&a;
    ptr[1]-&b;
    ptr[2]=&c;

    /* Value of pointer variable is accessed  */

    printf("\na = %d ",*ptr[0]);
    printf("\nb = %d ",*ptr[1]);
    printf("\nc = %d ",*ptr[2]);

    printf("\n Address of a   = %u",&a );
    printf("\n Value of ptr[0]= %u",ptr[0] );
}
```

Output:

```
    A=10
    B=20
    C=30
    Address of a      = 12042
    Value of ptr[ 0 ] = 12042
```

In the above program **ptr[0]** holds the address of variable **a**. So **&a** and **ptr[0]** contains the same values (i.e., address).

## 7.17 CALLING FUNCTIONS USING POINTERS

Normally functions are invoked by specifying its name with the necessary arguments. Now we are going to invoke the function using pointers. The address of variable can be obtained as follows.

```
    int a;
    printf("\nAddress = %u ",&a);
```

The output of the above would be the address of the variable **a**. It may be **1240**, which is not always the same. Address of the function can also obtained as illustrated below.

```
/* Obtaining the address of function */
main( )
{
   int test( )

   printf("\nAddress  function  test  = %u ",test);
}
```

This program returns the address of function **test( )**. This address can be assigned to a pointer of the function variable as shown below.

```
int test( );    /* Function prototype declaration */
int (*ptr)( ); /* Pointer to function */
```

Address of function **test()** is assigned to the pointer variable **ptr** as

$$ptr = test;$$

The function can be invoked using pointer as below:

```
(*ptr)( );    /* Similar to calling as test( ) */
```

The following is a complete program, which illustrates the above discussion like how the functions are called using the pointers.

```
/* Illustrating the function calling using pointers  */
main( )
{
   void test( );
   void (*ptr)( );

   ptr = test;      /* Address  assignment  */
   (*ptr)( );       /* Function calling     */
}

void  test( )
{
   printf("\nHello");
}
```

## 7.18  THE NEED FOR DYNAMIC MEMORY ALLOCATION

What is meant by dynamic memory allocation? The memory can be allocated in the following two ways:

1. Static memory allocation
2. Dynamic memory allocation

What we have discussed in the previous chapters, is only about static memory allocation.

That is, once we declare a variable like array, we cannot extend or shrink the array size. For example, in the following declaration

```
char a[15];
```

At the time of execution, **15** bytes will be reserved for the above declaration, because each character occupies one byte of memory. If we use all the memory area effectively to store the data, then there is no problem. The problem will occur only when the data size (memory utilization) exceeds the available memory size.

In the variable **a** we can store **15** characters as **"Mr. KARTHIKEYAN"** and no problem in the variable utilization. Suppose if we are going to store the value as **"KARTHI"**, only **6** characters are stored and the remaining memory is wasted. On the other hand, if we want to store the value like **"KARTHIKEYAN IS A GOOD BOY"**, there is no memory to store this value. Because it requires **24** bytes of memory.

If we are dealing with small amount of memory it is OK. But when we want to store hundreds and thousands of data items, the only way is **dynamic memory** allocation. In this type, the memory will be allocated only at the time of execution, not in the compile time.

## 7.19 HOW TO ALLOCATE MEMORY DYNAMICALLY?

The library function **malloc( )** is used to allocate the memory dynamically. The format of this function is as follows:

```
void * malloc(size)
```

where the **size** is the number of bytes to be allocated. If there is a sufficient memory for the request, it returns starting address of the allocated memory block. If it fails, a **NULL** value will be returned.

For example, the statement **malloc(10)** will allocate **10** bytes, memory and returns the starting address. This address can be assigned to a pointer variable and used.

```
int *ptr ;
ptr = malloc(10);
```

Instead of a constant number of bytes like **10**, we can use a variable number of bytes. The type of data also should be defined. Otherwise, memory is assigned but not able to identify which type of data is going to be stored. So, the type of data that is going to be stored in memory should be specified during allocation.

The type of memory reference should be defined explicitly as follows:

```
ptr = ( int * ) malloc( 10 );
```

Explicit type conversion

Here **malloc( 10 )** will allocate only **10** bytes of memory and **( int *)** is an explicit type conversion and which identifies it as integer type. The following program illustrates the idea of dynamic memory allocation.

```
/* Example for Dynamic memory allocation */
main( )
{
   int   n ,  i;
   int   *ptr ;

   printf("\nHow many values");
   scanf("%d",&n);

   ptr=malloc(sizeof(int) * n);
               /* Dynamic memory Allocation */

   printf("\nEnter %d values ",n);
   for(i=0;i<n;i++)
      scanf("%d",(ptr+i));

   for(i=0;i<n;i++)
   printf("%d\n",*(ptr+i));
}
```

What a fantastic program? Without mentioning the size of the array. The size will be determined at the time of execution. Here **malloc( )** will return a block of memory depending upon the value of **n**, which is user-defined. The **sizeof (int)** is **2** bytes and if user supplies a value of n as **10** then **20** bytes will be allocated. So that it can comfortably hold **10** **integer** values.

You will find it interesting to test the following program, which is an entirely new method to sort the set of numbers using **pointers, function and dynamic memory allocation**.

### *Example:*

```
/* Sorting—Using pointers, functions and
    Dynamic memory allocations */
#include <stdio.h>
main()
{
int *a,i,n;

clrscr();
printf("\nHow many elements : ");
scanf("%d",&n);
     /* Dynamic memory allocation */
a = (int *) malloc(n * sizeof(int));

printf("\nEnter %d elements   ",n);
for(i=0;i<n;i++)
     scanf("%d",a+i);
```

```
printf("\nElements Before Sorting\n");
for(i=0;i<n;i++)
    printf("%5d",*(a+i));

sorting(a,n);

printf("\nElements After Sorting\n");
for(i=0;i<n;i++)
    printf("%5d",*(a+i));

getch();
}

sorting(int *p,int n)
{
    int i,j,temp;

    for(i=0;i<n-1;i++)
        for(j=i+1;j<n;j++)
            if (*(p+i) > *(p+j))
            {
                temp = *(p+i);
                *(p+i) = *(p+j);
                *(p+j) = temp;
            }
}
```

**Output:**
```
How many elements : 5
Enter 5 elements
    55
    22
    44
    11
    33
Elements Before Sorting
    55 22 44 11 33
Elements After Sorting
    11 22 33 44 55
```

## 7.20   RETURNING ADDRESS

The previous section provides an idea about the function and pointers that indirectly return the address. But we can return a memory address to the calling function like a normal function return type. Look at the following code:

**int Read()**    => The function returns an integer value

**char Read()**   => The function returns a character value

**void Read()**   => The function returns nothing

**int * Read()**   => Now the function returns memory address.

The following example program illustrates the idea of returning an address from the function. The program read the array elements in the function and returns the base address of the array to the **main()** function. Later the address will be used in further process in **main()** function.

## Example:

```
/* Program which read value in function Read() and return the address
to the main() function   */

#include <stdio.h>
#include <conio.h>

int * Read(int);
main()
{
int *a,n,i;

clrscr();
printf("\nEnter the size of the array :");
scanf("%d",&n);
a = Read(n);
printf("\nArray elements are \n");
for(i=0;i<n;i++)
   printf("%5d",*(a+i));

   getch();
}

int * Read(int m)
{
int *p,i;
p=(int *) malloc(sizeof(int) * m);
printf("\nEnter %d values ",m);
for(i=0;i<m;i++)
   scanf("%d",(p+i));

return p;
}
```

Output:
```
Enter the size of the array : 5

Enter 5 values
11
22
33
44
55

Array elements are
11     22     33     44     55
```

## REVIEW QUESTIONS ✍

1. What is the need of pointers in a program?
2. What is the disadvantage of function?
3. How to declare pointer variables?
4. What are the operators associated with the pointer variables?
5. How to obtain the address of a variable?
6. Write short notes on pointer arithmetic
7. Write short notes on pointers and function
8. Explain the role of pointers in string with an example
9. Call by value and Call by reference. Explain.
10. How to pass the whole array to the function?
11. Write short notes on pointers and two-dimensional array
12. Prove that how the array elements are stored in consecutive memory locations
13. How do we use array of pointers? Explain
14. Can we call a function using pointers? If so how?
15. What is the need of Dynamic memory allocation?
16. How to allocate memory dynamically?
17. Why we have to release the memory and how?
18. Try to pass two-dimensional array to the function.
19. What is the disadvantage of malloc( )?
20. What is the size of pointer variables?

# Chapter 8
# Structures and Unions

## 8.1 WHAT IS A STRUCTURE?

Array is a collection of data items and all the data items must be of same type. In very large applications, some data items may be related to others or group of data items may be related. Let us consider the college and the information related to the student such as name; roll number, age, marks, etc. are heterogeneous types. These items cannot be grouped using array. To group these kinds of data items, another feature of C called **structure** can be used. Structure means that related data items may be grouped under a name. By grouping related items under one name called structure name, we could write programs well.

For example, the information about an employee like employee name, department, designation, and salary details can be grouped by one name like **emp_record**.

## 8.2 HOW TO DECLARE THE STRUCTURE

How to declare the variable? We are already familiar about the declaration of simple, array variables in the earlier chapters. But structure declarations somewhat differs from the conventional declarations, as in the following:

```
struct <tag>
   {
      member-1;
      member-2;
      ...
      member-n;
   };
```

```
struct [<tag>]
    {
        member-1;
        member-2;
        ...
        member-n;
   }sv1,sv2...;
```

⇨ **struct** is a keyword to indicate that structure variable.

⇨ member-1, member-2 are the variables of the structure.

⇨ In the first option the **<tag>** name is a must because using this **<tag>** only we can create new structure variable as follows. The structure variable is defined in the following format only.

```
struct <tag> sv1,sv2...;
```

This declaration is just like in **int a,b,c ...;** In the second option **sv1** and **sv2** are the structure variables. The structure ends with semicolon like others.

The information about students such as name, roll number and marks are grouped and declared as follows:

```
struct stu
   {
      char name[16];
      int rollno, marks;
   };

struct stu s1,s2;
```

Here, by using the tag name **stu** the structure variable **s1** and **s2** are created. Alternative way to declare the structure variable is as follows.

```
struct stu
   {
      char name[16];
      int rollno, marks;
   }s1,s2;
```

Now without using tag name the variables **s1** and **s2** are created. So we can use any one of the above declarations.

## 8.3 REFERRING THE DATA IN STRUCTURE

The aim of the array and structure is basically same. In array, the elements are referred by specifying array name with index like a[5] to refer the fifth element. But in structure, the members are referred by entirely new method as mentioned below:

```
structure-name. variable name;
```

The dot (.) operator is used to refer the members of the structures. For example if we wish to access the members of the previous structure, the following procedure have to be followed:

```
s1.name, s1.marks, s1. rollno
```

## 8.4 ASSIGNING THE VALUES TO THE STRUCTURE VARIABLE

The values may be assigned for the array while declaring it as follows:

```
int a[5]={10,20,30,40,50};
```

In the same manner, we can assign the values for the members of the structure as follows:

```
struct stu
   {
      char name[15];
      int rollno, marks;
   } s1= {"Karthi",1000,76};
```

Here the string value **"Karthi"** will be assigned to the member **name**, **1000** will be assigned to the member **rollno** and **76** will be assigned to **marks**. The following program is a first one using structure and sees how the members of the structure are being referred.

**Example:**

```
/* Example for structure reference and assignment */
main( )
{
   struct stu
   {
      char name[15];
      int rollno, marks;
   }s1 = {"Karthi",1000,76};

   printf("\nName    = %s ",s1.name);
   printf("\nroll no  = %d ",s1.rollno);
   printf("\nMarks    = %d ",s1.marks);
}
```

**Output:**

```
Name     : Karthi
roll no : 1000
Marks    : 76
```

Suppose all the values of one structure are necessary for another structure variable. The values can be copied one-by-one as usual. Here the structure that supports the whole structure can be assigned using = operator. Assume **s1** and **s2** are the structure variables and the contents of **s1** should be copied in **s2** also as shown in the following program:

```
strcpy(s2.name, s1.name);
s2.rollno = s1. rollno; /* copying one by one*/
s2.marks = s1. marks.
     (or)
s2 = s1;
   /* Copying entire structure to another structure */
```

The second one is the best way of programming approach to copying structures. An example program to prepare a pay slip for the employee using the structure.

### Example:

```
/*To find the net pay of the employee, using structure */
main()
{
   struct emp
   {
      char name[25];
      float bp,hra,pf,da,np;
      int empno;
   }e;

   printf("\nName of the employee : ");
   gets(e.name);
   printf("\nEmployee No : ");
   scanf("%d",&e.empno);
   printf("\nBasic Pay   : ");
   scanf("%f",&e.bp);

   if (e.bp>5000)
      {
         e.da  = 1.25 *  e.bp;   /* 125 %  DA  */
         e.hra =  .25 *  e.bp;   /*  25 %  HRA */
         e.pf  =  .12 *  e.bp;   /*  12 %  PF  */
      }
   else
      {
         e.da  = 1.0 *  e.bp;    /* 100 %  DA  */
         e.hra =  .15 * e.bp;    /*  15 %  HRA */
         e.pf  =  .10 * e.bp;    /*  10 %  PF  */
      }
   e.np = e.bp + e.da + e.hra - e.pf;

   printf("\n\tKarthik  Systems pvt. ltd., \n");
   printf("\nName : %s  Employee No :  %d
                     \n",e.name,e.empno);
   printf("\nBasic Pay   D.A       H.R.A     P.F
                     Net Pay\n");
   printf("\n%5.2f    %5.2f  %5.2f  %5.2f  %5.2f ",
            e.bp, e.da, e.hra, e.pf, e.np);
}
```

Output:
```
Name of the employee : karthikeyan
Employee No : 12000
Basic Pay    : 5500
```

```
Karthik  Systems pvt. ltd.,

Name   :  karthikeyan    Employee No.   12000
Basic Pay    D.A        H.R.A    P.F      Net Pay
5500.00      6875.00    1375.00  660.00   13090.00
```

## 8.5  ARRAY OF STRUCTURES

The above example is only for manipulating a single record, that is, only one employee information. Suppose if we want to prepare more records, we can use the array of structures. Array of structure is defined as simple as ordinary arrays as below:

`struct emp e[100];`

The above declaration indicates that **e** is an array of structure variable and we can store **100** employee information.

The reference of members is also similar to the array reference. So, first we have to specify the index of the structure and necessary variables. To refer the first employee's information we have to use the notations

`s[0].name, s[0].np etc.`

Likewise all the employees' information is referred and processed. The following example illustrates the array of structures.

```c
/* To find the class of the students  */
main()
{
   struct stu
   {
     char name[25];
     int rollno,marks;
   }s[50];

   int n,i;
   char result[15];

   printf("\nHow many students  : ");
   scanf("%d",&n);
   printf("\nEnter %d  students information\n",n);
   for(i=0;i<n;i++)
   {
     printf("\nEnter %d persons name : ",i+1);
     scanf("%s",s[i].name);
     printf("\nRoll No: ");
     scanf("%d",&s[i].rollno);
     printf("\nMarks: ");
     scanf("%d",&s[i].marks);
   }
```

```
      printf("\nResult of the students ");
      for(i=0;i<n;i++)
      {
         if (s[i].marks >= 60)
            strcpy(result,"First");
         if ((s[i].marks >= 50)  && (s[i].marks <60))
            strcpy(result,"Second");
         if ((s[i].marks >= 40) && (s[i].marks<50))
            strcpy(result,"Third");
         if (s[i].marks < 40)
            strcpy(result,"Fail");

      printf("\nResult = %s class ",result);
      }
}
```

What is the output of the previous program? I leave for your execution. Test it and see how this kind of programs help in real-life applications.

As we know that the elements of an array are stored continuously. In structure also the members will be stored in consecutive memory locations, one after another. This is illustrated in the following program. It has a structure **stu** and the size of single structure is **17** bytes. (**2** for age and **15** for name, so **2+15=17** bytes).

**Example:**

```
/* Array of structures  */
struct
{
   int  age;
   char name[15];
}stu[5];

main()
{
   int i;

   for(i=0;i<5;i++)
      printf("\nAddress is : ",&stu[i]);
}
```

Output:
```
Address is : 1200
Address is : 1217
Address is : 1234
Address is : 1251
Address is : 1268
```

From this output, it is found that the elements in structure are also stored in the consecutive memory locations.

## 8.6  NESTED STRUCTURE

In case of nested **if,** the statement part will have another **if** statement. In case of nested looping also, the statement portion has another looping statement. So the nested structure also will have another structure variable as a member.

There is no data type for maintaining date related information. Now we are going to create a user-defined data type using structure and it can be used as a data type for date.

```
struct
{
   int dd,mm,yy;
}d;

struct
{
   char name[15];
   struct d dob;
}stu;
```

The first structure **d** has three fields to represent a date by using three variables, dd (day), mm(month) and yy(year). The second structure **stu** has two member fields. They are **name** and date of birth (**dob**), which is declared using the structure **d.**

We have an idea about the reference of values of the structure variable. Here to access the **name** is very simple and to access the **dob** is differ. The **dob** structure members are accessed by as follows:

stu.d.dd,  stu.d.dd and stu.d.dd

To refer the member **dob,** it is enough specify **stu . dob**. But **dob** is not an ordinary variable, which is another structure variable with three members. If we made any reference directly via **dob,** we can refer by **dob.members**. But if reference is through the **stu,** we have to use the **stu.d.dd,** etc. A complete program for nested structure is given below:

***Example:***

```
/* Example for Nested structure */

struct dob
{
   int dd,mm,yy;
};

struct
{
   char name[15];
   struct dob db;
}stu;
```

```
main()
{
    clrscr();
    printf("\eEnter the name :");
    scanf("%s",stu.name);
    printf("\nEnter the age (dd/mm/yy) :");
    scanf("%d%d%d",&stu.db.dd,&stu.db.mm,&stu.db.yy);
    printf("\nYour Name is  : %s ",stu.name);
    printf("\nDate of Birth : %2d-%2d-%2d",
                stu.db.dd,stu.db.mm,stu.db.yy);

}
```

**Output:**

```
Enter the name : Karthi
Enter the age  (dd/mm/yy)  : 3 4 1974

Your name is  : Karthi
Date of Birth : 3-4-1974
```

## 8.7 STRUCTURES AND POINTERS

The features of pointers are not limited to simple application. It is used in the structure also. The declaration of structure pointer is as follows:

```
struct structure-tag * structure-pointer;
```

Proceed with the following example and see how ordinary variables and pointer variables are used in the program.

```
struct stu *s1; /* s1 is structure pointer */

struct
    {
        char name[15];
        int rollno;
    }s1, *s2;
```

In the above declaration, **s1** is an ordinary structure variable, but **s2** is a pointer to structure variable. The members of the structure **s1** will be referred using dot (.) operator. But the members of pointer to structure variable will be accessed using an operator called an arrow operator (→). In simple definition, instead of dot(.) operator, we have to use the arrow operator. So the members of **s2** are referred as **s2→name** and **s2→rollno**. The following program illustrates our discussion and may be clarified easily.

```
/* Example for pointers and structures */
main()
{
    struct stu
    {
        char name[25];
        int rollno;
    };

    struct  stu s1, *s2;

    printf("\nName of the student  : ");
    scanf("%s",s2->name);
    printf("\nRoll No.            : ");
    scanf("%d",&s2->rollno);
    printf("\nName: %s\nRoll No. :%d ",s2->name,s2->rollno);
}
```

## 8.8  STRUCTURES AND FUNCTIONS

The role of **function** in a program and how it can be used were discussed in Chapter 6. Passing and returning various parameters and returning various values, etc., also given. Now let us see, how the functions are used in structures also. In a simple function call, we have to mention the name of the function with necessary parameters as given below to pass one integer argument.

`void display(int a);`

Now we need to pass the structure to the function. One solution is passing the members of the structure one by one. But it is not convenient when there are large members in a structure. Otherwise look the following:

`void display(struct stu s)`

The above declaration is simple and easy to understand because instead of conventional variable, structure variable **s** is mentioned. The complete program which illustrates the above declaration is given below:

### *Example:*

```
/* Passing structure to the function  */
struct stu /* structure is declared as global  */
{
    char name[25];
    int rollno;
};
main( )
```

```
{
    struct stu s1;   /*s1 is only local to main( )   */

    printf("\nName of the student  : ");
    scanf("%s",s1.name);
    printf("\nRoll No.              : ");
    scanf("%d",&s1.rollno);

        display(s1);
            /* Calling function using structure variable */
}
/* Structure stu must be declared as global otherwise we cannot
use this name as in the following parameter declaration */

void display( struct stu s2)
{
    printf("\nYour  information is \n");
    printf("\nName    : %s ",s2.name);
    printf("\nRoll No : %d ",s2.rollno);
}
```

**Output:**

```
Name of the student  : karthi
Roll No.             : 1000

Your  information is
Name    : karthi
Roll No.: 1000
```

## 8.9  PASSING POINTER OF THE STRUCTURE TO THE FUNCTION

In the previous topic we discussed the functions and structures. But if we made any changes in the function, it will not affect the **main( )**. To achieve this, pointer is the only solution. Instead of sending the structure variable to the function, pass the address of the structure variable. Now we have the address and so our problem is solved. Everywhere about the pointer the address is enough. If we get the address, the remaining things are very easy for us. The following example gives the brief view of passing pointer of the structure to the function.

***Example:***

```
/* Passing pointer of the structure to the function  */
    struct emp
    {
        char name[25];
        float bp,da,pf,np;
    };
```

```
main()
{
   struct emp e1;
   input(&e1);
   calculate(&e1);
        display(&e1);
}

void input(struct emp *e2)
{
   printf("\Employee Name : ");
   scanf("%s",e2->name);
   printf("\nBasic Pay    : ");
   scanf("%f",&e2->bp);
}

void calculate(struct emp *e2)
{
   e2->da = 1.25 * e2->bp;
   e2->pf = .12  * e2->bp;
   e2->np = e2->bp + e2->da - e2->pf;
}

void display(struct emp *e2)
{
   printf("\n    Karthik Systems Pvt Ltd.,\n\n");
   printf("\nName       : %s    ",e2->name);
   printf("\nBasic Pay  : %5.2f ",e2->bp);
   printf("\nD. A       : %5.2f ",e2->da);
   printf("\nP. F       : %5.2f ",e2->pf);
   printf("\nNet Pay    : %5.2f ",e2->np);
}
```

**Output:**

```
Employee Name : Sanjai
Basic Pay     : 5000
Karthik Systems Pvt Ltd.,
Name       : Sanjai
Basic Pay  : 5000.00
D.A.       : 6250.00
P.F.       : 600.00
Net Pay    : 10650.00
```

This program is a basic idea about how the pointers, structures and functions are used in the program. Pointers have a large number of applications mostly in data structures such as in linked list, tree traversal, etc.

## 8.10  MISCELLANEOUS APPLICATIONS OF STRUCTURES

The structure is used to store different types of values and all the variables are stored continuously as shown in the diagram on page 172, and the following program illustrates this.

### *Example:*

```
/* To find the address and size of a structure */
main( )
{
   struct
      {
         int a, b;
      } test;

   printf("\nBase address of structure  : %u ",&test);
   printf("\nAddress of first member 'a': %u ",&test.a);
   printf("\nAddress of second member 'b' : %u ",&test.b);
   printf("\nSize of the structure 'test' : %d bytes ",sizeof(test));
}
```

Output:

```
Base address of structure      : 3354
Address of first     member 'a' : 3354
     /* 2 bytes for int   */
Address of second member 'b' : 3356
Size of the structure 'test' : 4 bytes
/* So 2+2=4  bytes   */
```

Starting address of the structure **test** is **3354.** The address of the first structure variable **a** is also same, i.e. **3354.** The next variable **b** is stored in the next memory location. (i.e. **3354+2 = 3356, int**eger needs **2** bytes memory)

The size of the structure is **4** bytes, because of two integer variables (**2+2 = 4** bytes). The memory representation of array of structures is also same for simple arrays and it will be cleared in the following program:

```
/* Addresses of the elements in the array of structures */

main( )
{
   struct
      {
         char name[16];
         int rollno,marks;
      }s[5];             /* five structures   */

int i;

for(i=0;i<5;i++)
   printf("\nAddress of structure S[%1d]= %d ",i,&s[i]);
```

```
printf("\nSize of the entire structure = %d bytes",sizeof(s));
```

```
Address of structure S[0]   =   8650
Address of structure S[1]   =   8670
Address of structure S[2]   =   8690
Address of structure S[3]   =   8710
Address of structure s[4]   =   8730

Size of the entire structure =   100 bytes
```

In the above program the structure **s** is declared as array of structure with the size **5**.

⇨ Address of the first structure (s[0]) is **8650** and the next is at **8670**, etc.
⇨ Size of the single structure is **20** bytes (**16 + 2 + 2 = 20**).
⇨ So for **5** structures **100** bytes were needed.

| 1st structure | 2nd structure | 3rd structure | 4th structure | 5th structure | ..... |
|---------------|---------------|---------------|---------------|---------------|-------|
| 8650          | 8670          | 8690          | 8710          | 8730          |       |

Here each structure occupies **20** bytes of memory and single structure is stored in the memory as follows:

| name (16 bytes) | rollno ( 2 bytes) | marks (2 bytes) |
|-----------------|-------------------|-----------------|

## 8.11 UNIONS

Union is the best gift for the C programmers. The general declaration of union is similar to the structure variable. Instead of the key word **struct**, the keyword **union** is used. The members of **union** also referred with the help of (.) dot operator.

The union variable has been mainly used to set/reset the status of the hardware devices of the computer system and it plays an important in the system software development.

For example, the register has **16** bytes and they are named as low byte and high byte. The changes in the low or high byte the will affect the full word of the register, will be clearly explained in the forthcoming chapter.

## 8.12 DIFFERENCE BETWEEN THE STRUCTURE AND THE UNION

In case of structure, all the members occupy different memory locations depending on the type, which it belongs to. In union, memory will be allocated only for the larger size variable of the group, and no other memory allocation will be made. Now, allocated highest memory will be shared by all the remaining variables of the union. The declaration of a union and its format are as follows:

General format:                                    Example:

```
union                              union
   {                                  {
       member-1;                          char name[15];
       member-2;                          int rollno;
       member-3;                          float marks;
       ...                            } stu;
       member-n;
   } union-variable;
```

We may think that the size of the union variable is **21** bytes **(15+2+4)**. But it is not correct. Because of union, only the larger memory request is considered for allocation. No independent memory for the other members will be allocated. The following program gives the clear picture of our previous discussion.

## *Example:*

```
/* Example for the union variable */
main( )
{
   union
   {
      char name[15];
      int rollno;
      float marks;
   } s;

printf("\nSize of the union  : %d ",sizeof(s));
}
```

**Output:**

```
Size of the union : 15
```

In this program, the maximum memory request is **15** (char name [15]). So all the remaining members of the union **rollno, marks** will share the same memory area.

Let us consider a **union** variable with two members one is **int** and another one is **float.** In general, **int**eger requires 2 bytes and **float** requires 4 bytes. But in union only the memory for **float** will be allotted and this is also shared by **int** variable. This discussion is illustrated in the following diagrams:

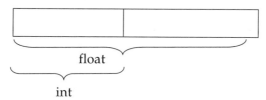

## 8.13   MEMORY IS SHARED—A PROOF

The following program illustrates the idea of memory sharing discussed in the previous subsection. The largest memory area will be shared by the other members. But be clear that when two values will be accessed, changes in one results in changes in the other one. The following program explains how memory is shared in the union.

**Example:**

```
/* A proof of union-sharing memory */
main( )
{
    union
    {
        char c;
        int  a;
    }s;

        s.c= 'z';
        printf("\nC = %c   ",s.c);
        printf("\nA = %d   ",s.a);

        s.a = 65;
        printf("\nNew C = %c   ",s.c);
        printf("\nNew A = %d   ",s.a);
        getch();

}
```

Output:

```
C = z
A = 122    /*This is not same for all executions*/
New C = A
New A = 65
```

First time the union variable **a** has some unexpected data. After changing its value, the character variable **c** value also has been changed as from **'z'** to **'A'**. This is enough to prove whether the memory in the union is shared or not.

## 8.14   typedef  (Type Definition)

This is also a user-defined data type used to set a new name for the existing data types. The **typedef** statement is used to create a new user-defined data type. That is we can give a new name for the data types like **int, float** etc. The declaration is similar to the simple variable declaration. The general format of the declaration is

```
typedef    data-type new-name;
```

In feature to declare the same kind of data type we can use the **new-name** instead of old **data-type**. Look at the following example:

```
typedef  int  number;
```

Here **number** is declared as an **int**eger data type and it is equivalent to the data type **int**. Now we can use **number** to declare the variable of integer type.

```
number a,b,c;
```

By using the **typedef** the new data type **string** will be created as follows with the example. There is no provision for declaring string directly.

***Example:***

```
/* Example for typedef declaration */
main( )
{
   typedef  char string[80];
   string  name;
   /* name is string type data  */
   printf("\nEnter a name : ");
   scanf("%s",name);
   printf("\n'%s' welcome to all",name);
}
```

`Output:`

```
Enter a name : Sanjai
'Sanjai' welcome to all
```

## 8.15 ENUMERATED DATA TYPE

Enumeration is also another type of user-defined data type, for which we are allowed to specify the possible values for the test. We can utilize this feature to keep some names instead of values. In some cases remembering the numeric value is difficult. String or Word is always better instead of the numbers.

For example, in C programming language, the numeric value **0** (zero) is treated as **FALSE** and **1** is treated as **TRUE**. When we use these values like **0** or **1**, we may confuse little bit. If the number increases the problems also increase.

One more example, suppose we have 5 choices like **1-INSERT, 2-DELETE, 3-JOIN, 4-REVERSE** and **5-LIST**. When we use the numbers like 1,2,3,4 and 5 to represent the choices, it is difficult to identify the purpose.

Which type of representation is your preference? Number or Word. Yes. Word. I also prefer word. Ok. How to define? Format of the Enumerated definition is:

```
enum tag
   {
      Constant-Name1=Value1,
      Constant-Name2=Value2 ...
   } variable(s);
```

The following is a simple example,

```
enum status
{
    FALSE,TRUE
};
```

Here the user defined data type **status** is created and its value may be **FALSE** or **TRUE**. In this case, as I mentioned in the introduction the value of FALSE is actually 0 and the value of TRUE is 1.

We can change the value by specifying its value explicitly. For example, the declaration

```
enum status
{
    TRUE=1,FALSE=2
};
```

Here TRUE will be interpreted as value 1 and FALSE as 2. One more example, to keep the days of the week. The days are mentioned like SUN, MON, TUE, ..., SAT. But there is no constant values like this for our representation. We have to use some values like 0 to represent SUN, 1 to represent MON, 2 to represent tue, etc.

Another way of keeping the days of the week is as follows using the enumerated declaration.

```
enum days
{
    SUN,  MON,  TUE,WED,THU,FRI,SAT
}dow;
```

Here the variable dow (day of the week) may contain any one of the given values (SUN, MON ... ) and their actual interpretation is 0, 1, 2, ..., etc.

The following is a simple program to check the value of the constant name in the enumerated data type.

```
/* Example for enumerated type */

enum status
    {
        TRUE,FALSE
    };

main()
    {
        enum status value;
        printf("%d",TRUE);
    }
```

## REVIEW QUESTIONS ✍

1. Define structure? Discuss the necessity of structure in a program.
2. How to declare structure? Example.
3. How are the members of structure are accessed?
4. Write short notes on array of structure.
5. Write short notes on nested structure.
6. Explain about how the structure variables are passed to the function.
7. Explain with example how the memory allocation is made for structure.
8. What is the advantage of union?
9. Differentiate structure and union with an example.
10. Write short notes on typedef.
11. Write short notes on enumerated type.
12. _____ operator is used to refer the members of pointer to the structure.
13. Write a simple program to illustrate pointers and structures.
14. What is the difference between arrays and structures.
15. Design an example program to prepare Electricity Bill using array of structures.

# Chapter 9
# Files

## 9.1 INTRODUCTION

A file is the most familiar item in our daily life. A file is used to store information for future use. Our C programming language too has files, which help us in storing the data. Before we take a journey in to the concepts of files in C, do think as what happens to the input data in the programs that we have discussed in the earlier chapters. Suppose the program requires one/two input data, we could supply at any time without any difficulty. Imagine the details of student in a very large institution. If we need to prepare a mark statement for all of them, we have to enter the whole details every time. It requires large manpower and computational resources. When we are allowed to store the data permanently and referred later, we will be very happy.

The program upon execution will require some data as input to be processed to yield the results. As the data are stored temporarily, the data has to be reentered to see the results. Imagine, if the volume of the data is high like 1000 records, is it possible for us to reenter the voluminous amount of data each time. This is the major draw back of previous programs. This can be overcome by using files.

The file-based programs are used to store the data permanently and can be referred in the future. **FILE** is a predefined structure, which maintains all the information about the files we create. Information such as the location of buffer, the pointer to the character in the file, the end of file and mode of the file, etc. We may perform the following operations in a file

1. Read data from the file
2. Write data into the file

The operation of reading and writing may be performed either character by character or word by word or line by line or record by record.

## 9.2 HOW TO DECLARE FILE TYPE VARIABLE?

We already know **FILE** as a predefined structure. The file pointer is declared as follows:

```
FILE *file-pointer;
```

where **file-pointer** is a pointer variable, which points to the first character of an opened file. For example:

```
FILE *fp;    /* fp is a file pointer */
```

Here **fp** is a **file-pointer,** which points to the first character of the file (Starting address of the file). If we know the starting address then we can access all the data of file using the features of pointers by adjusting into its next locations.

## 9.3 HOW TO OPEN/CLOSE THE FILE?

The purpose of using a file may be to read or write data. To do any of the two functions first we must open the file. The file can be opened by using the library function **fopen( )** and its format is

```
fopen(filename, mode);
```

⇨ Where **filename** is the name of the file to be opened
⇨ **mode** is the purpose of opening a file such as read/write/append.

Whenever this function is success, it returns the starting address of the file otherwise it returns **NULL.** For example

```
fopen("stu.dat","r");
```

⇨ **stu.dat** is the name of the file
⇨         **r** is mode of opening the file ("**r**" indicates the read mode).
⇨ If success, it returns the starting address of **stu.dat** file. This address will be assigned to the above said file pointer for further usage. The complete declaration is as follows.

```
FILE *fp;
fp=fopen("stu.dat","r");
```

The file may be opened depending on the any one of the following modes:

| Mode | Description |
|------|-------------|
| w | Create a new file for writing |
| r | Open the available file for reading |
| a | Open the file for appending |
| w+ | Create the new file for both operations (read & write) |
| r+ | Open the available file for both operations (read & write) |
| a+ | Open the available file for both (read & write) operation with append |

**Note:**
⇨ If an existing file is opened in write mode, the contents of the file will be destroyed and new file will be created with the same name.
⇨ If an existing file is opened in append mode the contents of will not be lost and a new information can be added to the existing data.

Examples with different type of opening modes are given below; assume the result is assigned to a pointer variable of type **FILE**.

1. `fopen("stu.dat","r")`
   ⇨ The file **stu.dat** will be opened for reading the data if the file exist.
   ⇨ If no such file exists, it returns **NULL** value.
2. `fopen("stu.dat","w")`
   ⇨ The file **stu.dat** will be created for writing the data
   ⇨ Every time a new file will be created with the same name
   ⇨ Content of the file will be overwritten
3. `fopen("stu.dat","a")`
   ⇨ The file **stu.dat** is opened for appending data at the end of file
   ⇨ If no such file, new file is created for writing
   ⇨ New data will be added to the end of existing data
4. `fopen("stu.dat","r+")`
   ⇨ The file is opened for both purposes (Reading and Writing).
5. `fopen("stu.dat","w+")`
   ⇨ The file is created for both purposes (Reading and Writing).
6. `fopen("stu.dat","a+")`
   ⇨ The file is opened for both purposes. If the file is not existing new file is created.

The complete relationship between the file pointer and assignment of file to it is illustrated below:

```
FILE *fp;
fp=fopen("test.dat","r");
   or
FILE *fp=fopen("test.dat","r");
```

The following is a program to test the availability of the file, which is mentioned.

```
/* Example for testing the availability of the file */
main()
{
    FILE   *fp;
    fp = fopen("test.dat","r");

    if (fp== NULL)
        {
            printf("\nNo such file in the directory.");
            exit(1);    /*To exit from the running program  */
        }
    fclose(fp);
}
```

**Note:**

Suppose the file to be opened is not in the current working directory, the path should be clearly specified. For example, if the working directory is in C drive, but the file to be opened is in D drive (**D:\EKARTHI\test.c**), then to access the file the **fopen( )** function is written as given below.

```
fopen("d:\\ekarthi=\\test.c","r");
```

Now this function will return the starting of the file successfully. One more point is that, double \\ are a must, otherwise it is treated as an escape sequence character.

## 9.4 `fclose( )` (TO CLOSE THE FILE)

The file may be opened for performing the reading/writing operations, but once the process is completed, it must be closed. If the file is not properly closed, the file pointer may be somewhere in the file and it may cause some problem when we start our next execution. If the file is properly closed, the pointer will successfully initialized to the starting of the file. The function **fclose ( )** is used to close one of the opened files and **fcloseall( )** function is used to close all the opened files. The general format of these functions is as follows:

```
fclose (file-pointer);
      fcloseall ( );
```

**Example:**

1. `fclose(fp);`
   ⇨ It will close only the specified file.
2. `fcloseall( )`
   ⇨ It will close all the opened files.

## 9.5 READING/WRITING CHARACTER IN A FILE

In this section, we are going to discuss how to read/write characters in a file. The library functions such as **fgetc( )**, **fputc( )**, **getc( )**, **putc( )** are used for the above said operations, the formats and their usage are listed here.

getc()     - To read a character from the file and adjust the file pointer to the next character of the file automatically.

fgetc()    - to read a character from a file.

putc()     - to write a character into the file.

fputc()    - to write a character into the file.

The general formats of the **getc( )** and **fgetc( )** functions are as follows.

```
char getc(file-pointer);
char fgetc(file-pointer);
```

These two functions read one character at a time from the file. After every read operation, the file pointer will be automatically adjusted to the next location in the file. By this way we could read all the characters from the file one by one. This method is called as sequential operation. The character fetched from the file can be assigned to a character variable and used further as below.

```
ch = fgetc(fp); /* Getting character from file */
putch(ch);      /* Displaying it in the screen */
```

**Note:**
File pointer will be automatically adjusted to the next location.

## 9.6 feof( ) (TO CHECK END OF FILE)

As said above, we can read character by character from a file. Then, how do we stop the read operation? What is the condition to exit from the read? In case of string, the **NULL** character is used to identify the end of string. Is there any special character like this? Yes. All the files are have a special character **end-of-file** or **EOF** to stop the read operation. The function **feof( )** is used to test whether we reached the end of the file or not. Suppose the file pointer is now pointing to the last character or the end of the file, the function returns **TRUE** indicates that we reached the end of the file. Otherwise it returns **FALSE**. The pseudo code for our idea is given here.

```
FILE *fp=fopen("test.dat","r");
result=feof(fp);
```

If the file reaches the end, the value in **result** is **TRUE** otherwise the value in **result** is **FALSE**. Now we can make use of any looping statement to repeat the read operation until we get **FALSE** from **feof()** as follows.

```
while( !feof(fp))
{
    /* Statements */
}
```

The following is a complete program to illustrate the above idea that how to read the content of file.

```
/* Reading characters from a file */
#include <stdio.h>

main()
{
    FILE *fp;
    char ch;

    fp=fopen("test.txt","r");
    if (fp == NULL)
    {
        printf("\nNo such file this name");
        exit(0);
    }

    while (!feof(fp))
    {
        ch = getc(fp);
        putch(ch);
    }
}
```

In this program the file **test.txt** has been opened for reading data. Using the function **getc(fp)** the characters are read, and displayed in the screen using **putch( )**. The function **feof( )** is used to check the occurrence of end of file. The process will be terminated when end of file is reached.

The function **putc( )** and **fputc( )** are used to write a character into a file, the format is as follows.

```
putc (character , file-pointer);
fputc (character , file-pointer);
```

⇨ Here the **character** denotes the character to be written
⇨ **file-pointer** indicating the file which receives the character.

For example

```
fputc('a', fp);
```

Now the character **'a'** will be stored in a file pointed by the file pointer **fp**. The following is an example which illustrates the **putc( )** function.

```
/* Creating New file by reading characters */
#include <stdio.h>
main()
{
   FILE *fp;
   char ch;
   fp=fopen("test.txt","w");
   if (fp==NULL)
      {
         printf("\nNo such file");
         exit(0);
      }
   while((ch=getch( )) != 'z' )
   {
      putc(ch,fp);
      putch(ch);
   }
      fclose(fp);
}
```

When we execute this program, we are allowed to type number of characters and for every key press, the same will be stored in a file. Since we specified the condition as **until z**, as soon as we press **z** the process of read will be stopped. Let us consider that we have supplied the following characters.

**No gain without pain z**

After completion of the above input, check the file and its content using any editor or previous program. Now we are going to design a small application that is used to copy the content of one file to another. The functions **getc( )** is used to fetch a character from a file and **putc( )** is used to write the characters fetched via **getch( )** as illustrated below.

*Example:*

```
/* Copy the content of one file to another  */
#include <stdio.h>

main()
{
   FILE *fps,*fpd;    /* source and destination */

   char ch, sfile[15], dfile[15];

   clrscr();

   printf("\nSource file    : ");
   scanf("%s",sfile);
```

```
printf("\nDestination file : ");
scanf("%s",dfile);
fps=fopen(sfile,"r");
        /*source file should be opened for read  */
fpd=fopen(dfile,"w");
        /* This file should be opened for write  */
if (fps= =NULL)
{
   printf("\nNo source file in the directory");
   exit(0);
}
while(!feof(fps))
{
   ch=getc(fps);
   putc(ch,fpd);
}
fcloseall( );    /* Closes  all the opened files */
}
```

Output:
```
      Source file      :   ek.c
      Destination file :   mahi.c
```

After the execution, the content of file **ek.c** is copied into the file **mahi.c** successfully. Use type command/first program of this chapter to ensure the success of the program.

## 9.7  READ/WRITE A LINE OF CHARACTERS

In the previous section we discussed a few programs about how to read/write characters in a file. Now we are going to discuss how we could read/write a group of characters at a time instead of single characters at a time. The function **fputs( )**, **fgets( )** are used for this purpose and the format of the functions is as follows.

```
fputs(string, file-pointer);
fgets(string-variable, size,file-pointer);
```

⇨ **String** contains the characters to be written into the file using file-pointer.
⇨ **String-variable** is the variable denoting the string
⇨ **Size** is the number of characters to be read

Mostly these functions are used for line-by-line process and few examples are

1. `fputs("Abdul  Kalam",fp);`
   ⇨ Here the string **"Abdul Kalam"** is written in to the file **fp**.
2. `fgets(str,80,fp);`
   ⇨ Here **80** characters will be retrieved from the file and copied into the string variable **str**.

The following program is used to count the number of lines in the specified file, each line is considered as 80 characters.

```
/* To count number of lines from the file  */
#include <stdio.h>

main()
{
    FILE *fp;
    int c=0;
    char ch, str[80];

    fp=fopen("test.txt","r");
    if (fp==NULL)
       {
           printf("\nNo source file in the directory");
           exit(0);
       }
    while(!feof(fp))
     {
           fgets(str,80,fp);
           c++;
           puts(str);
     }
    printf("\nNo. of lines :   %d ", c);
    fclose(fp);
}
```

In the above program, for every execution, **80** characters will be picked up from the file **"test.txt"**, and the counter variable **c** will be incremented. Finally, the number of lines can be obtained from the variable **c**.

## 9.8  FORMATTED INPUT/OUTPUT STATEMENT IN FILE

The reader is already experienced by using formatted input and output functions such as **scanf( )** and **printf( )**, which we discussed in the earlier chapters. Now the same is going to be used to read/write formatted data from the file with small modification, as given below.

```
fscanf(file-pointer , format-string, variables);
fprintf(file-pointer , format-string, variables);
```

The function **fscanf( )** reads data from the file, and each field is formatted according to the format specifier passed to **fscanf( )**. Finally **fscanf( )** stores the formatted input at an address passed to it as an argument following the format. The user is not necessary to supply any input here.

The function **fprintf( )** accepts a sequence of arguments (variables) and applies it to the format specifier, which is in the format string and redirect the formatted output to the specified file. The **printf( )** function redirect the data to the screen, but **fprintf( )** redirect the data to the file. Look the following few example to understood how the formatted data is stored/retrieved from a file.

1. `fprintf (fp,"Welcome to My India");`
   ⇨ Here the string value **Welcome to My India** will be redirected to the file
2. `char name[]={"I Love India"};`
   `fprintf (fp," %s ",name);`
   ⇨ Here the format string get replaced by the value **I Love India** and stored in the file.
3. `fprintf(fp,"name=%s a=%f=%d",name, a, b);`
   ⇨ Here format string has been combined with different data type and as usual they are written in the file **fp**.
4. `fscanf(fp,"%d",&n);`
   ⇨ Here the data is obtained from the file and stored in a variable **n**.
   ⇨ While reading the data we should take care when more data types
   ⇨ If the format string does not exactly match, then wrong data will be retrieved from the file.

The program below illustrates the preparation of electricity bill and the utility of **fprintf( )** can be visualized.

*Example:*

```
/* To prepare Electricity Bill for the consumer  */
#include <stdio.h>

main()
{
    FILE *fp;
    int serno;
    char name[50];
    float amt, pr, cr, units;

    fp = fopen("eb.dat","w");

    printf("\nConsumer  Name : ");
    gets(name);
    printf("\nConsumer  No.  : ");
    scanf("%d",&serno);
    printf("\nPrevious reading :");
    scanf("%f",&pr);
    printf("\nCurrent  reading : ");
    scanf("%f",&cr);
    units = cr - pr;

    amt = units * 1.25;
            /*Cost per  unit is  assumed  1.25  */
```

```
/* Write the result in the file  */
fprintf(fp,"\t\tELECTRICITY  BLL\n");
fprintf(fp,"\nName : %s \tService No.: %d
                   \n",name,serno);
fprintf(fp,"\n----------------------------------------");
fprintf(fp,"\nPrevious  Current   Units       Amount");
fprintf(fp,"\nReading   Reading   Consumed    Rs. ");
fprintf(fp,"\n----------------------------------------");
fprintf(fp,"\n%5.2f\t %5.2f   %5.2f  %5.2f",pr,cr,units,amt);
fprintf(fp,"\n----------------------------------------");

fclose(fp);
}                /*  End of file    */
```

**Output:**

```
Consumer  Name   : Vivekanandar
Consumer  No.    : 1000
Previous reading : 650
Current  reading : 950
```

After reading the data, calculation will be made and the formatted result will be stored in the file **eb.dat,** we can check it by opening the file and it will have the result as below.

```
                       ELECTRICITY BLL
Name : Vivekanandar     Service No. : 1000
------------------------------------------------
Previous        Current       Units        Amount
Reading         Reading       Consumed     Rs.
------------------------------------------------
650.00          950.00        300.00       375.00
------------------------------------------------
```

If you complete the testing of the above program, the idea for reading and writing formatted data item in a file is clearly understood. This program is for only one customer and can't be used for more bill preparation. When there are number of customers, the necessary input data items must be stored in a file. At the time of execution, the stored data will be retrieved and processed.

How to prepare a mark list for number of students? The student file **stu.dat** have the information as given below. They will be read from the file in order to calculate the class of each student. First we must create a data file by typing the content in a file.

```
Sathya          1000 75
Karthi          1001 35
murugappan      1002 56
mahesh          1003 99
```

*Example:*

```
/* Read data and calculate the class, display them    */
/* Example for fscanf ()     function   */

#include <stdio.h>
main( )
{
   FILE *fp;
   int rollno, marks;
   char name[50],rank[15];

   fp = fopen("stu.dat","r");

   if (fp==NULL)
      {
         printf("\nSorry.  No such file ");
         exit(0);
      }

   printf("\nName        Rollno    Marks    Class\n");

   while (!feof(fp))
   {
      fscanf(fp, "%s %d %d", name, &rollno, &marks);

      if (marks>=60)
         strcpy(rank, "First");
      if ((marks>=50) && (marks < 60))
         strcpy(rank,"Second");
      if ((marks>=40) && (marks <50 ))
         strcpy(rank, "Third");
      if (marks<40)
         strcpy(rank, "Fail");

      printf("\n%s\t  %6d  %5d  %s",name,rollno,marks,rank);
   }
   fclose(fp);
}
```

Output:

| Name | Rollno | Marks | Class |
|------|--------|-------|-------|
| Sathya | 1000 | 75 | First |
| Karthi | 1001 | 35 | Fail |
| murugappan | 1002 | 56 | Second |
| mahesh | 1003 | 99 | First |

When the above program is executed the input is obtained from the file not from the user.

## 9.9   READ/WRITE RECORD IN THE FILE

In the previous section, we did some example programs—reading character, words, lines and formatted data. OK. Good. But when there are a number of variables in a function such as **fscanf( )/fprintf( )**, we need to specify the number of format specifiers carefully. This is very difficult when there are more variables. To avoid this kind of problems, C supports to read/write a group of variables at a time that is we could read/write a structure from a file. Structure may have more variables with different types of values. The two functions **fread()** and **fwrite( )** are used for this purpose and their format are given below.

```
fread(pointer-to-structure, sizeof structure, number of records,
file-pointer);

fwrite(pointer-to-structure, sizeof structure, number of records,
file-pointer);
```

Both the functions take the same number (four) of arguments. They are:

1. Pointer to the structure variable
2. Size of the structure
3. Number of structures to read/write
4. File pointer

Let us consider the structure and its elements

```
struct
   {
      int rollno;
      char name[20];
   } stu;
```

If we need to write the values of the structure, we have to use the formatted output statement as below.

```
fprintf(fp,"%d %s",&stu.rollno, stu.name)
```

But the same statements can be re-written as follows:

```
fwrite(&stu, sizeof(stu),1,fp);
```

For every execution, the content of the whole structure will be stored in a file specified via **fp.** Here **&stu** is a pointer to the structure, **sizeof(stu)** specifies the memory size of record/structure, the number of the structure is **1** and file is **fp.** The following is a program to illustrate how **fread( )** and **fwrite( )** are used in an application. First half of this program reads the data and second half processes the same.

## Example:

```
/* Example for read/write structure in a file */
#include <stdio.h>
#include <process.h>
#include <string.h>

struct
{
    int rollno;
    char name[15];
    float avg;
}stu;

main( )
{
    FILE *fp;
    int n,i;
    char res[10];

    clrscr();
    fp=fopen("test.dat","w");
    if (fp==NULL)
    {
        printf("\nCan't create file");
        exit(0);
    }

    printf("\nNo. of students :");
    scanf("%d",&n);
    printf("\nEnter the details\n");


for(i=1;i<=n;i++)
    {
        printf("\nRoll No.      :");
        scanf("%d",&stu.rollno);
        printf("\nName          :");
        scanf("%s",stu.name);
        printf("\nAverage       :");
        scanf("%f",&stu.avg);
        fwrite(&stu,sizeof(stu),1,fp);
    }

fclose(fp);
clrscr();

fp=fopen("test.dat","r");
```

```
printf("\n-------------------------------------------");
printf("\nRollNo.   Name           Average    Result");
printf("\n-------------------------------------------");

fread(&stu,sizeof(stu),1,fp);

while(!feof(fp))
     {
        if (stu.avg>=40)
           strcpy(res,"Pass");
        else
           strcpy(res,"Fail");

        printf("\n%4d",stu.rollno);
        printf("\t%-15s",stu.nam
        printf("\t%5.2f ",s
        printf("\t   %s"

        fread(&stu,sizeof(stu),1,fp.
     }

    printf("\n-------------------------------------------");

    fclose(fp);
    getch();
}
```

Output:

```
No. of students :2
Enter the details
Roll No. :1001
Name      :karthi
Average   :35.50
Roll No. :1002
Name      :sabari
Average   :50.75

-------------------------------------------
Roll No.   Name          Average    Result
-------------------------------------------
1001       karthi        35.50      Fail
1002       sabari        50.75      Pass
-------------------------------------------
```

If the testing of the above program is successfully completed, you can develop a real-time application using files.

## 9.10 RANDOM FILE OPERATION

In a file we can store the data permanently and we may go for read/write operation. The programs we discussed in the earlier section are based on the sequential operation (one by one). Let us consider that we have 10000 records and we need to access 4500th record. If we use the earlier idea, we can reach this record after travelling from 1st record to 4499th record. The process is sequential and we have to spend more time to reach a particular record. This is not good for an application.

Now C helps us to process any record in a file randomly! Yes. Without spending more time we can reach a particular location in a file. This is called as random file access. The following are the few functions, which will help in accessing the records randomly.

1. fseek ( )
2. ftell ( )
3. fgetpos ( )
4. rewind ( )

## 9.11 fseek (TO SET THE FILE POINTER)

The function **fseek( )** is used to set the file pointer at the specified location, the format is as follows.

```
result fseek (file-pointer, location, from-where);
```

⇨ Here **result** tells whether the operation is successful or not
⇨ **file-pointer** is a pointer, which points to the opened file
⇨ **location** is the number of the location to be adjusted
⇨ **from-where** specifies from where the process starts

The **from-where** may be any one of these values.

**SEEK_SET** => Seeks from beginning of the file
**SEEK_CUR** => Seeks from current location
**SEEK_END** => Seeks from the end of the file

While opening the file for the first process, the file pointer always points to the first location of the file. Now the file pointer may be placed in any file as given in the following examples.

1. fseek (fp, 10,SEEK_SET);
   ⇨ From the first location of file, the pointer is placed at 10th location, because count begins from 0th location.
2. fseek (fp, -5,SEEK_END);
   ⇨ From the end of file or the last location of file, the pointer is placed at 5th location.

For example, the file "**test.dat**" contains the following data and its locations are illustrated as

| Location | 0 | 1 | 2 | 3 | 4 | 5 | 6 | 7 | 8 | 9 | 10 | 11 | 12 |
|----------|---|---|---|---|---|---|---|---|---|---|----|----|----|
| Value | I | | L | O | V | E | | I | N | D | I | A | **EOF** |

The total number of characters in the file is **13** including the end of the file (**EOF**). EOF is a single character. After the statement, **fp = fopen("test.dat","r")**, the file pointer **fp** is pointed to the first location and is

| Location | 0 | 1 | 2 | 3 | 4 | 5 | 6 | 7 | 8 | 9 | 10 | 11 | 12 |
|----------|---|---|---|---|---|---|---|---|---|---|----|----|----|
| Value | I | | L | O | V | E | | I | N | D | I | A | **EOF** |

fp

After the statement **fseek( fp, 5 , SEEK_SET)**, the **fp** is adjusted to the 5th location from the beginning of the file and is

| Location | 0 | 1 | 2 | 3 | 4 | 5 | 6 | 7 | 8 | 9 | 10 | 11 | 12 |
|----------|---|---|---|---|---|---|---|---|---|---|----|----|----|
| Value | I | | L | O | V | E | | I | N | D | I | A | **EOF** |

fp

After the statement **fseek( fp, –4 , SEEK_END)**, the **fp** is adjusted to the 9th location from the end of the file (last character is **EOF**, so 4th location from the last is **N**).

| Location | 0 | 1 | 2 | 3 | 4 | 5 | 6 | 7 | 8 | 9 | 10 | 11 | 12 |
|----------|---|---|---|---|---|---|---|---|---|---|----|----|----|
| Value | I | | L | O | V | E | | I | N | D | I | A | **EOF** |

fp

The following is a program to be used to display the remaining characters from the user-specified location. For example, if the user supplies **5** as input and all the remaining characters from 5th location will be displayed.

**Example:**

```
/*To display the characters from the user given location */
#include <stdio.h>

main( )
{
    FILE *fp=fopen("c:\\temp\\ek.dat","r");
    char ch;
    int n;
```

```
    printf("\nNo. of characters from first : ");
    scanf("%d",&n);
    printf("\nRemaining of file  : \n");

    fseek(fp, n , SEEK_SET);
      /* Adjusted to the nth location */

    while(!feof(fp))
    {
       ch=fgetc(fp);
       printf("%c",ch);
    }
}
```

Output:

```
No. of characters from first : 3
Remaining of file :
OVE INDIA
```

This program will display the remaining portion of the file depending on the value of **n**.

## 9.12 `ftell( )` (TO FIND THE LOCATION OF THE FILE)

The function **ftell( )** is used to find the location of the file pointer in a file. We can use the **fseek( )** function to set the file pointer and it can be ensured by this function, its format is

```
long ftell(file-pointer);
```

For example, **fseek(fp, 5, SEEK_SET)** places the file pointer at 6th location from the beginning of the file. How to check whether it is really in the 6th location or not? Look at the following pseudo code

```
int location;
fseek(fp,10,SEEK_SET);
location = ftell(fp);
```

Check the value stored in the variable **location.** Use the following program and find the advantage of this **ftell( )** function in applications.

```
/* To display the content of the file with its actual location in a file */
#include <stdio.h>
main( )
{
    FILE *fp=fopen("ek.dat","r");
    char ch;
    long l;

    while(!feof(fp))
    {
        printf("\n%c stored at location  %d ",fgetc(fp),ftell(fp));
    }
}
```

**Output:**

```
I      stored at location    0
       stored at location    1
L      stored at location    2
O      stored at location    3
V      stored at location    4
E      stored at location    5
       stored at location    6
I      stored at location    7
N      stored at location    8
D      stored at location    9
I      stored at location   10
A      stored at location   11
EOF    stored at location   13
```

The **EOF** is only for user identification. The end of file is marked by the character –1. So, whenever the EOF appears, the process is terminated from the **while** loop.

## 9.13 SIZE OF THE FILE—A SIMPLE WAY

To find the length of the file, one way is to travel to the end of the file. Another way is to obtain the length of the file is using the feature **ftell( )** function.

```
/* Finding the size of the file */
#include <stdio.h>

main()
{
    FILE *fp=fopen("ek.dat","r");
    char ch;
    long l;
```

```
        fseek(fp,0,SEEK_END);
        l=ftell(fp);
        printf("\nLength is = %d characters",l);
    }
```

Output:

```
    Length is = 13 characters
```

## 9.14  REVERSING THE CONTENT OF A FILE

We can display the content of a file as we discussed in the earlier sections. Is it possible to travel or display the content of a file in reverse? Yes, we can reverse. Use the **fseek( )** function to set the file pointer and check the same using **ftell( )** function. For every execution, the pointer will be placed from the end up to the beginning of the file.

If calculated everything, the file pointer is adjusted from the end using the **fseek(fp,–i, SEEK_END)** function. Here **fp** is a file pointer, **i** is the location variable and **SEEK_END** is the place to start the process.

*Example:*

```
/* Reversing the content of the file */
#include <stdio.h>
main( )
{
    FILE *fp;
    int n,i=0;
    char ch;

    fp = fopen("ek.dat","r");
    fseek(fp,0,SEEK_END);   /*Adjusted to the end */
    n=ftell(fp);            /* Getting the location */
    printf("\n File in Reverse\n");

    while(i<=n)
    {
        fseek(fp,-i,SEEK_END);
            /* Adjusted to each character */
        i++;
          ch=fgetc(fp);  /* Reading the  character */
          printf("%c",ch);
    }
}
```

Output:

```
    File in Reverse
    AIDNI EVOL I
```

## 9.15 `rewind( )` (ADJUSTED TO THE BEGINNING)

In the random file organization, once the necessary record is accessed, the file pointer may be somewhere inside the file. Suppose we need to start a new search/process from the beginning of the file, we have to use **fseek( )** to set the pointer. This is also obtained by using the function **rewind( )**, which places the file pointer in the beginning of the file.

Suppose we have thousands of records, which are processed very often. Normally the data can be processed as in the previous programs. We are in the need of searching the items and the item is in a different place. How to search them? Start searching from the beginning of file and continue until the end of file. Once again for the new set of data, we have to search the entire file. What we have to do is the file pointer should be adjusted to the beginning of file by using **fseek(fp,0,SEEK_SET)**. This task can be achieved by a simple function called **rewind( )**. Wherever this function occurs, the specified file pointer is going to be readjusted to the beginning of file. The general format of rewind function is

```
void rewind (file-pointer);
```

The input for this function is just a file pointer. The following is a simple program that finds the occurrence of a character repeatedly.

### Example:

```c
/* Example for rewind function */
#include <stdio.h>

main()
{
    FILE *fp;
    int count,choice;
    char ch1,ch2;

    fp=fopen("ek.dat","r");
    do
    {
        printf("\nDo you want to check (0 - Exit)");
        scanf("%d",&choice);

        fflush(stdin);
          /* To remove the characters from buffer if any */

        if (choice!=0)
        {
            printf("\nCharacter to check :");
            scanf("%c",&ch1);

            count=0;

        while(!feof(fp))
```

```
        {
          ch2=fgetc(fp);
          if (ch1==ch2)
            count++;
        }
        printf("\n%c has  occured  %d times  ",ch1,count);
        rewind(fp);
      }
    }while(choice!=0);
  getch();
}
```

**Output:**

```
KARPAGAM COLLEGE

Do you want to check (0 - Exit)1

Character to check: A

A has occured  3 times
Do you want to check (0 - Exit).1

Character to check: L

L has  occured  2 times
Do you want to check (0 - Exit) 0
```

## REVIEW QUESTIONS ✍

1. What is the role of files in a program?
2. What do you mean by file pointer?
3. How to declare file pointer type variable?
4. Write a function to open a file.
5. What are the various modes of opening a file?
6. What is the difference between write and append mode?
7. Explain the file with character processing.
8. How to find the end of the file?
9. Discuss about the formatted I/O statements associated with file.
10. How to read/write records?
11. What is the advantage of random file access methods?
12. Discuss the functions to be used in random files.
13. How to use **ftell( )** function in a file program?
14. Write a program to perform read, write operation in a file.
15. How to delete a record from a file?

# Chapter 10

# *Preprocessor*

## 10.1 INTRODUCTION

In general, the execution of any C program starts from **main( )** function. Now the preprocessor will allow us to include various statements to the compiler and will get the compiled first. Some possible applications are including the content of new file, defining symbolic constants and macros, conditional compilation, etc. All the preprocessor directives begin with # symbol. This is not considered as a statement of C program, so it does not end with semicolon (;).

## 10.2  #define   (MACRO DEFINITION)

The **#define** preprocessor directive defines an identifier and the set of characters that will be replaced for every occurrence of the identifier in the program. Suppose if a group of characters appear in the program many times, we have to spend a lot of time for typing lengthy statements. But this kind of definition allows having alternative short names, instead of a group of characters. It is also called as macro definition, which is similar to the function. In case of function, the function call will transfer the control to the function, but here the set of characters will be replaced. Another advantage of macro definition is that suppose we need to change the set of characters in the program, we need to do changes only in the macro definition, and the remaining will automatically change. The following is a format of this definition.

```
#define   identifier   string
```

In the program, when there is an identifier, it will be replaced by the set of characters or a string. Even we are allowed to have a simple function. Let us see some examples about the definition and its usage.

1. #define MAX 100
   In this definition, we defined the MAX as 100. For every occurrence of MAX in the program, MAX will be replaced by the value 100.

2. `#define name "Dr. A.P.J. Abdulkalam"`

Here we defined the set of characters and we can use the identifier **name** instead of the string **Dr. A.P.J. Abdulkalam** in our program. At the time of execution, the actual string will replace the **name**.

```
#define name "Dr. A.P.J. Abdulkalam"
main ()
{
    printf(name);
}
```

Some of the other simple examples for macro definition are given below:

```
#define  cls        clrscr()
#define  nl         printf("\n")
#define  getInt(n)  scanf("%d", &n)
```

In programs, we use **clrscr( )** very often. Now this is simplified as **cls,** which is more convenient than the actual one. In the last declaration, instead of complex **scanf( )** statement, **getInt( )** can be used.

Another use of **define** is to reduce the size of the program. But it takes more steps to implement in the program. By using the macro, the small function can be written easily as below.

```
/* Example for Macro with function */
#define big(a,b)  a>b?a:b
void main()
{
    int a=210,b=20;
    printf("\nBig : %d ",big(a,b));
}
```

When we use the **big(a,b)**, it will be replaced by the statement **a>b?a:b** So, it can be used for defining simple functions.

A macro allows to declare more than one statement as below. Here the **line(n)** definition contains a group of statements.

```
int n,i;

#define line(n) for(i=1;i<n;i++)printf("*");
#define string "\nKarpagam Arts and Science College"

void main()
{
    line(35);
    printf(string);
    line(35);
    getch();
}
```

A macro allows declaring more than one statement as below. Here the **line(n)** definition contains a group of statements with multiple line declarations.

```
int n,i;
#define line(n) for(i=1;i<n;i++)    \
{ printf("*"); printf("Karthikeyan");}

void main()
{
    line(35);
    getch();
}
```

## 10.3  # include  (INCLUDING THE CONTENT OF ANOTHER FILE)

Suppose there is an application program using function which is designed for all the students of a class of 50, the same function has to be written 50 times for 50 students. Using a common function reduces the size of the program. In this case, we write a single function and it is stored in one file. Any number of people can include this file and the necessary function. It is like designing a library function.

For example, the function namely **test( )** is a common function for all the members and the program looks like follows.

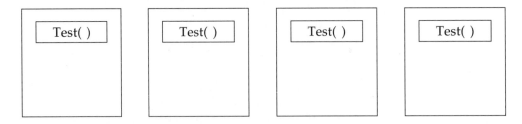

In the above kind of program, the function **test( )** appears throughout the program. It can be reduced by using the common function as follows.

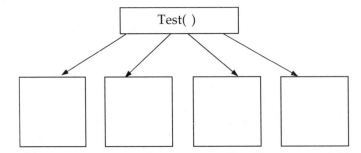

How to add the function by using the program structure? We have the feature **#include**, to include the contents of another file to any necessary file.

```
/* Test() is defined in the program called common.h */

void test( )
{
   /* Content of function test( ) */
}
```

The following is a program which uses the function **test( )** that is defined in another program as below.

```
#include <common.h>
void main()
{
   test( ); /* Invokes the function in common.h */
}
```

**Note:**
The file can be included into the current file by using any one of the formats.

```
#include "test.h"
#include <test.h>
```

The first type searches the availability of the file in the current working directory and if it is there, it includes the file. Otherwise searches its path and includes it if available. But in the second type, the file must be in the current working directory.

Apart from the above, some other preprocessor directives are also available, such as conditional compilation (**#if, #else, #elif** and **#endif**). These directives allow us to select a code at the time of execution that is mostly used in the software products.

**Format–1**
```
#if <constant-expression>
   // Statements-1
#else
   // Statements-2
#endif
```

**Format–2**
```
#if <constant-expression>
   // Statements-1
#elif <constant-expression>
   // Statements-2
#elif <constant-expression>
   // Statements-3
   . . .
#endif
```

The above conditional preprocessor directives are like the control statements that we discussed in Chapter 3. In case of Format-1, whenever the constant expression is TRUE, the Statements-1 will be compiled, otherwise Statements-2 part will be processed. The Format-2, is like a **switch-case** ladder. If the constant expression is TRUE, its corresponding statements will be processed. Look at the following examples.

```
#define TAMIL 1
main()
{
   // Code to decide the Language characteristics
   #if (TAMIL)
      printf("Language is Tamil");
   #else
      printf("Language is English");
   #endif
}
```

*Note:*

The expression must be a constant expression.

#undef

The defined macro can be disabled using **#undef**, as given below.

$$\#undef \quad identifier$$

Test the following code and find the role of **#undef** in a program

```
#define MAX 100
main()
{
   printf("\nMaximum Size is : %d ", MAX);
   #undef MAX
   printf("\nMaximum Size is : %d ", MAX);
}
```

This program causes an error, because the #undef preprocessor directives remove the previously defined macro.

## 10.4 COMMAND LINE ARGUMENTS

### 10.4.1 What is Meant by Command Line?

Operating system is actually a collection of programs, which control the operations of the whole computer system. These pre-written programs are also called **commands**. A good example is LINUX programs developed by using C programming language.

How are we allowed to execute these programs or commands? The file types such as **.COM, .BAT** and **.EXE** can be executed from the command prompt just entering a command. This is the place where the commands can be given to the operating system or the program to be executed, as shown below.

In DOS

```
C:\  _                   // For C drive
```

Cursor

Prompt

Other drive or operating systems prompt appears as

```
A:\  _                   // For A drive-floppy drive
H:\  _                   // May be networks
$    _                   // In Unix
```

The commands or programs are executed from the command line as given below.

```
                        C: \ dir
```

Here the command **dir** is invoked from the command line (C:\) and it displays all the files in the current working directory. If we have any executable file (**.EXE**), it can also be executed from the command line. For example, if we have an executable file **test.exe**, it will be executed from the command prompt as below.

```
        C:\test      // test must be an executable file
```

After the completion of the above, depending upon the actual code of the program **test** you will get the result.

## 10.4.2  What are Command Line Arguments?

Argument! We discussed the function and arguments in the earlier chapters with various forms of passing arguments to the function. Look at the simple code which illustrates the idea of passing arguments to the function.

```
/* Example for calling and passing arguments */
main( )
{
   display(100);
}
void display(int x)
{
   printf("\nX = %d ",x);
}
```

In this program, the function **display( )** is invoked from the **main( )** with argument **100**, as **display(100)** and it will be received by the function.

The actual arguments provided at the command prompt along with the name of the executable file are called command line arguments.

For example, consider the **TYPE** command, which is used to display the content of the specified file will be given as below.

```
            C:\ TYPE test.c
```

Here **test.c** is the name of the file to be displayed and **TYPE** is a command. Both **TYPE** and **test.c** are called command line arguments. Can we pass arguments to our program from command line? Yes, we can. We are allowed to pass arguments to the **main( )** function, because this is the first function that starts executing. In the earlier programs of **main ( )** we have not mentioned any argument to the **main( )** function. Suppose if we pass the arguments to the function, how the function declaration looks? Look at the new form of **main( )** function.

```
main(int count, char *s[15])
```

⇨ Here the **count** will have the number of arguments
⇨ Character array variable **s** has the values of arguments.

Look at the following code, which illustrates how to pass command line arguments. These arguments are copied into the string variable in sequence.

```
C:\ test abc def
```

Here **test** is the name of the file to be executed, **abc** is the first argument and **def** is the second argument to the **main( )** function. How to process these arguments? The number of arguments is obtained from the variable **count**, and the values of arguments are in the character array variable **s**. The arguments **test**, **abc** and **def** are available in **s[0]**, **s[1]** and **s[2]**. Test all the theoretical ideas implemented in the following program.

```
/* Example for Command Line Arguments  */
main(int count,char *s[10])
{
   int i;

   printf("\nNo. of arguments : %d ",count);
   printf("\nList of arguments");

   for(i=0;i<count;i++)
      printf("\nArgument %d  is %s ",i , s[i]);
}
```

Type the above program and save in the file **"test.c"**. After compilation, convert the same into an **EXE** file (By Pressing F9). Finally exit from the editor and type execute the program as given below.

```
C:\ekarthi\c>test abc def

No. of arguments : 3
List of arguments
Argument 0 is C:\EKARTHI\C\TEST.EXE
Argument 1 is abc
Argument 2 is def
```

I hope you are satisfied about the command line arguments. Here is another example program to display the content of file page-wise (it is a command like **cat** in Linux). Each page will be displayed after a key press. Assume that the source file is "**test.txt**" has the following content.

> No gain without pain
> All that glitters is not gold
> Be Indian and Buy Indian
> Be a Candle not be a Wax
> Karpagam Arts and Science College
> Department of Computer Science
> Coimbatore

### Example:

```
/* Example for displaying the content of file page-wise */
#include <stdio.h>

main(int count, char *s[10])
{
   char ch;
   int c=0,page=1;
   FILE *fp=fopen(s[1],"r");

   if (fp==NULL)
      {
         printf("\nSorry. No. such file");
         exit(0);
      }

   head(page);   /* To print the heading */
   while(!feof( fp ) )
   {
         ch=fgetc(fp);
         printf("%c",ch);

         if (ch= ='\n')
             c++;
         if (c= =5)      /* Assume 5 Lines per Page */
         {
            c=0;
            page++;
            printf("\nPress any key to next page ...");
            getch( );
            head(page);
         }
      }
   fclose(fp);
}
```

```
/* Function to print the heading */
head( int  p )
{
   printf("\nPage No. : %d \n",p);
}
```

**Output:**

```
Type the following command
   C:\EKARTHI\C>cmd test.txt

   Page No. : 1
   No gain without pain
   All that glitters is not gold
   Be Indian and Buy Indian
   Be a Candle Not be a Wax
   Karpagam Arts and Science College

   Press any key to next page ...
   Page No. : 2
   Department of Computer Science
   Coimbatore
```

The name of the file to be processed is passed from command line that is available in **s[1]** and using this name the file is opened. To illustrate the above program, we take **5** lines per page. Whenever the new line character '**\n**', encounters in the program, the counter variable **c** will be incremented by one. If it reaches to **5**, some header will be displayed like press any key to continue and after a key press next page will be displayed.

**Note:**
The **main( )** function will also be allowed to have a third argument, which indicate the configuration details

*Example:*

```
/* To find the third argument of command line */
#include <stdio.h>

main(int cc, char *s[15], char *ss[15])
{
   printf("\nFirst  argument  : %s ",ss[0]);
   printf("\nSecond argument  : %s ",ss[1]);
   printf("\nThird  argument  : %s ",ss[2]);
   printf("\nFourth argument  : %s ",ss[3]);
   printf("\nFifth  argument  : %s ",ss[4]);
   getch();
}
```

Output:

```
First   argument  :  TMP=C:\WINDOWS\TEMP
Second  argument  :  TEMP=C:\WINDOWS\TEMP
Third   argument  :  PROMPT=$p$g
Fourth  argument  :  winbootdir=C:\WINDOWS
Fifth   argument  :  COMSPEC=C:\WINDOWS\COMMAND.COM
```

### 10.4.3  Sending Data to the Printer

The standard output device is a visual display unit, so that all the output of the earlier programs were displayed on the monitor. As I told you about the features of C programming language in many places.

Can we send data to the printer directly from our program? Yes, we can send data to the printer via our program. Instead of conventional file stream in the **fprintf( )** function, specify **stdprn,** which redirects the output to the printer instead of file. The following is a very simple idea for sending data to the printer.

```
fprintf(stdprn , "Hello Good Morning");
```

Now the message **"Hello Good Morning"** will get printed in the printer. Look at the following program, which gives complete idea of sending the whole file to the printer.

```
/* To Send data to the printer  */
#include <stdio.h>
main(int count,char *s[10])
{
   char ch;
   FILE *fp=fopen(s[1],"r");
   int n,i;

   printf("\nHow many copies");
   scanf("%d",&n);
   if (fp==NULL)
      {
         printf("\nSorry. No. such file");
         exit(0);
      }
   /* N represents the no. of  copies  */
   for(i=0;i<n;i++)
   {
      while(!feof(fp))
      {
         ch=fgetc(fp); /*Redirect the ch to the printer*/
         fprintf(stdprn, "%c", ch);
      }
         rewind(fp);
   }
  fclose(fp);
}
```

The program can be used to take one or more printouts of the given file. After completion of whole file, the function **rewind( )** is used to reposition the file pointer at the first location.

## REVIEW QUESTIONS ✍

1. What is a macro?
2. What is the advantage of macros/preprocessors?
3. Explain **#define** directives.
4. How to create our own header file? Explain with an example.
5. Write short notes on command line arguments.
6. Can we use **function** in macros? If so how?
7. First argument in command line argument refers to _____.
8. Discuss the advantage of creating header file.
9. What is the difference between #include < > and #include "    ".
10. Write short notes on conditional directives.

# Chapter 11

# Data Structures and Algorithms

## 11.1 SEARCHING

Search is a technique to find whether the given item is available in the list or not. For example, to check whether a student is available or not in the information book. The information can be searched traditionally in two ways. One is sequential search and another is binary search.

### 11.1.1 What is a Sequential Search?

Sequential searching is a very simple technique to find the information and process one-by-one. In this model, the element is searched from the first to the last element of the list and the elements may be in any order. The drawback of this system is that it takes a long time if the necessary element is far away from the first.

A simple program to find the availability of a number from the list of elements. In this program, travel from the first to the last and if the number is found in the list, just the variable **found** is initialized with **true**.

***Example:***

```
/* Program for Sequential Searching */
enum bool{false,true} found;
main()
{
int i,n,m,a[10];

clrscr();
printf("\nHow many elements : ");
scanf("%d",&n);
printf("\nEnter %2d elements ",n);
for(i=1;i<=n;i++)
   scanf("%d",&a[i]);
```

```
printf("\nElements to be searched : ");
scanf("%d",&m);
/*Searching the element*/
found=false;
for(i=1;i<=n;i++)
  if (m==a[i])
    found=true;

if (found)
  printf("\n%d is found in the list",m);
else
  printf("\n%d is not found in the list ",m);
getch();
}
```

**Output:**
```
How many elements : 5
Enter 5 elements 10 20 30 40 50
Elements to be searched : 40
40 is found in the list
```

Here the value **40** is identified after **4** searches. So the time will proportionally increase with the number of searches.

### 11.1.2  What is Binary Search?

In the binary searching technique, the elements should be in the sorted order. For every comparison, the set of elements are divided into two halves. The next process may be first half or second half. So it takes less time than the sequential searching. Because the comparison and the number of elements will be reduced by half for every iteration.

***Note:***
Disadvantage of Binary Search is—All the elements must be sorted before search begins.

*Algorithm:*
1. Initialize the value as low=1, high=n
   (1-First, n-Last)
2. Read the element to be searched, m
3. While low <= high
       mid= (low+high)/2
       if a[mid]=m then  print "found" and exit
       if a[mid]>m then
         high=mid-1
       else
         high=mid+1
     done

***Example:***

| Given elements | : 10 | 20 | 30 | 40 | 50 |
|---|---|---|---|---|---|

Element to be searched is    : 40

| Location: | 1 | 2 | 3 | 4 | 5 | low | high | mid |
|---|---|---|---|---|---|---|---|---|
| Pass 1: | 10 | 20 | 30 | 40 | 50 | 1 | 5 | 3 |
| | low | | mid | | high | | | |
| Pass 2: | | | | | | | | |
| | 10 | 20 | 30 | 40 | 50 | 4 | 5 | 4 |

low mid high

Element is found at the fourth location. So with the two iterations, the element has been checked.

***Example:***

```c
/* Program for Binary Search */
main()
{
    int i,j,n,m,l,h,t,mid,a[15];
    clrscr();
    printf("\nHow many values ");
    scanf("%d",&n);
    printf("\nEnter %2d sorted values ",n);
    for(i=0;i<n;i++)
       scanf("%d",&a[i]);

    /*If the elements are not sorted, sort them here*/
    printf("\nElement to searched : ");
    scanf("%d",&m);
    /* Searching Part */
    l=0;h=n-1;
    while(l<=h)
    {
       mid=(l+h)/2;
       if ( a[mid]==m )
          {
             printf("\n%d is found at : %d",m,mid+1);
             break;
          }
       if (a[mid]< m)
          l=mid+1;
       else
          h=mid-1;
    }
    getch();
}
```

```
Output:
    How many values 6
    Enter 6 sorted values
    11    22    33    44    55    66
    Element to be searched : 33
    33 is found at : 3
```

## 11.2  STACK

Stack is a one-dimensional array and is very important in the procedure oriented programming techniques. The operations on stack are inserting, removing and traveling to the elements. The name of the operation may vary as

1. Push—Inserting an element
2. Pop—Removing an element

The operation is like a normal operation such as insert and delete an item. But the process end is different from the array. In stack, all the operations are only at one end called **top,** points to the top element of the stack or to the last element of the stack. From the value of **top**, we can identify the location of the next operation at which location. Stack operation is also called **Last In First Out** (LIFO).

### *Push operation*

1. Check the value of **top**
2. If top = MAX the stack is **FULL** and not able to insert
3. If top = 0, the stack is **EMPTY** and can insert.
4. Otherwise, the new item can be inserted by
   top = top + 1
   Stack [ top ] = item

### *Pop operation*

1. Check the value of **top**
2. If top = 0 , the stack is **EMPTY** and no more elements to remove
3. Otherwise, the item is removed by decrementing the top by 1
   item = stack [ top ]
   top = top − 1

A simple example for stack operation is illustrated here.

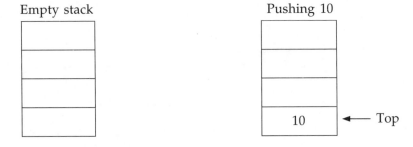

Empty stack                          Pushing 10

After pushing 20                                    After popping 20

### Relationship with function calling and stack?

In general, the function can be invoked by specifying its name. While invoking the function, the control is transferred from the calling function to the called function. Before transferring the control, system should do some process which is necessary for latter use. The system keeps the status of the calling function, and it is kept in the stack. After completion of the execution in the called function, control is returned to the calling function and continues the execution by taking the status of the resumed process from the stack.

For example, consider a function **test( )** , called by **main( )**.

```
/* Example for calling function */
main ( )
{
   int a = 10;

   test ( a );
   printf("\n a = %d ",a);
}
void test( int b )
{
   printf("Hello ! Welcome ");
}
```

Here, execution starts from the **main( )** function and it calls one user-defined function namely **test( )**. Before calling the function, the value of **a** is assigned as **10**. While calling, the control is transferred to the function **test( )**. Before jumping to the function, the program keeps the status of the last process i.e., **main( )** function status. When the process is completed in **test( )** it is returned back to **main( )**. Now there is a confusion, that is from where the execution starts?

Process is continued from where it has stopped. This information was already stored as status. So, there is no confusion at all.

**What is the role of stack in function?** We know that function calling is in sequence and return is in reverse. This is illustrated below:

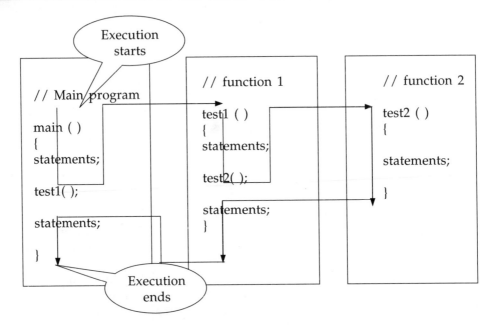

In the above figure, **main( )** calls a function **test1( )**. Now the status of **main( )** function is pushed into the stack. The function **test1( )** calls another function **test2( )**. Once again the stack's push operation and status of **test1( )** is pushed into the stack. Now the stack contains the statuses of the two functions, one is **main( )** and the other is **test1( )**, and the top is pointed to the status of **test1( )**.

When the process is completed in the **test2( )**, control is returned to its parent program, i.e., **test1( )**. Now **test1( )** continues its process by popping the status of its last processes available in stack, the top of the stack.

In general, when the function is called, the status is pushed into the stack and released. The status is taken from the stack for further process.

How to implement the stack operation? By using the array or linked list, we can process the functionality of the stack. Here array is taken for our discussion.

There is a variable called **MAX** defined as macro which keeps the maximum size of the stack and bottom of the stack is identified by '−1'.

*Example:*

```
/* Stack program with all operations */
#define MAX 100
int i,n,ch,item;
int stack[MAX], top = -1;

main()
{
    do
    {
        printf("\n1.Push 2.Pop 3. List 4. Exit");
        printf("\nSelect an operation : ");
```

```
      scanf("%d",&ch);
      switch(ch)
      {
        case 1: push( ); break;
        case 2: pop( ); break;
        case 3: list( ); break;
        case 4: printf("\nThanks ");
      }
   }while(ch!=4);
}

void push( )
{
     if ( top = = MAX )
     {
        printf("\nStack is full");
        return;
     }
   else
      {
        if ( top = = -1)
           printf("\nStack is empty ");

        printf("\nItem to insert :");
          scanf("%d",&item);

        top ++;
        stack[ top ] = item;
      }
}

void pop( )
{
   if (top = = -1)
   {
     printf("\nStack is empty. No elements in stack");
     return;
   }

   item = stack[top];
   top—;
   printf("\nRemoved item : %d ",item);
}
```

```
void list( )
{
   printf("\nList of items in stack ");
   for(i=top;i>=0;i--)
     printf("\n %d ",stack[i]);
}
```

**Output:**
```
    1. Push  2. Pop  3. List  4. Exit
    Select an operation : 1
    Stack is empty
    Item to insert :10
    1. Push  2. Pop  3. List  4. Exit
    Select an operation : 1
    Item to insert :20
    1. Push  2. Pop  3. List  4. Exit
    Select an operation : 1
    Item to insert :30
    1. Push  2. Pop  3. List  4. Exit
    Select an operation : 3
    List of items in stack
      30
      20
      10
    1. Push  2. Pop  3. List  4. Exit
    Select an operation : 2

    Removed item : 30
    1. Push  2. Pop  3. List  4. Exit
    Select an operation : 3

    List of items in stack
      20
      10
    1. Push  2. Pop  3. List  4. Exit
    Select an operation : 1

    Item to insert :100
    1. Push  2. Pop  3. List  4. Exit
    Select an operation : 3
    List of items in stack
      100
      20
      10
    1. Push  2. Pop  3. List  4. Exit
    Select an operation : 4
```

Functions **push( )**, **pop( )** and **list( )** are used to perform the operations like inserting, removing and listing of values respectively. Very important variable in the stack is top of the stack and the bottom of the stack.

## 11.3  QUEUE

Queues are found in real life near ticket centres, entries into halls, etc. Queue is a first in first out system (FIFO).

**The important of queue is that m**ost processes in the computer system are based on queue. For example, if we press the keys continuously, the inputs are received in sequence.

The Windows operating system and GUI work based on the message queue. Any information from the user and the interrupt are treated as messages. For example, while moving mouse, the messages like WM_MOUSEMOVE and pressing the key WM_CHAR, etc, are received as messages and processed sequentially.

Operations on the queue include insertion and deletion of an item. In stack, all the operations are performed only at one end. But in a queue the operations can take place at any end.

There are two pointers called **front** and **rear**, which keeps the status of the queue. The pointer **front** points to the first element of the queue, and the pointer **rear** points to the last element of the queue. A sample queue with pointers is as follows:

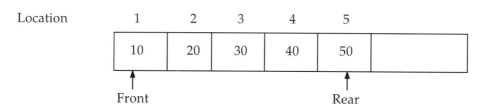

New element will be **inserted** in the queue at the **rear** end and elements are **removed** from the queue from the **front** end. So the queue is also called FIFO (First In First Out).

To represent the program, initially the **front** and the **rear** are initialized to **0**. *Actually the front points one position before its actual first location.*

### Insertion Operation

1. Check the availability of space, If **rear** = **MAX**, then the QUEUE is **FULL**.
2. Check the **front** and the **rear** values.
   If both are **0**, QUEUE is empty and start insertion
3. Insertion can be done by making
   rear = rear + 1
   QUEUE [ rear ] = item

### Deletion Operation

1. Check the value of **rear**. If it is **0**, the QUEUE is empty. So, we cannot perform the remove operation.
2. If **front=rear**, the QUEUE has no more elements to process
3. The removed item can be collected by
   item = QUEUE[front]
4. Element is removed by adjusting **front** as
   front = front + 1

### List Operation

1. The elements are between **front** & **rear**.
2. They are processed as
   for (**i** = **front+1** to **rear**) print **i**

To insert the item **10**, the front has to be incremented by **1** and the new queue list is

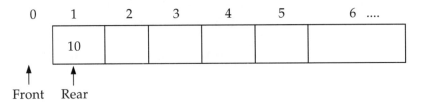

After inserting the items 20, 30 and 40, the QUEUE is

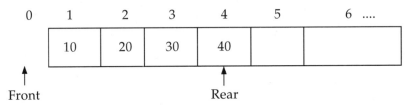

After removing the item 10, the QUEUE is

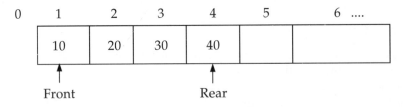

***Example:***

```
/* QUEUE Operation using arrays */
#define MAX 10

int front= -1, rear=-1, queue[MAX], item, ch, i;
main()
{
   do
      {
         printf("\n1.Ins 2.Del 3. List 4.Exit");
         printf("\nSelect a choice ...");
         scanf("%d",&ch);

         switch(ch)
         {
            case 1: insert() ; break;
            case 2: remov() ; break;
            case 3: list() ; break;
            case 4: printf("\nThanks. Queue operation is over");
         }
      } while(ch!=4);
   getch();
}


void insert()   /* Insertion function */
{
   if (rear= =MAX)
   {
     printf("\nQueue is empty. Insertion is not possible");
     return;
   }

   if ((front= = -1) && (rear= = -1))
      {
         printf("\nQueue is empty.");
         rear=front=0;
      }
   else
        rear ++;

   printf("\nItem to insert :");
   scanf("%d",&item);
   queue[rear]=item;
}
```

```
void remov()   /* Deletion function */
{
   if (front = = -1)
   {
   printf("\nQueue is empty. Deletion is not possible");
   return;
}

item = queue[front];
printf("\nRemoved item : %d ",item);

if (front==rear)
   front= rear = -1;
else
   front++;
}


/*Function to display the content of queue */
void list()
{
   if (front != -1)
      {
         printf("\nList of item in the Queue\n");
         for(i=front;i<=rear;i++)
         printf("\n%d ",queue[i]);
      }
}
```

**Output:**
```
1. Ins  2. Del  3. List  4. Exit
Select a choice ...1

Queue is empty.
Item to insert :10
1. Ins  2. Del  3. List  4. Exit
Select a choice ...1

Item to insert :20
1. Ins  2. Del  3. List  4. Exit
Select a choice ...1

Item to insert :30

1. Ins  2. Del  3. List  4. Exit
Select a choice ...
```

```
List of item in the Queue
10
20
30
1. Ins  2. Del  3. List  4. Exit
Select a choice...2

Removed item : 10
1. Ins  2. Del  3. List  4. Exit
Select a choice...2
Removed item : 20
1. Ins  2. Del  3. List  4. Exit
Select a choice...3

List of items in the Queue
30
1. Ins  2. Del  3. List  4. Exit
Select a choice...2

Removed item : 30
1. Ins  2. Del  3. List  4. Exit
Select a choice...2
Queue is empty. Deletion is not possible
1. Ins  2. Del  3. List  4. Exit
Select a choice...4

Thanks. Queue operation is over
```

## 11.4  CIRCULAR QUEUE

Queue is an ordered list in which insertions are made at one end called 'rear' and deletions will be done at another end called 'front'. When we implement this idea in real-time applications using arrays, there are some problems.

Let us consider that the queue is full, but there are some locations that are free in front. So to insert an element in the queue, we need to move all the elements one location forward. It looks very simple, but it takes some amount of time whenever the size of the queue is large.

The circular queue solves the problem and there is no need to move elements for new insertions. The two pointers such as the front and the rear are circularly moved round the queue. There must be room to find the front and the rear in the circular queue. So the **maximum number of elements in the circular queue is N–1.** The procedures for the operations insertion and deletion for a circular queue are given below.

### *Insertion Operation*

1. Check the availability of space by
   If (rear +1) % MAX = front, **then** QUEUE-FULL.
2. Empty C-Queue is checked by
   **If front = rear,** then **QUEUE-EMPTY**
3. If the C-Queue is empty
   **rear = (rear + 1) % MAX**
   **QUEUE [ rear ] = item**

### *Deletion operation*

1. Check the value of **rear** and **front**
   **If front=rear** then **QUEUE-EMPTY**
2. Element is removed by adjusting **front** as
   front = (front + 1) % MAX

Let us consider that the maximum size of the circular queue is **4,** the **front** and the **rear** are initialized by **0**. The insertions and deletions are illustrated in the following figure. To insert the item **10,** rear will be incremented by **1** and the new queue list is

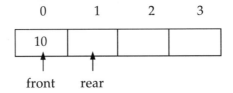

After inserting the items 20 and 30, the QUEUE looks as shown below

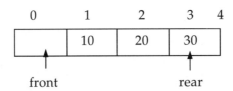

Now if we try to insert an element in the circular queue it will fail, because there must be one empty room. As mentioned earlier, we can store $N-1$ elements when the size of the queue is $N$. If we remove one element (10) from the queue, the new queue is

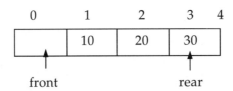

Now look at the value at rear. It reaches the maximum limit. We were not able to insert in the earlier case. But because of the property of the circular queue, now **rear** will

be moved to its next location (actually 0) and the new element can be inserted as shown below.

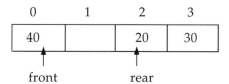

What is happening here? The front and rear are in different orders. The rear may follow the front. By this way, we can make use of the queue efficiently without moving the elements further.

### Example:

```c
/* Program for circular queue operations */
#include <stdio.h>
#include <conio.h>
#define MAX 5
void main()
{
int cqueue[MAX],i,data,front,rear,ch;

clrscr();
front=rear=0;
do
{
printf("\nSelect Your Option ");
printf("\n1. Insert 2. Delete 3. Display 4. Exit ");
scanf("%d",&ch);
switch(ch)
{
   case 1:
      printf("\nCircular Queue Insertion ");
         if (front==rear)
        printf("\nOh! Circular Queue is Empty");

      if ((rear+1)%MAX==front)
        {
           printf("\nSorry ! Queue Full");
        }
      else
      {
         rear=(rear+1)%MAX;
         printf("\nEnter your data to insert : ");
            scanf("%d",&data);
            cqueue[rear]=data;
      }
      break;
```

```
      case 2:
        printf("\nCircular Queue Deletion ");
        if (front==rear)
          printf("\nSorry ! Queue is Empty");
        else
        {
            front=(front+1)%MAX;
            printf("\nDeleted Data Item is : %d",cqueue[front]);
        }
        break;
      case 3:
        printf("\nData items in the Circular Queue \n");
        for(i=front+1;i!=(rear+1)%MAX;i=(i+1)%MAX)
          printf("%5d",cqueue[i]);
        break;
    }
  }
  while(ch<4);

  }
```

Output:
```
  Select Your Option
  1. Insert  2. Delete  3. Display  4. Exit 1
  Circular Queue Insertion
  Enter your data to insert : 10

  1. Insert  2. Delete  3. Display  4. Exit 1
  Circular Queue Insertion
  Enter your data to insert : 20

  1. Insert  2. Delete  3. Display  4. Exit 1
  Circular Queue Insertion
  Enter your data to insert : 30

  1. Insert  2. Delete  3. Display  4. Exit 3
  Data items in the Circular Queue
  10  20  30

  Select Your Option
  1. Insert  2. Delete  3. Display  4. Exit 2
  Circular Queue Deletion
  Deleted Data Item is : 10

  Select Your Option
  1. Insert  2. Delete  3. Display  4. Exit 3
  Data items in the Circular Queue
  20  30
```

```
Select Your Option
1. Insert  2. Delete  3. Display  4. Exit 1
Circular Queue Insertion
Enter your data to insert : 40

Select Your Option
1. Insert  2. Delete  3. Display  4. Exit 3
Data items in the Circular Queue
20  30  40

Select Your Option
1. Insert  2. Delete  3. Display  4. Exit 4
```

## 11.5  POLYNOMIAL ADDITION

### What is a polynomial?

Polynomial is an algebraic equation, which is a collection of coefficients and exponents. Each term contains one coefficient and its exponent. A simple polynomial is given below.

$$A(x) = 5x^3 + 3x^2 + 6x + 10$$

In the polynomial, we perform the simple arithmetic operations like addition, subtraction, multiplication, etc. The information about the polynomial is going to be stored using the arrays. The array contains the sequence of terms. The first value of the array contains the maximum value of the exponent, followed by the coefficient of the first term and its exponent and it is continuous for all the terms. In the above polynomial, $A(x)$ is represented as

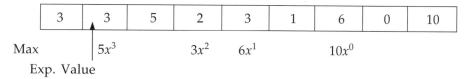

And the values can be stored in the array as (3, 3, 5, 2, 3, 1, 6, 0, 10).

### How to make the addition operation?

The addition operation in the polynomial is very simple. For this operation, two polynomials are necessary. Take, for example, $A(x)$ and $B(x)$ which are two polynomials and find the $C(x)$, which is $A(x) + B(x)$.

Start the operation by checking the exponent values of the equations. Suppose that the exponent values of both the equations are equal, respective coefficients are summed and the result is stored in the $C$ array with its exponent value. This process will continue until no more elements.

While comparing the exponent values of polynomials, there is a possibility of mismatching and the result of comparison may be greater or less than the expected value.

So what is the solution in this case? A simple solution is that, the coefficient of the highest exponent will be copied into C with its exponent.

The number of terms in the polynomial is also considered, when the function contains less than the second polynomial terms. In this case, all the remaining elements of the polynomial are copied into C.

Simple example: $A(x) = 5x^3 + 3x^2 + 5x$
$B(x) = 4x^3 + 5x^2 + 2x$

And the summation $C(x) = 9x^3 + 8x^2 + 7x$

| A(x) | 3 | 3 | 5 | 2 | 3 | 1 | 5 |
|------|---|---|---|---|---|---|---|
| B(x) | 3 | 3 | 4 | 2 | 5 | 1 | 2 |

| C(x) | 3 | 3 | 9 | 2 | 8 | 1 | 7 |
|------|---|---|---|---|---|---|---|

**Algorithm:**
1. Check the exponent values of the equations
2. If it is equal, corresponding coefficient value is added
3. If the exponent of the first equation is higher than the second one, the items of the first equation are copied into C.
4. If steps 2 and 3 fail, copy the contents of the second equation into C.
5. Steps 1 through 4 will continue until any one of the equations becomes empty, and no more elements to process.
6. In some cases, one equation items may or may not be in both.
7. In this situation, all the remaining items of the corresponding equation are copied into C.

**Example:**

```
/* Addition of two Polynomial Equations */
#define MAX 20

void main()
{
    int i,p,q,m,n,a[MAX],b[MAX],c[MAX+MAX];
    int t=1;
    clrscr();

    printf("\nHighest Exponent of the first eqn. (Max) :");
    scanf("%d",&m);
    a[0]=m;
    t=2*(m+1);

    printf("\nEnter the Coefficient and Exponent eqn. ");
    for(i=1;i<=t;i++)
        scanf("%d",&a[i]);
```

```c
    printf("\nHighest Exponent of the second eqn. (Max) :");
    scanf("%d",&n);
    b[0]=n;

    t=2*(n+1);
    printf("\nEnter the Coefficient and Exponent eqn.");
    for(i=1;i<=t;i++)
        scanf("%d",&b[i]);

    printf("\nFirst Equation is : ");
    for(i=1;i<=t;i++)
        {
            printf("%+dx",a[i]);
            printf("%d ",a[++i]);
        }
printf("\nSecond Equation is : ");
for(i=1;i<=t;i++)
    {
        printf("%+dx",b[i]);
        printf("%d ",b[++i]);
    }

p=2;q=2;
while((p<=2*(m+1)) && (q<=2*(n+1)))
{
    if (a[p]==b[q])
        {
            c[p-1]=a[p-1] + b[q-1];
            c[p]=a[p];
            p+=2;q+=2;
        }


if (a[p]>b[q])
    {
        c[p-1]=a[p-1];
        c[p]=a[p];
        p+=2;
    }

if (a[p]<b[q])
    {
        c[q-1]=b[q-1];
        c[q]=b[q];
        q+=2;
    }
}
```

```
while(p<=2*(m+1))
{
    c[p-1]=a[p-1];
    c[p]=a[p];
    p+=2;
}

while(q<=2*(n+1))
{
    c[q-1]=b[q-1];
    c[q]=b[q];
    q+=2;
}
printf("\nResult is : ");
for(i=1;i<=t;i++)
    {
        printf("%+dx",c[i]);
        printf("%d ",c[++i]);
    }

getch();
}
```

**Output:**
```
    Highest Exponent of the first eqn. (Max) : 2
    Enter the Coefficient and Exponent eqn.
    3  2  5  1  3  0
    Highest Exponent of the second eqn. (Max) : 2
    Enter the Coefficient and Exponent eqn.
    2  2  7  1  2  0

    First Equation is  : + 3x2 + 5x1 + 3x0
    Second Equation is : + 2x2 + 7x1 + 2x0
    Result is          : + 5x2 + 12x1 + 5x0
```

## 11.6  POSTFIX CONVERSION

### What is an expression?

An expression is a collection of operators and operands. Operands are simple variables. Here is an example of the expression: $C = A + B$. The operator is + and the operands are $A$, $B$ and $C$. We used to give the expression as above and it is not going to be executed directly. The expression should be any of the three formats: **infix**, operator is between the operands ($A + B$), **postfix**, operator is followed by the operands ($AB+$), and **prefix**, operator is preceded by the operands ($+AB$).

The traditional expression is in the infix format. The compiler converts this expression into the postfix format and it performs the execution. Why we have to convert into the postfix format? The postfix expression is the only way to perform the operation properly with its priority. So, all the expressions have to be converted into postfix format for evaluation.

## What is priority and why?

The expression is evaluated by using the priority of the operators. The simple priority table is given below.

| Operator | Priority |
|----------|----------|
| * and / | 1 |
| + and – | 2 |

So, the operator * and / are given the highest priority than + and –. If there are two operators like * and + in the expression, * will be executed first and next +.

## How to convert infix to postfix?

We have to set the priority for the operators explicitly as in the above table. The following is an algorithm for this conversion using the priority table. Stack is used for inserting and removing operators.

Take the individual characters from the expression and perform the necessary operations. If the character of the expression is

1. **Operand**, copy the operand into the postfix array.
2. **Operator**
   If the stack is empty
       Push the operator into the stack
   Else
       Check the operator's priority.
   If the **Priority (Stack[top]) > Priority (In-coming operator)**
       Pop the operators and add to the postfix array.
   Else
       Push the operator into the stack.
3. If there is no other character in the expression,
   Pop all the operators from the stack and into postfix array.

## Note:

If the characters (and) are included in the expression, we have to keep different priorities for them (highest priority when it comes from the expression, Lowest priority if it is in the stack).

The following is a program for converting infix expression into postfix expression.

***Example:***

```
/* Converting Infix To Postfix expression */
#include <stdio.h>
#include <conio.h>
int i=0,top=0;
char stack[10],expr[15],postfix[15];

void push(char);
char pop();
int priority(char ch);

void main()
{
   char ch;
   int x,j=0;

   clrscr();
   printf("\nEnter the Infix Expression : ");
   scanf("%s",expr);

   while((ch=expr[i])!='\0')
   {
      if ((ch>='a') && (ch<='z'))
        postfix[j++]=ch;
      else
        if (top==0)
            /*Push directly if it is the first character */
          push(ch);
        else
        {
        if (priority(ch) > priority(stack[top]))
          push(ch);
        else
        {
   while((priority(ch)<=priority(stack[top]))&& (top!=0))
      postfix[j++]=pop();

   push(ch);
        }
      }
      i++;
   }

   /* Pop the remaining elements from the Stack */

   while (top!=-1)
      postfix[j++]=pop();

   postfix[j]='\0';
```

```
    clrscr();
    printf("\nInfix Expression : %s ",expr);
    printf("\nPostfix Expression : %s",postfix);
    getch();
}

void push(char ch)
{
    top++;
    stack[top]=ch;
}

char pop()
{
    return(stack[top--]);
}

/* To check the priority */
int priority(char ch)
{
    switch(ch)
    {
      case '*':
      case '/': return 2;
      case '+':
      case '-':return 1;
    }
}
```

**Output:**
```
    Enter the Infix Expression : a+b*c-d
    Infix Expression : a+b*c-d
    Postfix Expression : abc*+d-
```

## 11.7  LINKED LIST

### The need of Linked List/Problems in the Array

Array is used to keep a number of elements and all the elements are of same data types. For simple applications array is good. But it has many drawbacks, such as, when the user wishes to add an element to the array or coishes to remove an element from the array, the array elements should be shifted and this takes more time.

### Dynamic Memory Allocation

Dynamic memory allocation is a technique used to allocate the memory dynamically at the time of execution of the program. For example, there is a declaration **int a[100]** and is used to allocate memory for **100** elements (100 * 2 = 200 bytes). Suppose, if we are going to use less than declared size say, **25** elements, what about the remaining **75**? All the remaining 75 * 2 = 150 bytes in the location remain unused and wasted. So here, we are wasting the memory.

Another problem is suppose we need to store more than the defined range of 100, say **200** elements, we are not able to store because of lack of memory. The only solution is to change the program code as **int a[200]**. But this is not a convenient way to store the values whenever the size changes.

The solution to this problem is allocating memory dynamically. That means memory is allocated at the time of execution of the program. The size may be **10** or **100** or **1000**, etc.

### Note:
Size does not matter in the Dynamic Memory Allocation

### Problems in Dynamic Memory Allocation

While allocating memory, either statically or dynamically, the memory is reserved sequentially from the first to the last element (continuous memory locations) of the array. We are clear in the array definition like the memory locations are same. This is illustrated in the following two examples both static and dynamic memory allocation.

```
/* Example using static memory allocation */
main()
{
    int n,i,a[5];
    clrscr();
    printf("\nAddresses of elements");
    for(i=1;i<=5;i++)
        printf("\n%u",&a[i]);
}
```

Output of the above program is as follows. It produces only the addresses of the array elements which are allocated statically by using **int a[5]**.

Addresses of elements

1000    1002    1004    1006    1008

The following is a program to test the addresses of the array elements, which are allocated dynamically at the time of execution.

```
/* Example of using dynamic memory allocation */
main()
{
    int n,i;
    int *ptr;

    clrscr();
    printf("\nEnter the size : ");
```

```
    scanf("%d",&n);
    ptr=(int *) malloc(sizeof(int) * n);
    printf("\nAddresses of elements ");
    for(i=1;i<=n;i++)
        printf("\n%u",ptr++);
}
```

This program also generates the sequential addresses as follows, where even the memory is allocated dynamically using the statement

```
    ptr=(int *) malloc(sizeof(int) * n);
```

and the output is

```
Enter the size : 5
Addresses of elements
1050    1052    1054    1056    1058
```

### What is the problem here?

The problem occurs when there is not enough space for the elements. For example, the following is the memory with 24 cells.

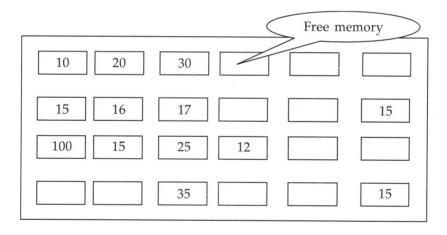

Now we would like to store **5** elements and the declaration is

```
int a[5]={11,22,33,44,55};
```

In general, the memory for this array variable will be allocated continuously. But in the array, there are no five consecutive memory locations even though we have **11** free spaces. The only solution for this type of problem is the *linked list*. Using the linked list, we can store the elements anywhere in the memory. It is okay for keeping the elements, but how to process them? For this purpose, all the elements should have one additional information called link (pointer) to its next element.

Look at the following diagram and all the elements are successfully accommodated in the memory with the link.

```
int a[5]={11,22,33,44,55};
```

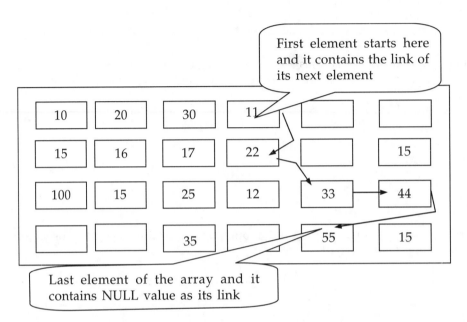

So, without wasting a single memory location, all the free areas can be utilized using the linked list.

Another problem in the array is that, inserting or removing an element from it. For example, we have **100** elements in continuous memory. Now we have to insert a new element inside the array, at the 25th location. To insert this element, all the elements from **25** to **50** are adjusted to their next locations like **25** to **26**, **26** to **27**, ..., **50** to **51**. This complexity is simplified and removed using the linked list. New element can be inserted in the middle or front or last easily in lesser time and fewer movements.

Linked list is a collection of one or more nodes. The single node contains minimum of two informations, one is data and another one is link, which points to the next node's location. The general structure of the node is

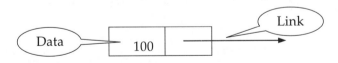

How to represent this node in the computer format? We can use the feature of structure. So a structure contains data and self-referential pointer to the structure. The declaration of a single node can be

```
struct node
{
   int data;               /* Data */
   struct node *link;      /* Link to the next node */
};
```

Here the declaration **struct node * link** is used to keep the address of the next node in the list. Before developing a program, it is better to have a general overview on the linked list and the next few pages will bring the related information about it.

To perform the operations in the linked list, here I am taking sample list with four nodes and its data are 10, 20, 30 and 40. Using this list we are going to perform the operations like Insertion and Deletion on the list.

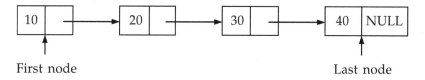

First node                              Last node

## Insertion

In this case the new node is going to be inserted and it may be anywhere in the list Front, End or Middle. This is a great advantage over the array. In array, the insertion and deletion of elements in the middle is very difficult. But here with less transaction, the elements can be inserted at any place.

**Front Insertion:**
1. Create a TEMPorary node and assign its value as 100
2. Establish a link from TEMP to FIRST as TEMP→link = FIRST
3. Reassign the FIRST to TEMP node as FIRST=TEMP.

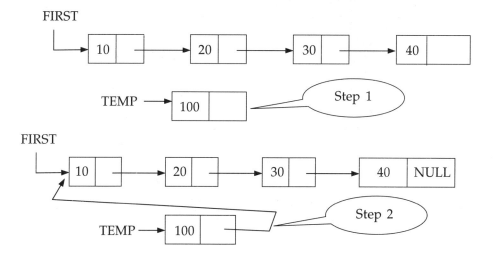

After adjusting the FIRST, the list is

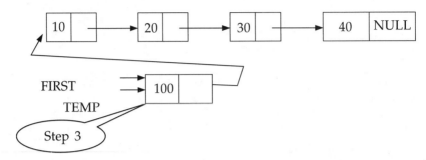

After completion of the insertion, the list becomes 100, 10, 20, 30 and 40. So, the value 100 is successfully inserted in the front.

### End Insertion:
1. Create a node TEMP, with value 100 and fill its link as NULL, because of the last node of the list
2. Let CUR=FIRST
3. Travel up to the end of the list using while as
   while(CUR→link != NULL)
   CUR= CUR→Link
4. Replace the NULL link of CUR node by
   CUR→link = TEMP

Initial Stage of the list is as follows:

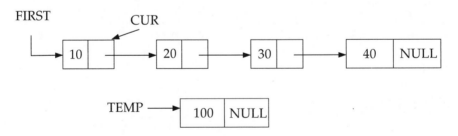

After travelling to the end, the list looks like:

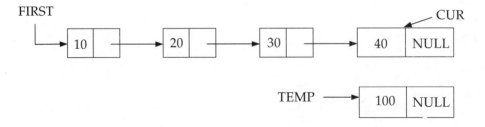

After inserting at the end using CUR->link = TEMP, the list is:

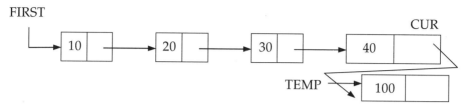

Now the node with the value 100, is appended at the end of list and the sequence of the list is 10, 20, 30, 40 and 100.

### Insert in the middle after some Element

It is a very good feature over arrays. In array, the insertion in the middle is very difficult as I mentioned above. The new node is inserted in the middle of the list easily. Middle in the sense, after a particular (or a matching element) of the list.

1. Create a node TEMP, and fill the value as 100.
2. Let CUR=FIRST, CUR represents Current node
3. Travel until the matching of element or end of the list as
   while (CUR→data != ele )
   CUR= CUR→link;
4. If the element is found, then do
   TEMP→link = CUR→link
5. CUR→link = TEMP

Assume that the new node is going to be inserted after the element 30. In this case, after searching the number 30, the the new element is inserted.

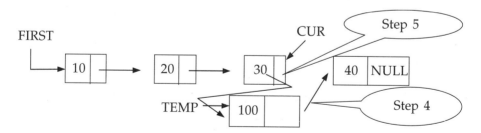

After the insertion of the new node with value 100, the list contains the values in the order as 10, 20, 30, 100 and 40.

### *Deletion*

The elements in the list can be removed anywhere from FRONT/END/MIDDLE easily.

**Deletion of the first element**

The simplest operation on the linked list is to delete a node in the front. In this case, node FIRST is adjusted to the next node, since, the previous node has no links with others, it is removed from the list automatically.

Initial Stage with four nodes and their values are as below:

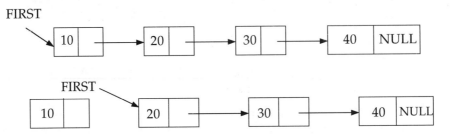

Now the node with a value 10 is removed from the list, by adjusting the **FIRST** to its next.

**Deletion of the last element**

Removing the last element is a bit difficult compared to removing the element from the front. A pointer **CUR** is used to keep the current element in the list and one more temporary **TEMP** is used to keep the previous of **CUR**. When **CUR** reaches the end, it is identified by **NULL** and the **TEMP** points to the second element from the last or previous of **CUR** node.

1. Assign CUR=FIRST
2. Travel until the matching of element or end of the list as
   while (CUR != NULL )
   {
       TEMP = CUR;
       CUR= CUR→link;
   }
3. Make TEMP's link as NULL, and automatically the CUR, which is now pointed to the last node, is removed from the list.

After travelling to the last node, the pointers FIRST, CUR and TEMP are pointed as follows:

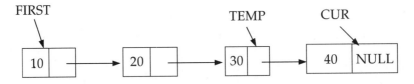

In simple, the link of **TEMP** is filled by **NULL**. The node, which is named as **CUR** is removed from the list, because it has no communication with others and its diagram is as follows:

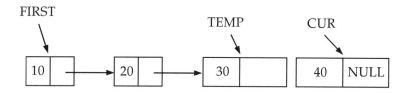

So the element 40 is successfully removed from the list. A complete program with all the possible operations is given in the following program. Initially the list contains nothing and is specified by **first = NULL**.

***Example:***

```
/* Program for Singly Linked List */
#include <stdio.h>
#include <conio.h>

struct node
{
   int data;
   struct node *link;
};
void main()
{
   int n,ch,ch1,ele;
   struct node *first, *temp, *cur;

   clrscr();
   first = NULL; /* Empty on first */

   do
   {
   printf("\nSelect operation\n1.Add 2.Del 3.List4.Exit\n");
   scanf("%d",&ch);
   switch(ch)
   {
     case 1:
        printf("\nEnter the data : ");
        scanf("%d",&n);

        if (first==NULL)
        {
           printf("\nList is empty");
           first=(struct node *)malloc(sizeof(struct node));
           first->data=n;
           first->link=NULL;
           break;
        }
     else
```

```
{
printf("\nWhere to insert\n1.Front2.End3.Middle ");
scanf("%d",&ch1);
switch(ch1)
{

case 1:
   temp=(struct node *)malloc(sizeof(struct node));
   temp->data=n;
   temp->link=first;
   first=temp;
   break;

case 2:
   cur=first;
   while(cur->link!=NULL)
     cur=cur->link;
   temp=(struct node *)malloc(sizeof(struct node));
   temp->data=n;
   temp->link=NULL;
   cur->link=temp;
   break;

case 3:
   cur=first;
   printf("\nInsert after the element :");
   scanf("%d",&ele);
   temp=(struct node *)malloc(sizeof(struct node));
   while(cur->link!=NULL)
   {
       if (cur->data==ele)
       {
          temp->data=n;
          temp->link=cur->link;
          cur->link=temp;
       }
     cur=cur->link;
   }
 }
 break;
case 2:
   printf("\nWhere to remove\n1.Front 2.End");
   scanf("%d",&ch1);
```

```
      if (ch1==1)
      {
         printf("\nRemoved item is : %d ",first->data);
         first=first->link;
         break;
      }

      if (ch1==2)
      {
         cur=first;
         while(cur->link!=NULL)
         {
            temp=cur;
            cur=cur->link;
         }
            printf("\nRemoved item is : %d ",cur->data);
            temp->link=NULL;
         }
         break;
      case 3:
         printf("\nList of nodes\n");
         cur=first;

         while(cur!=NULL)
         {
            printf(" %5d ",cur->data);
            cur=cur->link;
         }
         break;
      }
   }
   }while(ch!=4);
}
```

**Output:**

```
Select operation
1. Add  2. Del  3. List  4. Exit
1
Enter the data : 10
List is empty
Select operation
1. Add  2. Del  3. List  4. Exit
1
Enter the data : 20
Where to insert
```

```
1. Front  2. End  3. Middle
1
Select operation
1. Add  2. Del  3. List  4. Exit
1
Enter the data : 30
Where to insert
1. Front  2. End  3. Middle 2
Select operation
1. Add  2. Del  3. List  4. Exit
3

List of nodes
  20  10  30
Select operation
1. Add  2. Del  3. List  4. Exit
1
Enter the data : 40
Where to insert
1. Front  2. End  3. Middle 3
Insert after the element: 20
Select operation
1. Add  2. Del  3. List  4. Exit
3
List of nodes
  20  40  10  30
Select operation
1. Add  2. Del  3. List  4. Exit
2
Where to remove
1. Front  2. End1
Removed item is : 20
Select operation
1. Add  2. Del  3. List  4. Exit
2
Where to remove
1. Front  2. End 2
Removed item is : 30
Select operation
1. Add  2. Del  3. List  4. Exit
3
List of nodes
  40  10
Select operation
1. Add  2. Del  3. List  4. Exit
4
Thanks
```

## 11.8 LINKED STACK

In the stack, we can perform the operations such as insertion and deletion. But these operations are restricted to be at one end called top. So, all the operations are based on the value of top, which always points to the top of the stack.

Implementing the stack using linked list is very easy if we have some idea about the operations on linked lists. By making the operations on the first node of the linked list, we can implement the stack (here, the first element can be taken as top of the list).

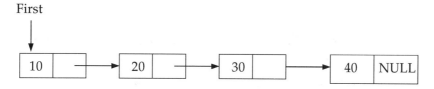

The new element 100 is going to be pushed into this list by inserting the new node at the first and it looks like

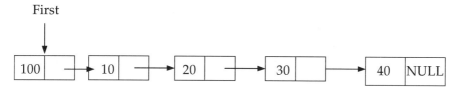

To remove the element, just adjust the first to its next location and the first element is automatically removed from the list as

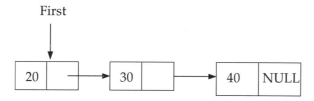

Here, the element 10 is removed at the front, so the pop operation is successfully implemented. The complete program to implement the stack operation using linked list is illustrated below.

### *Example:*

```
/* Program for a Stack using Linked List*/
#include <stdio.h>
#include <conio.h>
#include <malloc.h>
struct node
{
    int data;
    struct node *link;
};
```

```c
void main()
{
   int n,ch;
   struct node *first, *temp, *cur;

   clrscr();
   first = NULL; /* Empty on first */

do
{
printf("\nSelect operation\n1.Push 2.Pop 3.List 4.Exit\n");
scanf("%d",&ch);
   switch(ch)
   {
      case 1:
      printf("\nEnter the data : ");
      scanf("%d",&n);

      if (first==NULL)
      {
         printf("\nStack is empty");
         first=(struct node *)malloc(sizeof(struct node));
         first->data=n;
         first->link=NULL;
      }
   else
      {
         cur=first;
         while(cur->link!=NULL)
            cur=cur->link;

         temp=(struct node *)malloc(sizeof(struct node));
         temp->data=n;
         temp->link=NULL;
         cur->link=temp;
      }
         break;


      case 2:
         if (first==NULL)
            {
               printf("\nSorry! Stack is empty.");
               break;
            }
         cur=first;
         while(cur->link!=NULL)
```

```
            {
               temp=cur;
               cur=cur->link;
            }
         printf("\nRemoved item is : %d ",cur->data);
         temp->link=NULL;
         free(cur);
      break;

      case 3:
         printf("\nList of nodes\n");
         cur=first;

         while(cur!=NULL)
         {
            printf(" %5d ",cur->data);
            cur=cur->link;
         }
      }

      }while(ch!=4);
}
```

**Output:**
```
Select operation
1. Push  2. Pop  3. List  4. Exit
1
Enter the data : 10
Stack is empty
Select operation

1. Push  2. Pop  3. List  4. Exit
1
Enter the data : 20
Select operation
1. Push  2. Pop  3. List  4. Exit
1
Enter the data : 30
Select operation
1. Push  2. Pop  3. List  4. Exit
2
Removed item is : 30
Select operation
1. Push  2. Pop  3. List  4. Exit
3
List of nodes
10   20
Select operation
1. Push  2. Pop  3. List  4. Exit
4
```

## 11.9 CONCATENATION OF LINKED LISTS

One more simple application in the linked list is concatenation of two linked lists or joining of two lists (Take **X** and **Y**, the new list is **Z**). For this, just establish the link of the last node of the **X**, to the first node of the second list **Y**. The new list **Z**, contains the concatenated list of nodes.

In some cases, first ensure the nodes of two lists **X** and **Y** respectively, whether they contain any node or not. Sometimes they may be empty.

If the first node of X is empty, just do the following assignment

$$Z = Y;$$

If the second node is empty, the assignment is

$$Z = X;$$

If both X and Y are not empty, then follow the below given process

Travel to the end of the list **X** and now just establish the **NULL** link of **X** to the first node of **Y**.

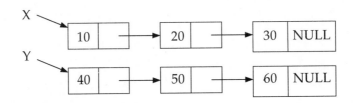

Use one temporary variable **P**, to travel to the end of the list **X**, and when it reaches the end, new link of **P** (Now it is NULL) will be established that points to the first node of **Z** as

$$X \rightarrow link = Z;$$

New concatenated list **Z**, is as follows and the sequence is 10, 20, 30, 40, 50 and 60.

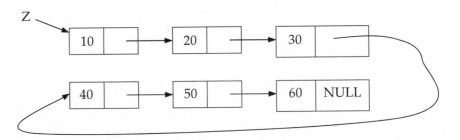

Concatenation of two linked lists is illustrated in the following program:

***Example:***

```
/* Concatenation of two linked lists */
#include <stdio.h>

struct node
{
   int data;
   struct node *link;
};

struct node *head1,*head2,*head3,*temp,*cur;

void main()
{
   int ch,ch1,t,i;
   head1=head2=NULL;

   clrscr();
   /* Each List contains 3 nodes */
   for(i=1;i<=3;i++)
   if (head1==NULL)

     {
        printf("\nFirst list is empty\n");
        head1=(struct node *) malloc(sizeof(struct node));
        printf("Data to insert :");
        scanf("%d",&head1->data);
        head1->link=NULL;
     }
     else
     {
        temp=(struct node *) malloc(sizeof(struct node));
        printf("Data to insert :");
        scanf("%d",&temp->data);
        temp->link=NULL;

        /* At the end */
        cur=head1;
        while(cur->link!=NULL)
           cur=cur->link;

        cur->link=temp;
   }
   for(i=1;i<=3;i++)
     if (head2==NULL)
        {
           printf("\nSecond list is empty\n");
           head2=(struct node *) malloc(sizeof(struct node));
```

```
        printf("Data to insert :");
        scanf("%d",&head2->data);
        head2->link=NULL;
    }
    else
    {

    temp=(struct node *) malloc(sizeof(struct node));
    printf("Data to insert :");
    scanf("%d",&temp->data);
    temp->link=NULL;

    /* At the end */
    cur=head2;
    while(cur->link!=NULL)
       cur=cur->link;

    cur->link=temp;
}

printf("\nData items in first list : ");

temp=head1;
while(temp!=NULL)
    {
       printf("%5d",temp->data);
       temp=temp->link;
    }

printf("\nData items in second list : ");
temp=head2;
while(temp!=NULL)
    {
       printf("%5d",temp->data);
       temp=temp->link;
    }
printf("\nData items in Jointed List : ");

cur=head1;

while(cur->link!=NULL)
    cur=cur->link;

    cur->link=head2;

    cur=head1;

    while(cur!=NULL)
```

```
    {
        printf("%5d",cur->data);
        cur=cur->link;
    }
    getch();
}
```

**Output:**

```
First list is empty
Data to insert :10
Data to insert :20
Data to insert :30

Second list is empty
Data to insert :40
Data to insert :50
Data to insert :60

Data items in first list : 10 20 30
Data items in second list : 40 50 60
Data items in Joined List : 10 20 30 40 50 60
```

## 11.10  REVERSING THE LINKED LIST

Reversing linked list is a little bit complex compared to the previous discussions. Here, we are going to use three temporary nodes, **t1**, **t2** and **t3**. Initially **t1** points to the **first** node, **t2** points to the **second** and **t3** to the **third**. For every operation, all the three pointers are adjusted to their next locations. The traveling process will stop when **t2** reaches the end. The following is a list, which contains five nodes in the sequence of 10, 20, 30, 40 and 50. Now we are going to reverse this sequence as 50, 40, 30, 20 and 10.

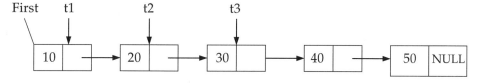

Set the first node's link as **NULL**, because it will be the last node of the new list by using the statement **t1->link=NULL** and the list is

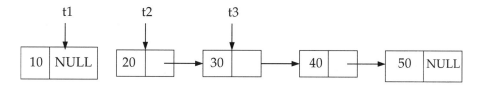

To reverse, the first, set the **t2's** link to **t1**, as **t2->link=t1**. Now second node points to the first node is reversed. Next adjust each of **t1**, **t2** and **t3** to its next node. The new list looks like

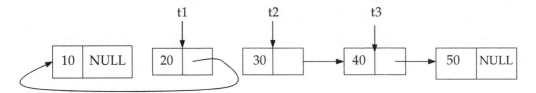

Travel to all the nodes until the **t2** reaches to **NULL** and the following is the new list after traveling to the last node.

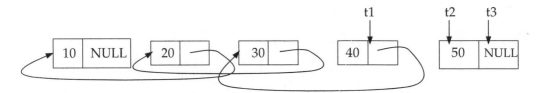

Now, the node **t2** reaches the end of the list, because of **NULL**. So stop further process and just establish the new link of the last node as

$$t2->link = t1;$$

A completely reversed list is

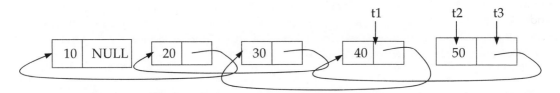

If we try to travel in the linked list, **first** can be set in the **t2's** location and using this we can travel to the last node. The sequence is now, 50, 40, 30, 20 and 10. Process will stop at 10, because of **NULL**.

The following is a program to reverse the content of the linked list.

***Example:***

```
/* Reverse the Content of Linked List */

#include <stdio.h>
#include <conio.h>
#include <malloc.h>
```

```
struct node
{
   int data;
   struct node *link;
};

struct node *head,*temp,*cur;
struct node *f1,*t1,*t2,*t3;

void main()
{
   int n,t,i;

   head=NULL;
   printf("\nHow many nodes : ");
   scanf("%d",&n);
   clrscr();
   for(i=1;i<=n;i++) /*Create a list with 5 nodes*/
   if (head==NULL)
   {
      printf("\nList is empty\n");
      head =(struct node *) malloc(sizeof(struct node));
      printf("Data to insert : ");
      scanf("%d",&head->data);
      head->link=NULL;
   }
   else
   {
      temp=(struct node *) malloc(sizeof(struct node));
      printf("Data to insert :");
      scanf("%d",&temp->data);
      temp->link=NULL;

      /* At the end */
      cur=head;
      while(cur->link!=NULL)
         cur=cur->link;

         cur->link=temp;
   }

      clrscr();

   printf("\nData in the List ");
   cur=head;
   while(cur!=NULL)
```

```
   {
      printf("\n%5d",cur->data);
      cur=cur->link;
   }

// Reverse the Linked List

t1=head;
t2=t1->link;     /* Points to the second node */
t1->link=NULL;   /* First nodes link */
t3=t2->link;     /* Points to the third node */

while(t2->link!=NULL) /* Travel to end */
{
   t2->link=t1;
   t1=t2;
   t2=t3;
   t3=t3->link;
}
t2->link=t1;

getch();
printf("\nReverse of the List");
cur=t2;


while(cur!=NULL)
   {
      printf("\n%5d",cur->data);
      cur=cur->link;
   }
   getch();
}
```

**Output:**
```
How many nodes : 5
List is empty
Data to insert : 11
Data to insert : 22
Data to insert : 33
Data to insert : 44
Data to insert : 55

Data in the List
   11  22  33  44  55
Reverse of the List
   55  44  33  22  11
```

## 11.11  LINKSORT

```c
/* Sort the node of linked list */
#include <stdio.h>

struct node
{
   int data;
   struct node *link;
};

struct node *head,*temp,*cur,*t1,*t2;

void main()
{
   int ch,t,i,n;
   head=NULL;

   clrscr();
   printf("\nHow many elements : ");
   scanf("%d",&n);
   for(i=1;i<=n;i++)
   if (head==NULL)
   {
      printf("\nFirst list is empty\n");
      head=(struct node *) malloc(sizeof(struct node));
      printf("Data to insert :");
      scanf("%d",&head->data);
      head->link=NULL;
   }
      else
      {
         temp=(struct node *) malloc(sizeof(struct node));
         printf("Data to insert :");
         scanf("%d",&temp->data);
         temp->link=NULL;


      /* At the end */
      cur=head;
      while(cur->link!=NULL)
         cur=cur->link;

      cur->link=temp;

   }
   printf("\nData items in the List : ");
```

```
cur=head;
while(cur!=NULL)
   {
      printf("%5d",cur->data);
      cur=cur->link;
   }

   for(t1=head;t1->link!=NULL;t1=t1->link)
   for(t2=t1->link;t2!=NULL;t2=t2->link)
   if (t1->data>t2->data)
   {
      t=t1->data;
      t1->data=t2->data;
      t2->data=t;
   }
   printf("\nSorted Items :");
   for(t1=head;t1!=NULL;t1=t1->link)
   printf("\n%d",t1->data);

getch();
}
```

## 11.12  DOUBLY LINKED LIST

### *Disadvantage of Singly Linked List*

The advantages of singly linked list are realized in the previous section. Some of the advantages are, we can do insertion and deletion efficiently, use all the memory areas, etc.

Even though singly linked list has many advantages, it also has some disadvantages such as we can not travel back easily. If we introduce one more link in the node of a singly linked list and make it doubly linked list, we can solve the above kind of problems. Since each node in the doubly linked list has two links, one link (right link) pointing to the next node in the list and the other (left link) pointing to the previous node in the list. The node in the doubly linked list and the structure declaration are given below.

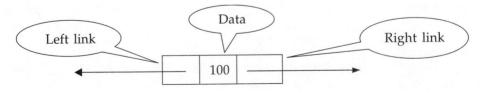

The following is a structure declaration of the single node in the doubly linked list.

```
struct node
{
    int data;    /* Data */
    struct node *rlink; /* Link to the next node */
    struct node *llink; /* Link to the previous node */
};
```

Here the declaration **struct node *rlink** is used to keep the address of the next node in the list and **struct node *rlink** is used to keep the address of the previous node in the list. The following is a list with three nodes in the doubly linked list. In case of doubly linked list, the left link of the first node and the right link of the last node are **NULL**.

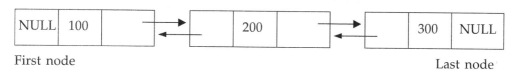

First node                                                            Last node

The operations in doubly linked list are similar to the singly linked list. Only thing is that for every operation, we need to consider two links instead of only one link.

## Insertion

Here also we can insert a new node at the first, last or in between. The following is a procedure for inserting a new node as a last node.

1. Create a **TEMP**orary node and assign its value as **10**
2. Fill its right link as **NULL** (Because this will be a new last node)
   TEMP→rlink = NULL
3. Find the last node in the list – by traveling till end
4. Fill the left link to the last node of the list
   TEMP→llink = CUR
5. Fill the right link of CUR to the TEMP
   CUR→rlink = TEMP

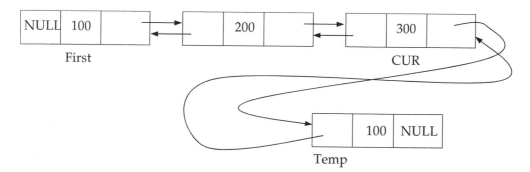

After inserting the new node with data value **10**, the list looks as above. Like this we could perform all possible operations on the doubly inked lists. If we are clear about the singly linked list, then there is no problem in doubly linked list. The following is a complete program, which illustrates the basic operations such as insertion, deletion and display the list of nodes in the list.

### Example:

```c
/* Doubly Linked List operations */
#include <stdio.h>
#include <conio.h>

struct node
{
   int data;
   struct node *llink;    /* Left Link */
   struct node *rlink;    /* Right Link */
};
void main()
{
   int n,ch;
   struct node *first, *temp, *cur;

   clrscr();
   first = NULL; /* Empty on first */

do
{
printf("\nSelect operation\n1. Add  2. Del  3. List  4. Exit\n");
scanf("%d",&ch);
switch(ch)
   {
   case 1:
      printf("\nEnter the data : ");
      scanf("%d",&n);

      /* Insert when the list is empty */
      if (first==NULL)
      {
         printf("\nList is empty");
         first=(struct node *)malloc(sizeof(struct node));
         first->data=n;
         first->llink=NULL;
         first->rlink=NULL;
         break;
      }
      /* Insert at end non-empty list */
   else
```

```
    {
       cur=first;
       while(cur->rlink!=NULL)
           cur=cur->rlink;
       temp=(struct node *)malloc(sizeof(struct node));
       temp->data=n;
       temp->rlink=NULL;
       temp->llink=cur;
       cur->rlink=temp;
       break;
    case 2:
       printf("\nDeleting Node \n");
       cur=first;
       while (cur->rlink!=NULL)
       {
          temp=cur;
          cur=cur->rlink;
       }
       printf("\nValue is : %d",cur->data);
       temp->rlink=NULL;
       break;
    case 3:
       printf("\nList of nodes\n");
       cur=first;

       while(cur!=NULL)
       {
          printf(" %5d ",cur->data);
          cur=cur->rlink;
       }
       break;
    }
    }
    }while(ch!=4);
}
```

**Output:**
```
Select operation
1. Add  2. Del  3. List  4. Exit
1
Enter the data : 10
List is empty
Select operation
1. Add  2. Del  3. List  4. Exit
1
Enter the data : 20
```

```
Select operation
1. Add  2. Del  3. List  4. Exit
1
Enter the data : 30
Select operation
1. Add  2. Del  3. List  4. Exit
3

List of nodes
  10  20  30
Select operation
1. Add  2. Del  3. List  4. Exit
2

Deleting node
Value is : 30
Select operation
1. Add  2. Del  3. List  4. Exit
3

List of nodes
  10  20
Select operation
1. Add  2. Del  3. List  4. Exit
1

Enter the data : 40

Select operation
1. Add  2. Del  3. List  4. Exit
3

List of nodes
  10  20  40
Select operation
1. Add  2. Del  3. List  4. Exit
4
```

## 11.13  SORTING

### 11.13.1  Insertion Sort

*Algorithm:*

In this sorting, we have to keep a minimum value at the first location and for every operation, the smallest element is inserted.

1. Keep minimum value in the first location ( 0 or –32767)

   $a[0] = 0$ or $a[0] = -32767$

2. For i = 2 to $n$

   If $a[i] < a[i - 1]$ then

   Travel towards the left side to find the smallest value.

Insert $a[i]$ into the next location of the smallest element.
Move all the elements to the next up to $(i - 1)$th location

| | | | | | | |
|---|---|---|---|---|---|---|
| 0 | 33 | 11 | 55 | 44 | 22 | Unsorted list. Start from 11 |
| 0 | 11 | 33 | 55 | 44 | 22 | Smallest in the left is 0. Insert 11 into the first location, move 33 to the next location |
| 0 | 11 | 33 | 55 | 44 | 22 | Take 55. No process, because 33 is < 55 |
| 0 | 11 | 33 | 55 | 44 | 22 | Take 44 and smaller is 33. So insert 44 into the next of 33 and move 55 to the next |
| 0 | 11 | 33 | 44 | 55 | 22 | Take 22 and smaller is 11. So insert 22 into the next of 11 and move 33, 44 and 55 to the next locations |
| 0 | 11 | 22 | 33 | 44 | 55 | All the elements are sorted |

Shaded portions are the processed elements of the array.

### Example:

```
/* Insertion sorting */
#include <stdio.h>
#include <conio.h>

main()
{
    int i,j,k,n,temp,a[10];
    clrscr();
    printf("\nHow many numbers :");
    scanf("%d",&n);
    printf("\nEnter %d numbers ",n);

    for(i=1;i<=n;i++)
        scanf("%d",&a[i]);

    a[0]=0;
    for(i=2;i<=n;i++)
    {
        j=i-1;
        while(a[i]<=a[j])
            j--;
```

```
            j++;
            temp=a[i];
            for(k=i;k>j;k--)
                a[k]=a[k-1];

            a[j]=temp;
        }
    printf("\nSorted Elements are \n");
    for(i=1;i<=n;i++)
        printf("\n%d",a[i]);
    getch();
}
```

**Output:**
```
    How many numbers:6
    Enter 6 numbers
    33  11  66  44  55  22
    Sorted Elements are
    11  22  33  44  55  66
```

## 11.13.2  Selection Sort

In this sorting technique, for every operation, we have to find the smallest number in the unsorted list and it has to be filled in the first element of the unsorted array.

1. Find the smallest element in the unsorted array.
2. Swap the smallest element and the first element of unsorted array.
3. Leave the smallest element and repeat the same process.

| | | | | | |
|---|---|---|---|---|---|
| 33 | 11 | 55 | 44 | 22 | Unsorted List |
| 33 | **11** | 55 | 44 | 22 | Min. is 11. Swap 33 and 11 |
| 11 | 33 | 55 | 44 | **22** | Min. is 22. Swap 33 and 22 |
| 11 | 22 | 55 | 44 | **33** | Min. is 33. Swap 55 and 33 |
| 11 | 22 | 33 | **44** | 55 | Min. is 44. Swap 44 and 44 |
| 11 | 22 | 33 | 44 | 55 | Sorted List |

***Note:***
Sorted part is shaded and minimum element is shown in bold face.

```
/* Selection Sort */
#include <stdio.h>
#include <conio.h>

main()
{
    int i,j,n,p,temp,min,a[10];
```

```
   clrscr();
   printf("\nHow many numbers:");
   scanf("%d",&n);
   printf("\nEnter %d numbers",n);
   for(i=0;i<n;i++)
      scanf("%d",&a[i]);

   for(i=0;i<n-1;i++)
   {
      min=a[i];
      p=i;
      for(j=i+1;j<n;j++)
         if (min>a[j])
            {
                min=a[j]; p=j;
            }
      temp=a[i];
      a[i]=min;
      a[p]=temp;
   }

 printf("\nSorted Elements are \n");
 for(i=0;i<n;i++)
    printf("\n%d",a[i]);
getch();
}
```

**Output:**
```
How many numbers: 5

Enter 5 numbers
33   11   55   44   22

Sorted elements are
11   22   33   44   55
```

### 11.13.3  Exchange Sort

1. Repeat the following process $n - 1$ times
2. Compare the nearest elements from the first to the last
    if $a[j] > a[j + 1]$
        then Swap the value of $a[j]$ and $a[j+1]$.
3. For each iteration, we will get the biggest of the unsorted array and it is not included for the next process.

A temporary variable, **temp** can be used to reduce the number of unnecessary repetetions.

| | | | | | | |
|---|---|---|---|---|---|---|
| 40 | 20 | 10 | 60 | 50 | 30 | Unsorted List |
| 40 | 20 | 10 | 60 | 50 | 30 | 40 & 20 are compared and swapped |
| 20 | 40 | 10 | 60 | 50 | 30 | 40 & 10 are compared and swapped |
| 20 | 10 | 40 | 60 | 50 | 30 | 40 & 60 are compared and not swapped |
| 20 | 10 | 40 | 60 | 50 | 30 | 60 & 50 are compared and swapped |
| 20 | 10 | 40 | 50 | 60 | 30 | 60 & 30 are compared and swapped |
| 20 | 10 | 40 | 50 | 30 | 60 | 60 is not included in the next process |
| 20 | 10 | 40 | 50 | 30 | | 20 & 10 are compared and swapped |
| 10 | 20 | 40 | 50 | 30 | | 20 & 40 are compared and not swapped |
| 10 | 20 | 40 | 50 | 30 | | 40 & 50 are compared and not swapped |
| 10 | 20 | 40 | 50 | 30 | | 50 & 30 are compared and swapped |
| 10 | 20 | 40 | 30 | 50 | | 50 is not included in the next process |
| 10 | 20 | 40 | 30 | | | 10 & 20 are compared and not swapped |
| 10 | 20 | 40 | 30 | | | 20 & 40 are compared and not swapped |
| 10 | 20 | 40 | 30 | | | 40 & 30 are compared and swapped |
| 10 | 20 | 30 | 40 | | | 40 is not included in the next process |
| 10 | 20 | 30 | 40 | 50 | 60 | Sorted List |

**Example:**

```
/* Exchange Sort.-Comparing Nearest Elements */
main()
{
int i,j,n,temp,a[10];

clrscr();
printf("\nHow Many numbers :");
scanf("%d",&n);
printf("\nEnter %d numbers ",n);

for(i=0;i<n;i++)
    scanf("%d",&a[i]);

for(i=0;i<n-1;i++)
    for(j=i+1;j<n;j++)
      if (a[i]>a[j])
         {
          temp=a[i];
          a[i]=a[j];
          a[j]=temp;
          }

      printf("\nSorted Elements are \n");
    for(i=0;i<n;i++)
      printf("\n%d",a[i]);

getch();
}
```

## 11.13.4  Quick Sort

Algorithm for QuickSort (first, last, A)

1.  Let Ref = a[first], i = first + 1, j = last
2.  Travel towards right side to find the bigger than Ref
    while Ref > a[i]
    i = i + 1
3.  Travel towards left side to find the smaller than Ref.
    while Ref < a[j]
    j = j – 1
4.  If i < j then
    SWAP (a[i] and a[j])
    Continue from Step 2.
    else
    SWAP a[first] and a[j]
    // a[first] is the exact location in the array. So in the next, leave the
    // value at the location a[j]

    Qsort(first, j–1, a) // First half
    Qsort(j+1, last a) // Second half

List of Numbers :  25  30  15  10  20  5

    p = 25, i = 2, j = 6

| 1 | 2 | 3 | 4 | 5 | 6 | P | I | J | Description |
|---|---|---|---|---|---|---|---|---|---|
| 25 | i<br>30 | 15 | 10 | 20 | j<br>5 | 25 | 2 | 6 | i < j. So swap a[i], a[j] |
| 25 | 5 | 15 | 10 | j<br>20 | i<br>30 | 25 | 6 | 5 | i > j. So swap a[j], P |

Now the set is divided into two sets

| | | | | | | | | | |
|---|---|---|---|---|---|---|---|---|---|
| 20 | 5 | 15 | 10 | 25 | 30 | | | | 25 is filled in its exact location. The second half contains only one element 30. So no need to sort. |
| 20 | i<br>5 | 15 | j<br>10 | | | 20 | 2 | 4 | New set of elements to sort |
| 20 | 5 | 15 | j, i<br>10 | | | 20 | 4 | 4 | i = j. So swap a[i], P |
| 10 | 5 | 15 | 20 | | | | | | Now 20 is filled in its actual location and the remaining elements are only considered |

| | | | | | | | |
|---|---|---|---|---|---|---|---|
| | | | New set of elements | | | | |
| 10 | j | i | | 10 | 3 | 2 | i > j. So, swap a[j], P |
| | 5 | 15 | | | | | |
| 5 | 10 | 15 | | | | | 10 is filled in its actual location. Now the first half and second half consist of only one element. So further process is not needed. |
| 5 | 10 | 15 | 20 | 25 | 30 | | Sorted list of elements |

**Example:**

```
/*Quick Sort using Recursive Function */
void main()
{
int l,r,i,j,n,a[10];
clrscr();
printf("\nHow many elements : ");
scanf("%d",&n);

printf("\nEnter %d elements ", n);
for(i=0;i<n;i++)
   scanf("%d",&a[i]);

printf("\nElements before sorting ");
for(i=0;i<n;i++)
   printf("%5d",a[i]);

l=0;r=n-1;
Quick(a,l,r);

printf("\nElements after sorting ");
for(i=0;i<n;i++)
   printf("%5d",a[i]);

getch();
}

Quick(int a[10],int l,int r)
{
int i,j,pivot,temp,k;
if (r>l)
{
   pivot = a[l];
   i=l+1;
   j=r;
```

```
do{
   while(a[i] < pivot && i<r)
      i++;
   while(a[j] > pivot && j>l)
      j--;

   if (i<j)
      {
         temp=a[i];
         a[i]=a[j];
         a[j]=temp;
      }
   } while(i<j);

   temp=a[l];
   a[l]=a[j];
   a[j]=temp;

   /* Sort the first Half */
   Quick(a,l,j-1);
   /*Sort the second first Half */
   Quick(a,j+1,r);
}
return;
}
```

**Output:**
```
How many elements: 6
Enter 6 elements 25
30
15
10
20
5

Elements before sorting:    25  30  15  10  20   5
Elements after sorting:      5  10  15  20  25  30
```

## 11.13.5  Heap Sort

Now, we have some idea about different ways of sorting the numbers. Heap sort is another way of sorting the set of numbers and it is based on the binary tree. Here the value of the parent should be greater than its children. General definition about the parent and its child relationship is that, if the parent is at location **I**, its children are at the locations **2∗I** and **2∗I + 1**. For example, if the parent is in the **2nd** location and its children must be at the **4th** and **5th** locations. Sometimes there may be only one child. The number of parents are identified by $n/2$, $n$ is the maximum number of nodes in the tree. For example, if there are **7** nodes in the tree, then there are **three (3)** parents ( **7/2 = 3.5 => 3**) in that tree.

*Algorithm:*
```
    1. If n > 1 then                // n is the number of elements
        If (n % 2 !=0)              // To check, whether n is odd or even
            OK = 1                  // If n is odd then set OK = 1

        NP = n/2                    // To half it and find the number of parents
        for j=1 to NP (number of parents)
            for i = NP to 1 Step –1
                Find the biggest of a[i], a[2 * i] and a[2 * i + 1]
                SWAP the parent and the biggest child value
```

Comparison will be started at the bottom of the tree towards the parent. This process will be continued as many times as the number of parents. After completion of the comparisons, the first and the last element of the list are swapped. The last element is the highest element in the tree and it is not going to be considered in the next iterations.

This process will continue until there are no more elements to compare. The following is an example for heap sort.

| 1 | 2 | 3 | 4 | 5 | |
|---|---|---|---|---|---|
| 15 | 5 | 10 | 25 | 20 | Compare the values of locations 2,4 and 5. For the parent 2, the children are at locations 4 and 5. Find the biggest of three, and then swap the corresponding child with parent |
| 15 | 25 | 10 | 5 | 20 | Compare values at locations 1, 2 and 3 |
| 25 | 15 | 10 | 5 | 20 | Compare values at locations 2, 4 and 5 |
| 25 | 20 | 10 | 5 | 15 | Compare values at locations 1, 2 and 3 |

Swap the first and the last location values and skip the last and start the next process.

| 15 | 20 | 10 | 5 | 25 | |
|---|---|---|---|---|---|
| 15 | 20 | 10 | 5 | | Compare values at locations 2 and 4 |
| 15 | 20 | 10 | 5 | | Compare values at locations 1, 2 and 3 |
| 20 | 15 | 10 | 5 | | Compare values at locations 2 and 4 |
| 20 | 15 | 10 | 5 | | Compare values at locations 1, 2 and 3 |

Next iteration is over. So swap the first and the last. Leave the last one for the next process

| 5 | 15 | 10 | 20 | | |
|---|---|---|---|---|---|
| 5 | 15 | 10 | | | Compare the values at locations 1, 2 and 3 |
| 15 | 5 | 10 | | | Swap the first and the last |
| 10 | 5 | 15 | | | |
| 10 | 5 | | | | Compare the values at locations 1 and 2 |
| 10 | 5 | | | | Swap the values at locations 1 and 2 |
| 5 | 10 | | | | |
| 5 | 10 | 15 | 20 | 25 | Sorted List |

***Example:***

```c
/* Heap Sort Program */

#include<stdio.h>
#include<conio.h>
#include<alloc.h>

void main( )
{
    int *x,i,n;
    int temp;
    void heap(int *,int);
    clrscr();
    fflush(stdin);
    printf("How many Numbers : ");
    scanf("%d",&n);
    x = (int *)malloc(n * sizeof(int));
    for(i=0;i<n;i++)
    {fflush(stdin);
        scanf("%d",&x[i]);
    }
    heap(x,n);

    for(i=n-1;i>=1;i--)
    {
        temp =  x[i];
        x[i] = x[0];
        x[0] = temp;
        heap(x,i-1);
    }

    printf("Sorted Elements");
    for(i=0;i<n;i++)
        printf("%d  ",x[i]);

    getch();
}


void heap(int *a,int n)
{
    int i,temp;
    for(i=n/2;i>=0;i--)
    {
        if(a[(2*i)+1] < a[(2*i)+2] && (2*i+1)<=n && (2*i+2)<=n)
```

```
            {
               temp = a[(2*i)+1];
               a[(2*i)+1] = a[(2*i)+2];
               a[(2*i)+2] = temp;
            }
         if(a[(2*i)+1] > a[i] && (2*i+1)<=n && i<=n)
            {
               temp = a[(2*i)+1];
               a[(2*i)+1] = a[i];
               a[i] = temp;
            }
      }
   }
}
```

**Output:**
```
How many Numbers : 6
44
11
55
33
66
22
Sorted Elements
11     22    33    44    55    66
```

## 11.13.6  Two-Way Merging

Merging means, combining two sorted arrays into one sorted array.

1. Let $a$ and $b$ are the two sorted arrays. $c$ is the merged array
2. $i = 1$, $m$ is the number of elements in $a$. $j = 1$ and $n$ is the number of elements in $b$
3. While $i <= n$ and $j <= m$
4. If $a[i] < a[j]$ then
      Copy $a[i]$ into $c[k]$
      $i = i + 1$
   Else
      Copy $a[j]$ into $c[k]$
      $j = j + 1$
5. If there are any more elements in $a$ or $b$ array, then copy all the remaining elements either from $a$ or from $b$ array into $c$.

| a | | | b | | | | c | | | | | | |
|---|---|---|---|---|---|---|---|---|---|---|---|---|---|
| 11 | 33 | 55 | 22 | 44 | 66 | 77 | 11 | | | | | | |
| 11 | 33 | 55 | 22 | 44 | 66 | 77 | 11 | 22 | | | | | |
| 11 | 33 | 55 | 22 | 44 | 66 | 77 | 11 | 22 | 33 | | | | |
| 11 | 33 | 55 | 22 | 44 | 66 | 77 | 11 | 22 | 33 | 44 | | | |
| 11 | 33 | 55 | 22 | 44 | 66 | 77 | 11 | 22 | 33 | 44 | 55 | | |
| 11 | 33 | 55 | 22 | 44 | 66 | 77 | 11 | 22 | 33 | 44 | 55 | 66 | |
| 11 | 33 | 55 | 22 | 44 | 66 | 77 | 11 | 22 | 33 | 44 | 55 | 66 | 77 |
| 11 | 33 | 55 | 22 | 44 | 66 | 77 | 11 | 22 | 33 | 44 | 55 | 66 | 77 |

## *Example:*

```c
/* Merging Two Sorted Arrays */
#include <stdio.h>
#include <conio.h>

void main()
{
int a[10],b[10],c[20],m,n,k,i,j;

clrscr();
printf("\nWhat is the size of the first array : ");
scanf("%d",&m);

printf("\nEnter %d elements (Sorted Order) ",m);
for(i=0;i<m;i++)
    scanf("%d",&a[i]);

printf("\nWhat is the size of the second array : ");
scanf("%d",&n);

printf("\nEnter %d elements (Sorted Order) ",n);
for(i=0;i<n;i++)
    scanf("%d",&b[i]);
i=j=k=0;

while(i<m && j<n)
{
if (a[i]<b[j])
    {
      c[k]=a[i];
      i++;k++;
    }
else
```

```
{
   c[k]=b[j];
   j++;k++;
}
}
/*Copying Remaining Elements of A */
while(i<m)
    {
      c[k]=a[i];
      i++;k++;
    }

/*Copying Remaining Elements of B */
while(j<n)
{
   c[k]=b[j];
   j++;k++;
}
printf("\nMerged Array \n");
for(i=0;i<k;i++)
   printf("%5d",c[i]);

getch();
}
```

**Output:**
```
What is the size of the first array: 3

Enter 3 elements (Sorted Order) 11
33
55

What is the size of the second array: 4

Enter 4 elements (Sorted Order) 22
44
66
77
Merged Array:
   11   22   33   44   55   66   77
```

# Chapter 12
# Additional Solved Programs

## Program to Generate Fibonacci Sequence up to the Range

```c
#include <stdio.h>
main()
{
int a=0,b=1,c,n;
clrscr();
printf("\nEnter the range : ");
scanf("%d",&n);
for(;;)
{
   c=a+b;
   a=b;b=c;
   if (c<n)
      printf("%5d",c);
   else
      break;
}
getch();
}
Enter the range : 10
   1   2   3   5   8
```

## Program to count the number of characters, words and lines of a file

```
/* To count the number of lines, characters and words in a file */

#include <stdio.h>
main()
{
FILE *fp=fopen("c:\\c\\ek.dat","r");
int c,l,w;
char ch;
c=l=w=1;

clrscr();
if (fp==NULL)
   {
      printf("\nSorry ! No such file");
      exit(0);
   }
while(!feof(fp))
{
   ch = getc(fp);
   c++;
   if ((ch==' ') || (ch=='\n'))
      w++;
   if (ch=='\n')
      l++;
}

printf("\nNumber of Characters : %d",c);
printf("\nNumber of Words      : %d",w);
printf("\nNumber of Lines      : %d",l);

getch();
}
```

## Suppose the following is the content of a file

```
I Love India
Better things in our life are little things we do for others
Dept. of Computer Science and Applications
```

**Output:**
```
Number of Characters : 117
Number of Words      : 21
Number of Lines      : 3
```

## Program to Implement SIN function

```
/* To compute SIN values */
#include <stdio.h>
#include <math.h>

main()
{
  float rad,x,result1;
  clrscr();
  printf("\nEnter the radius : ");
  scanf("%f",&rad);
  x = (3.14 * rad) / 180;
  result1 = SIN(x);
  printf("\nSIN ( %2.0f ) is %5.2f ",rad,result1);
  getch();
}

float SIN(float x)
{
  int i,sign=1;
  float sum=0;
  for(i=1;i<9;i+=2)
  {
     sum = sum + pow(x,i) / fact(i) * sign;
     sign=-sign;
  }
  return sum;
}

int fact(int n)
{
   int i,f=1;
   for(i=1;i<=n;i++)
      f = f*i;
return f;
}
```

**Output:**
```
Enter the radius :   30
SIN ( 30 ) is : 0.50

Enter the radius :   45
SIN ( 45 ) is :  0.71

Enter the radius :   60
SIN ( 60 ) is :  0.87
```

## Program to Implement COS function

```
/* To compute COS values */
#include <stdio.h>
#include <math.h>

main()
{
float rad,x,result1;

clrscr();
printf("\nEnter the radius :  ");
scanf("%f",&rad);

x = (3.14 * rad) / 180;

result1 = COS(x);
printf("\nCOS ( %2.0f ) is %5.2f ",rad,result1);
getch();
}

float COS(float x)
{
int i,sign=-1;
float sum=1;
for(i=2;i<9;i+=2)
{
   sum = sum + pow(x,i) / fact(i) * sign;
   sign=-sign;
}
return sum;
}

int fact(int n)
{
int i,f=1;
for(i=1;i<=n;i++)
   f = f*i;
return f;
}
```

Output:
```
Enter the radius :   30
COS ( 30 ) is :  0.87

Enter the radius :   45
COS ( 45 ) is :  0.71

Enter the radius :   60
COS ( 60 ) is : 0.50
```

## Program to find the number of palindromes in a given text

```c
/*To find the number of palindromes in a given text */

#include <stdio.h>
#include <string.h>
main()
{
int i=0,j=0;

char s[80];
char word[50];
clrscr();
printf("\nEnter a string : ");
gets(s);

while(s[i]!='\0')
{
   if (s[i]==' ')
      {
         word[j]='\0';
         j=0;i++;
         poly(word);
      }
   else
   {
     word[j]=s[i];
     i++;j++;
   }
}
word[j]='\0';
poly(word);

}
int poly(char *p)
{
int i,len,pol=1;
len=strlen(p);
for(i=0;i<len;i++)
   if (p[i]!=p[len-i-1])
     pol=0;

if (pol==1)
   printf("\nThe string '%s' is a palindrome ",p);
else
   printf("\nThe string '%s' is not a palindrome ",p);

getch();
}
```

```
Enter a string : madam speaks malayalam

The string 'madam' is a palindrome
The string 'speaks' is not a palindrome
The string 'malayalam' is a palindrome
```

## Program to find the number of occurrences of a character in a text

```c
#include <stdio.h>
#include <string.h>
void main()
{
    char ch,s[80];
    int i,l,c=0;

    clrscr();
    printf("\nEnter a text : ");
    gets(s);
    printf("\nEnter a character to check : ");
    scanf("%c",&ch);

    l=strlen(s);
    for(i=0;i<l;i++)
        if (s[i]==ch)
            c++;
    printf("\nThe character '%c' occurred %d times in the text ",ch,c);

    getch();
}
```

Output:
```
Enter a text : karthikeyananana
Enter a character to check : n
The character 'n' occurred 3 times in the text
```

## Program to find the Armstrong number

```c
#include <stdio.h>
#include <conio.h>

main()
{
    int n,m,k,sum=0;
    clrscr();
    printf("\nEnter a number : ");
    scanf("%d",&n);
    k=n;
    while(n!=0)
```

```
        {
            m=n%10;
            n=n/10;
            sum=sum + m*m*m;
        }

    if (k==sum)
        printf("\nThe number '%d' is an Armstrong number",k);
    else
        printf("\nThe number '%d' is not an Armstrong number",k);

getch();
}
```

**Output:**

```
Enter a number : 123
The number '123' is not an Armstrong number

Enter a number : 153
The number '153' is an Armstrong number
```

## *Program for implementing power function*

```
void main()
{
    int x,n,sum;

    clrscr();
    printf("\nEnter the value of x and n :");
    scanf("%d%d",&x,&n);
    sum=power(x,n);
    printf("\nPower(%d,%d) is : %d ",x,n,sum);

    getch();
}
int power(int x,int n)
{
    int i,temp=1;
    for(i=1;i<=n;i++)
        temp=temp * x;
    return temp;
}
```

**Output:**

```
Enter the value of x and n : 3   5
Power(3,5) is : 243
```

## Program to insert a string in a given text

```c
#include <stdio.h>
#include <string.h>

void main()
{
char s[100],str[10];
int i,j,len,loc;

clrscr();
i=j=0;
printf("\nEnter a text : ");
gets(s);
printf("\nEnter a string to insert : ");
gets(str);
printf("\nWhere to insert : ");
scanf("%d",&loc);

while(str[j])
{
len=strlen(s);

for(i=len;i>=loc;i−)
   s[i]=s[i-1];

   s[loc]=str[j];
   j++;loc++;
   s[len+1]='\0';
}

printf("\nNew string is : %s",s);
getch();
}
```

**Output:**

```
Enter a text : India is country

Enter a string to insert : my

Where to insert : 9

New string is : India is my country
```

## Program to find the prime numbers between two numbers

```c
#include <stdio.h>

main()
{
int i,j,m,n,prime;

clrscr();
printf("\nEnter the first number : ");
scanf("%d",&m);
printf("\nEnter the second number : ");
scanf("%d",&n);
printf("\nPrime numbers between %d and %d are \n",m,n);

for(i=m;i<=n;i++)
    {
       prime=1;
       for(j=2;j<i;j++)
          if (i%j==0)
             prime=0;

          if (prime==1)
             printf("%5d",i);

    }
getch();
}
```

Output:
```
Enter the first number : 5

Enter the second number : 30

Prime numbers between 5 and 30 are
    5    7   11   13   17   19   23   29
```

## Program to store Even numbers and Odd numbers in different files

```c
#include <stdio.h>

main()
{
   FILE *fodd,*feven;
   int m;
   fodd = fopen("odd.dat","w");
   feven = fopen("even.dat","w");
   clrscr();
   if (fodd==NULL || feven==NULL)
```

```
        {
            printf("\nSorry ! No file creation is made");
            exit(0);
        }
    do
    {
    printf("Enter a number (0 to terminate): ");
    scanf("%d",&m);
    if (m==0)
        break;

    if (m%2==0)
        putc(m,feven);
    else
        putc(m,fodd);
    }while(1);

    fcloseall();

    printf("\nContents of Odd File \n");
    fodd=fopen("odd.dat","r");

    while(!feof(fodd))
        printf("%3d",getc(fodd));

    printf("\nContents of Even File \n");
    feven=fopen("even.dat","r");

    while(!feof(feven))
        printf("%3d",getc(feven));
    getch();
    }
```

**Output:**
```
    Enter a number (0 to terminate): 1
    Enter a number (0 to terminate): 2
    Enter a number (0 to terminate): 3
    Enter a number (0 to terminate): 4
    Enter a number (0 to terminate): 5
    Enter a number (0 to terminate): 6
    Enter a number (0 to terminate): 7
    Enter a number (0 to terminate): 8
    Enter a number (0 to terminate): 9
    Enter a number (0 to terminate): 0

Contents of Odd File
    1   3   5   7   9
Contents of Even File
    2   4   6   8
```

## Program to generate a Calendar for one month

```c
#include<conio.h>

int day(int m1,int y1)
{
   int d;
   if(m1==1 || m1==3 || m1==5 || m1==7 || m1==8 || m1==10 || m1==12)
      d=31;
   else if(m1==4 || m1==6 || m1==9 || m1==11)
      d=30;
   else if((y1%100!=0 && y1%4==0) || y1%400==0)
      d=29;
   else
      d=28;
   return d;
}

void main()
{
   long unsigned int t;
   unsigned int y,y1,m,m1,d,da,i,j,k;
   char a[12][20]={"January","February","March","April","May","June",
      "July","August","September","October","November","December"};
   clrscr();

   printf("Enter the year: ");
   scanf("%4u",&y);
   printf("Enter the month: ");
   scanf("%2u",&m);
   clrscr();

   y1=0;
   t=0;
   while(y1<y)
   {
      if((y1%100!=0 && y1%4==0) || y1%400==0)
         t=t+366;
      else
         t=t+365;
      y1++;
   }
   m1=1;
   while(m1<m)
   {
      d=day(m1,y);
      t=t+d;
      m1++;
   }
```

```
d=t%7;
printf("\n\nCalendar for the Year: '%u' , Month : '%s'\n",y,a[m-1]);
printf("\n\n     Sun    Mon    Tue    Wed    Thu    Fri    Sat\n");

k=1;
for(i=1;i<=day(m,y);i++,k++)
{
   if(i==1)
   {
      if(d==0)
      {
         for(j=1;j<7;j++,k++)
            printf("%6s"," ");
      }
      else
      {
         for(j=1;j<d;j++,k++)
            printf("%6s"," ");
      }
   }
   printf("%6d",i);
   if(k%7==0)
      printf("\n");
}
getch();
}
```

**Output:**
```
    Calendar for the Year: '2007' , Month : 'March'

    Sun    Mon    Tue    Wed    Thu    Fri    Sat
                                  1      2      3
     4      5      6      7      8      9     10
    11     12     13     14     15     16     17
    18     19     20     21     22     23     24
    25     26     27     28     29     30     31
```

## Program to search the occurrence of string

```
/*Program to search the occurrence of a String */
#include <stdio.h>
#include <conio.h>
#include <string.h>

void main()
{
   int i,j,len,found=0;
   char s1[50],s2[50];

clrscr();
printf("\nEnter a text : ");
gets(s1);
printf("\nEnter a string to search in the text :");
gets(s2);
i=j=0;
len = strlen(s2);

while(s1[i])
{
   for(j=0;j<len;j++)
   {
     if (s1[i++]!=s2[j])
        {
        i—;
        break;
        }
   }
   if (j==len)
      found=1;
   i++;

}
if (found==1)
   printf("\nThe string '%s' appeared in the text",s2);
else
   printf("\nThe string '%s' did not appear in the text",s2);
getch();
}
```

**Output:**

Enter a text : I Love India

Enter a string to search in the text : Love

The string 'Love' appeared in the text

Enter a text : I Love India

Enter a string to search in the text : Leave

The string 'Leave' does not occur in the text

## Program to find decimal equivalent of a binary number

```
/*Program to find decimal equivalent of a binary number */
#include <stdio.h>
#include <conio.h>
#include <math.h>
void main()
{
   int m,n,c=0,sum=0;

   clrscr();
   printf("\nEnter binary number : ");
   scanf("%d",&n);
   printf("\nBinary number  : %d",n);
   while(n!=0)
   {
      m=n%10;
      sum=sum + m* pow(2,c);
      c++;
      n=n/10;
   }
   printf("\nDecimal number : %d",sum);
   getch();
}
```

Output:
Enter binary number : 1101
Binary  number   : 1101
Decimal number   : 13

## Program to find the determinant of a matrix

```
/*To find the Determinant of a Matrix */
#include <stdio.h>

void main()
{
float a[3][3],c,d;
int i,j,k,n;
clrscr();
printf("\nEnter the size of matrix : ");
scanf("%d",&n);
```

```
    printf("\nEnter %d x %d matrix  ",n,n);
    for(i=0;i<n;i++)
       for(j=0;j<n;j++)
          scanf("%f",&a[i][j]);
    printf("\nThe Matrix is \n");
    for(i=0;i<n;i++)
    {
       for(j=0;j<n;j++)
          printf("%5.1f",a[i][j]);
       printf("\n");
    }

    for(i=0;i<n;i++)
    for(j=0;j<n;j++)
    if(j!=i)
       {
          c=a[j][i] / a[i][i];
          for(k=0;k<n;k++)
          a[j][k] = a[j][k] - a[i][k] * c;
       }

    d=1;
    for(i=0;i<n;i++)
       d = d * a[i][i];
    printf("\nDeterminant of the Matrix is : %5.2f",d);
    getch();
    }
```

**Output:**
```
Enter the size of matrix : 3

Enter 3 × 3 matrix  -2
   2
  -3
  -1
   1
   3
   2
   0
  -1


The Matrix is
  -2.0   2.0  -3.0
  -1.0   1.0   3.0
   2.0   0.0  -1.0

Determinant of the Matrix is : 18.00
```

## Program to find the inverse of a matrix

```
/*To find Inverse of Matrix */
#include <stdio.h>

void main()
{
float a[3][3],c,r;
int i,j,k,n;
clrscr();
printf("\nEnter the size of matrix : ");
scanf("%d",&n);
printf("\nEnter %d x %d matrix   ",n,n);
for(i=0;i<n;i++)
   for(j=0;j<n;j++)
      scanf("%f",&a[i][j]);

printf("\nGiven Matrix is \n");
for(i=0;i<n;i++)
{ for(j=0;j<n;j++)
   printf("%5.2f\t",a[i][j]);
   printf("\n");
}

for(i=0;i<n;i++)
   for(j=0;j<n;j++)
      if(j!=i)
         {
            c=a[j][i] / a[i][i];
            for(k=0;k<n+n;k++)
              a[j][k] = a[j][k] - a[i][k] * c;
         }

   for(i=0;i<n;i++)
   {
      r = 1 / a[i][i];
         for(j=n+1;j<n+n;j++)
            a[i][j] = a[i][j] * r;
   }

printf("\nInverse of Matrix is \n");
for(i=0;i<n;i++)
{
   for(j=n+1;j<n+n;j++)
      printf("%5.2f\t",a[i][j]);

   printf("\n");
}
getch();
}
```

**Output:**
```
Enter the size of matrix : 3

Enter 3×3 matrix -2
  2
 -3
 -1
  1
  3
  2
  0
 -1


Given Matrix is
  -2.00    2.00   -3.00
  -1.00    1.00    3.00
   2.00    0.00   -1.00

Inverse of Matrix is
   2.00    0.00
  -0.00   -11.81
   0.01   -0.04
```

## Program for converting the numbers into words

```c
/*To convert the number into words */
void main()
{
char s1[21][10]={" ","One","Two","Three","Four","Five","Six","Seven",
"Eight","Nine","Ten","Eleven","Twelve","Thirteen","Fourteen",
"Fifteen","Sixteen","Seventeen","Eighteen","Nineteen"};

char s2[10][10]={" "," ","Twenty","Thirty","Forty","Fifty","Sixty",
"Seventy","Eighty","Ninety"};

char s3[10][10]={"Hundred","Thousand"};

int n,m,t;

   clrscr();
   printf("\nEnter a number (<10000): ",&n);
   scanf("%d",&n);
   printf("\nYour given number is : %d",n);
   printf("\nWord equivalent   is : ");
   if (n>1000)
   {
     m = n / 1000;
     n = n % 1000;
```

```
    if (m<19)
       printf("%s %s ",s1[m],s3[1]);
    else
       {
       t = m / 10;
       m = m % 10;
       printf("%s %s %s ",s2[t],s1[m],s3[1]);
       }
    }
    if (n>100)
    {
    m = n / 100;
    n = n % 100;
    printf("%s %s ",s1[m],s3[0]);
    }
    if(n>19)
    {
       m = n / 10;
       n = n % 10;
       printf("and %s ",s2[m]);
    }
    if (n<20)
       printf("%s",s1[n]);

getch();
}
```

**Output:**
```
Enter a number (<10000): 1234

Your given number is : 1234
Word equivalent    is : One Thousand Two Hundred and Thirty Four

Enter a number (<10000): 23456

Your given number is : 23456
Word equivalent is : Twenty Three Thousand Four Hundred and Fifty Six
```

### Program to find the Greatest Common Denominator (GCD) and the Least Common Multiplier (LCM)

```
#include <stdio.h>
#include <conio.h>

void main()
{
int m,n,i,gcd,lcm;
clrscr();
```

```
printf("\nEnter two numbers   ");
scanf("%d%d",&m,&n);

for(i=1;i<=m;i++)
   if ((n%i==0) && (m%i==0))
      gcd=i;

l cm = m * n / gcd;

printf("\nGCD (%d, %d) is %d",m,n,gcd);
printf("\nLCM (%d, %d) is %d",m,n,lcm);

getch();
}
```

Output:
```
Enter two numbers   2    8

GCD (2, 8) is 2
LCM (2, 8) is 8


Enter two numbers   2    8

GCD (2, 8) is 2
LCM (2, 8) is 8
```

## Program to display the status of the keyboard until a key press

```
#include <stdio.h>
main()
{
char far *kb=0x417;
clrscr();

do{
   if (*kb&64)
      printf("\nCaps is ON");
   else
      printf("\nCaps is Off");

      if (kbhit()) break;
}
while(1);

getch();

}
```

# Index